THE
NATIONAL GOVERNMENT
AND SOCIAL WELFARE

THE
NATIONAL GOVERNMENT
AND SOCIAL WELFARE

What Should Be the Federal Role?

Edited by
John E. Hansan and Robert Morris

AUBURN HOUSE
Westport, Connecticut • London

Library of Congress Cataloging-in-Publication Data

The national government and social welfare : what should be the
   federal role? / edited by John E. Hansan and Robert Morris.
      p.   cm.
   Includes bibliographical references and index.
   ISBN 0–86569–266–1 (alk. paper)
   1. United States—Social policy.   2. United States—Economic
policy.   3. Economic security—United States.   4. Social security—
United States.   5. Public welfare—United States.   I. Hansan, John
E.   II. Morris, Robert, 1910–   .
HN59.2.N37   1997
361.6'1—dc21   97–1468

British Library Cataloguing in Publication Data is available.

Library of Congress Catalog Card Number: 97–1468
ISBN: 0–86569–266–1

First published in 1997

Auburn House, 88 Post Road West, Westport, CT 06881
An imprint of Greenwood Publishing Group, Inc.

Printed in the United States of America

The paper used in this book complies with the
Permanent Paper Standard issued by the National
Information Standards Organization (Z39.48–1984).

10 9 8 7 6 5 4 3 2 1

Contents

Preface   ix

1. A Decade-Long Drift to Public "Conservatism" Redefining
   the Federal Roles in Social Welfare: Anticipating the Future
   and Preparing for It   1
   Robert Morris and John E. Hansan

2. Employment Challenges   17
   S. M. Miller

3. Policies to Improve Employment Outcomes for American
   Workers   29
   Robert I. Lerman

4. Reviving an Affirmative Concept of Corporate Duty:
   The Public Corporation   43
   Howard Schweber

5. Thinking About Social Security   71
   Alvin L. Schorr

6. Public and Private Approaches for Redesigning Social
   Security   81
   Yung-Ping Chen

7. Health Care: An American Report   91
   Rashi Fein

8. Thoughts on a New Government Role in Health Care
   Robert L. Kane   109

9. Outcome Measures for Persons with Disabilities as a
   Litmus Test for Quality in Managed Care   125
   Robert Griss

10. Housing: Reconstructing the Federal Government's Role
    and Responsibilities   135
    Michael E. Stone and Chester Hartman

11. Welfare Reform: Fixing the System Inside and Out   147
    Jared Bernstein and Irwin Garfinkel

12. Federal Role in Establishing National Income Security
    for Children   161
    Martha N. Ozawa

13. Redefining the Role of Government: A Work in Progress   179
    Robert Morris and John E. Hansan

Appendix: List of Participants at the Odyssey Forum Meeting,
    26–27 January 1996, Washington, D.C.   185

Index   187

About the Editors and Contributors   195

Preface

THE ODYSSEY FORUM IS LAUNCHED

In 1995, three colleagues began an exchange of papers and correspondence bearing on the question: what is an appropriate role for the national government in social welfare? They began to extend to other colleagues an invitation to join in this informal exchange of ideas. As more people responded favorably to the idea of participating in a "circle of correspondents," Odyssey Forum was created. It remains an informal association of approximately eighty social welfare advocates, policy experts, and scholars.

The uniqueness of Odyssey Forum is that it offers participants the opportunity to present views and recommend actions about social welfare issues unconstrained by agency identification, academic affiliation, or other special interests. Through Odyssey Forum, participants can share their knowledge and experience, and in that process bear witness to the effects of the careless, even brutal, shrinking of the safety net that is taking place. It is unhealthy to be quiet in these times, and Odyssey Forum is one means of sharing as widely as possible the humane and constructive ideas, recommendations, and proposals of informed professionals.

THE JANUARY 1996 MEETING

Encouraged by the response to the ideas and papers being circulated by mail, a meeting was planned for January 26–27, 1996 in Washington, D.C. To focus the discussion and allow more time for deliberations about specific proposals at the meeting, several participants were invited to prepare papers that could be circulated in advance. The papers in this volume are the fruit of that effort. Twenty-four participants took the time (and paid for their own travel!) to attend and discuss a set of issues face-to-face. Their deliberations resulted in substantial consensus on some fundamental issues, with sometimes strong disagreement on details. (A list of the participants at the January 26–27 meeting is included in the Appendix.)

The basic agreement reached by the participants at the meeting—hardly anticipated and without discernible dissent—may be set forth as follows:

1. In the United States, we yearn to be a part of a community, but at the same time, we value our individual freedoms. We are increasingly splintered on economic, political, and social issues.

2. Among our nation's difficulties is the fact that economic outcomes—profits and cost efficiency, for example—are regarded as the primary if not the sole criteria by which to judge policies. This is a profound error. We need a reasonable balance between satisfying economic *and* social needs.

3. The numerous issues underlying social policy are all closely related. Moreover, our political traditions and the current political environment do not encourage comprehensive planning. Effective policy making, therefore, requires an understanding of the complex relationships among seemingly disparate phenomena. For example, a growing economy depends on the availability of a healthy, educated labor force, yet continued lack of access to health care and good educational opportunities for large numbers of poor families adversely affects the quality of the labor force and, thus, the economy as well. Likewise, the lack of affordable and adequate child care decreases the access of single parents to employment, and limited work opportunities and low wages weaken incentives to work.

4. The national government is a necessary partner in dealing with the difficult problems of poverty, dependency, illiteracy, unemployment, delinquency, alienation, environmentally dangerous waste, and so forth. It would be reckless to dismiss those government institutions that can best help us cope with these matters.

5. The federal government ought to be actively involved in achieving our economic *and* social goals. The problem is not simply a matter of economic growth. In reality, productivity has increased twenty-five percent since 1973, yet median compensation has stagnated. Thus, growth is a necessary but not sufficient condition to meet our economic goals.

An economy growing at moderate rates (e.g., two percent per year) could produce important benefits if the gains were fairly shared. More equitable distribution of the gains from increased productivity could provide: *(a)* work opportunities for most able-bodied and interested adults, *(b)* wages sufficient to maintain a family above the poverty level, *(c)* a greater capacity of individuals and families to provide for most of their needs without recourse to public welfare, and *(d)* revenues government needs to fulfill its functions without excessive taxation.

The future requires economic growth *and* the appropriate distribution of the gains realized from this growth. Economic gains can be distributed through the workplace or by public programs. The success of either approach requires the private sector and the government to reinforce each other's efforts. Corporations need to reexamine their social responsibilities while preserving their profitability. Government encouragement and incentives can help. In turn, private enterprises can support government in the social welfare programs and tax policies which are its responsibilities.

THE ROLE OF THE NATIONAL GOVERNMENT IN SOCIAL WELFARE

This work addresses the efforts to redefine the social policy role of the federal government, which constitutes a central objective of political debate in the 1990s. The following chapters include twelve papers circulated to Odyssey Forum participants prior to the January meeting. They cover subject areas traditionally associated with social welfare issues: employment and wages, social security, health care, housing, and public assistance.

Redefining the Federal Roles in Social Welfare: Anticipating the Future and Preparing For It

Chapter 1 defines how the current federal roles evolved and the economic, demographic, social, and the political forces that have propelled the debate. It was written by the editors who, with Alvin Schorr, are the founders of Odyssey Forum. It presents the authors' views regarding the reasons that require a review and discussion of the role of the national government in social welfare at this time. It is their view that certain basic forces, among many, account for much of the changed national conditions we are experiencing. Recognition of these forces will help redefine the nature and extent of the roles for the national government. Among these forces are:

1. Economic changes, especially: (a) slow growth in aggregate gross domestic product (GDP), (b) unfair distribution of economic gains by the private sector (current patterns result in wage stagnation or an absolute drop in earned incomes for nearly half the population of both lower- and middle-income families, while incomes in the top five to ten percent of the population are increasing rapidly), and (c) job losses and job insecurity as a result of economic and corporate restructuring in a global economy.

2. Population changes, mainly in the expanding proportion of elderly persons, particularly the very old, and the increasing ethnic diversity of American society.

3. Public dissatisfaction with the worsening of social problems—despite extensive

public programs and expenditures for public welfare and rehabilitation—e.g., changing family composition, teenage pregnancy, drugs, violence, and abuse.

4. Loss of public confidence that the future will always be better than the past.

5. A growing proportion of children in low-income families—and minorities of all ages—who are acutely disadvantaged and experiencing daily a declining quality of life.

Work and Wages

Chapters 2, 3, and 4 examine some of the issues associated with the economy, employment, wages, and corporate responsibility. In "Employment Challenges," S. M. Miller provides the perspective that *"the most important social policy is national economic policy."* Invoking the seldom-discussed concept of "less eligibility," Miller describes why paid employment at adequate wages is a crucial component, if not the cornerstone, of effective social policy.

In Chapter 3, Robert I. Lerman reminds the reader that "the proportion of working-age Americans holding jobs is reaching all-time highs. While concerns about the state of the U.S. job market are widespread, the reality is a record that is very strong on the creation of jobs, though weak on wage growth and wage equality." Lerman goes on to describe four fundamental difficulties we need to overcome to reduce the gap between low- and high-wage earners, and he concludes with a list of feasible social policies designed to overcome these barriers.

For some readers, Howard Schweber's presentation, "Reviving an Affirmative Concept of Corporate Duty: The Public Corporation," in Chapter 4 may seem out of place in a book on social welfare policy. It is our view that the political emphasis on devolving federal responsibilities to other sectors of our society and increasing efforts to privatize some public programs and services, combined with recent documented evidence of corporate greed and irresponsibility, make it important to look at the nature of corporations and their contribution to American society. Schweber's review of the history of corporate law suggests the need and the potential for the revitalization of an affirmative notion of corporate duty and some steps we can take in the immediate future to foster a greater degree of corporate social responsibility.

Social Security

Chapters 5 and 6 focus on different aspects of social security. From their unique perspectives, Alvin Schorr and Yung-Ping Chen present powerful arguments for maintaining the integrity of our social insurance system while at the same time offering thoughtful proposals for what policy makers need to do to maintain fiscal solvency and public confidence. Schorr, in

"Thinking About Social Security," is very clear that "with or without the conservative tide that has come upon us, the social compact [i.e., the set of assumptions about what citizens and government owe each other] was going to have to change. Indeed, although the move to deconstruct the welfare state is usually phrased in ideological or money-saving terms (deficit reduction, tax cutting), underlying social and economic changes demand a revised social compact."

Yung-Ping Chen, in Chapter 6, provides a global perspective on the issues being debated about social security and how it needs to be reformed. He carefully reviews the World Bank's recent criticisms of social security programs and its proposal for a multipillar system of welfare payments and savings. It is Chen's view that "there is nothing basically wrong with the approach of social insurance that undergirds social security. Most of the seven factors which, according to the World Bank, have threatened so many publicly funded old-age security plans are attributable to plan designers and policy makers. They are not intrinsic to the social insurance model of social security."

Health Care

In this portion of the book, Rashi Fein, Robert Kane, and Robert Griss each present a different facet of the health care issue. In Chapter 7, Rashi Fein reviews the Clinton administration's failed health care reform initiative. In doing so, Fein provides a thoughtful backdrop for viewing the policy-making process in the United States. For example, he says, "while many factors contributed to the failure to enact any health care reform legislation (let alone meaningful reform) in the first two years of the Clinton administration, the overriding problem, as I see it, stemmed from America's individualistic orientation and deep skepticism, edging into antipathy, toward government." In what may appear to be a less than optimistic conclusion, Dr. Fein says, "Today, the American way of organizing and paying for health care reflects American values. If Americans are to change the former in fundamental ways, we shall have to be willing to depart from the latter."

Robert Kane's contribution directly addresses some of the difficult issues surrounding Medicare and Medicaid. For example, he asks, "Why won't anyone face up to the problems with the Medicare program? . . . Proposals to address Medicare's financial crisis by imposing across-the-board cuts or added beneficiary payments fail to recognize the extent of the current variation in Medicare costs." On Medicaid, Dr. Kane is equally forthright when he says, "The discussions about making all or part of Medicaid exclusively a state responsibility raise serious questions about whether geography should determine care. There is already considerable discrepancy from one state to another in terms of both eligibility and benefits. Transferring full responsibility for Medicaid to states under some form of block grant would widen the gap even further."

In Chapter 9, Robert Griss makes the case that, "With the rapid and largely unregulated transformation of the health care system toward corporatization, privatization, and managed care, people with disabilities have an important role to play as a litmus test for quality in managed care." He describes a set of measures that could be employed to ensure that publicly funded managed care organizations are in fact providing the range and quality of health care services they claim to be providing. In his conclusion, Griss says, "Only by combining civil rights, public health, and health care as a public utility will managed care contribute to the provision of publicly accountable health care that ensures equal access to appropriate services for the entire population."

Housing

Michael Stone and Chester Hartman, in Chapter 10, detail the record of federal financial housing assistance—social welfare—mainly benefiting housing developers, realtors, and upper-income home owners, while approximately one-third of the population remains "shelter poor." Stone and Hartman make the case that, for this to change, we will need to invest in what they term "nonspeculative" social ownership, or what is sometimes referred to as "forever affordable" housing.

Welfare Reform

In Chapter 11, Jared Bernstein and Irwin Garfinkel argue that "the key to reforming welfare lies not within the system but outside it—in the labor market and social institutions that are creating economic insecurity and fostering dependence on welfare." After briefly describing the history of public assistance in the United States, the authors effectively "close the loop" on the relationship between poverty and the economy—in particular jobs and wages. They conclude by saying, "increasing the minimum wage, strengthening unions, promoting full employment, and providing universal child care, national health insurance, child support assurance, and child allowances are the essential ingredients of real welfare reform."

Martha Ozawa's contribution, "Federal Role in Establishing National Income Security for Children," states up front that the condition of America's children is deteriorating, and that this, left uncorrected, presents a severe threat to the future of our economy and society. She describes why the current system of public transfers cannot be a means through which public resources are channeled effectively to children and then advocates for the direct involvement of the federal government in establishing income security for children.

A Work in Progress

Chapter 13 reflects the position that the times do not encourage undertaking great tasks of social engineering, centrally developed and administered within a hierarchical frame of rules and regulations—witness the rejection of the Clinton health care reform proposal and the devolution of the Aid for Families with Dependent Children (AFDC) program to the states. The editors believe that much of the current political debate and public discussion is based on an underlying assumption that we live in a privileged era of great capacities and can have all that everybody wants and quickly. Evidence about possible limitation of resources is obscured by evidence that the resources we do clearly have are poorly allocated and distributed. The result is a proliferation of voices raised in favor of expanding rights and wants that often conflict with each other, voices that pay little or no attention to the means for reconciling the needs and resources in a manner that is both equitable and consistent with freedom for all the interests.

After a forty-year span during which the necessity for making tough political decisions was postponed by a favored national economy and demographic conditions, we now have to examine our options and take available steps to balance human needs and wants against the social, economic, and demographic realities we confront. It is the editors' view that the ideas and recommendations in this volume are a very large step toward addressing the current complexity. The next step will be to move the ideas presented here into action. Odyssey Forum intends to be a part of that process.

Chapter 1

A Decade-Long Drift to Public "Conservatism" Redefining the Federal Roles in Social Welfare: Anticipating the Future and Preparing for It

Robert Morris and John E. Hansan

> The future cannot be a continuation of the past, and there are signs, both internally and externally, that we have reached a point of historic crisis.
>
> Eric Hobsbaum, *The Age of Extremes*

THE 1994–1995 CONTEXT

Recent national elections have transformed the perennial debate over how much of the national income should be allocated for social welfare, how broadly or narrowly the welfare responsibility of government should be defined, what populations or institutions should receive benefits or administer them, and how the costs should be divided. Today, the debate is over the nature of governance. Seriously proposed are plans to reverse the evolution in public policy which began with President Franklin D. Roosevelt's New Deal and the "revolution" of the 1930s in which major responsibility for individual and social or economic well-being was shifted from states and localities to the national government. The system that evolved over the past fifty years placed with the national government the management of about 30 percent of the gross national product (GNP) and fixed both the relationships among federal and state governments, business, and private organizations and federal responsibility for individual well-being through the taxing and cycling of $1.25 trillion annually into the economic lifestream of the nation.

It is not clear whether this new effort to radically change our existing social welfare system is sustained by deep and widespread voter and inter-est-group support, or whether the result will be return to a pre-1930 pattern or some radical reform of the existing system. Whatever the outcome, a period of uncertainty and even turmoil seems unavoidable as power rela-tionships are changed and as the flow of tax dollars into the economy is altered or reduced.

To anticipate our conclusions, we believe that the current review can best begin by understanding what the base was for the system we have today, which evolved in three stages over sixty-years' time:

1. The policies of the New Deal (1933–1941) and enactment of the Social Security Act of 1935 established the government's role in providing and protecting op-portunities for work at a living wage for able-bodied persons for limited emer-gency periods as an employer of last resort augmented by a worker/ employer-financed social insurance system to protect wage earners and their dependents against the total loss of income due to the involuntary and temporary unemployment, death, or retirement of the wage earner.

2. The "golden years" of exponential growth (1942–1970) expanded this base (for reasons discussed later) with: *(a) social benefit add-ons*, including housing sub-sidies for veterans and mortgage guarantees for the working and middle classes; education for veterans via the GI Bill of Rights; student loans, grants for local public education, and compensatory education for the developmentally disabled; disability insurance; Medicare; Medicaid; Supplemental Security Income, etc., *(b)* increased federal funding for *public goods*, including interstate highways; the construction of local hospitals, colleges, and universities; urban renewal; public housing; National Institutes of Health, etc., *(c)* institutionalization of *corporate welfare* in various forms, such as agricultural subsidies; economic development and small business loans; maintenance and support of defense industries; and federal financial aid for other industries deemed in need of funds for economic growth, such as the airlines and railroads.

3. The post–golden era (1975–1995) is marked by confusion about how to adapt to major changes in our economy and society. During this period there has been a shift in attitudes about the scope of government responsibilities (national, state, and local) fueled by growing uncertainty about government's ability to continue providing benefits to all who receive them and the sustainability of organizational structures developed to provide public benefits to different pop-ulations.

Extreme proposals for adapting to change seem to suggest rebuilding, almost from scratch, a social support system based mainly on local and private efforts. This would require a recasting of the foundations for com-munity life if the basic standards of human compassion and responsibility for the helpless and needy are to be retained. This task is not impossible, but it will not obviously save money—the driving force for the extreme position. Instead, it will only change how resources are mobilized. Is so radical a step unavoidable, or are there alternatives that reform the present system sufficiently to make it more effective, competent, and responsive to changing conditions? Various proposals are already circulating and more are in the pipeline. They range from suggestions about reforming specific sectors such as public assistance to narrowing the scope of national responsibility for individual welfare.

It is of course possible that there will be very little change once the parties confront the realities of what is proposed, the enormity of the dislocation proposed. We choose to discuss the issues as if the change movement is serious. This can be a time of opportunity. Welfare advocates can be at the cusp of change rather than adjusting after others do all the innovating. Developing an alternative-response strategy requires understanding of the underlying causes for voter dissatisfaction as well as of the way the current system has evolved. The issue is how to preserve basic national as well as community responsibilities while restructuring them to overcome the most serious flaws in a way that is consistent with an era of public demand for effective but limited government, fairness, and respect for constraints on public resources and public spending. This strategy could produce an alternative to more radical proposals to dismantle the present system or to deny the need for change.

The task is important because so much of the public debate has been about costs and waste, whereas the real problems are the changes in the underlying economic conditions that have persisted for at least twenty years, worsening the economic position of at least half the population—despite an overall optimistic outlook—obscured by the inappropriate use of averages to report national income distribution.

Thus far, welfare advocates have tended to take for granted public and political support for ever-expanding social programs. It is the purpose of this analysis to understand why that can no longer be taken for granted. First, we will examine the powerful pressures for change, especially the economic foundations. Then we will review how and why we achieved the past exponential increase in social welfare spending and why the increase has slowed. Finally, we will take a look at the basic core of principles regarding federal responsibility plus feasible areas for reconstruction that will not abandon those principles.

ECONOMIC FOUNDATIONS FOR DISCONTENT AND A DEMAND FOR CHANGE

The dominant belief of the voter in America is that of the production by the private sector of both jobs and adequate wage income as the essential foundation for opportunity to realize the aspirations of all citizens. Social welfare, which was originally designed to insure against deficiencies in this private function, has now been vastly expanded as a social welfare system, making it and government easy targets for criticism, thus diverting public attention and understanding from the root causes of economic discontent. It is essential that future social welfare strategy change its focus by addressing the root causes of inequity, including the defects in functioning of the private economic sector. Some facts pointing in this direction include:

1. For the past twenty years, the real incomes of family wage earners have declined at all levels—blue collar, white collar, and executive. For at least half the population, life has become less and less rewarding, or secure, or hopeful. Downward mobility now, or for children of the future, has become a common fear. The unanticipated growth in single-parent families with only one wage earner, usually a woman, has exacerbated the situation by further depressing average family incomes.

2. The workplace has become more uneven in the distribution of its rewards. Those with the highest skills, as defined by a service not a goods-manufacturing economy or by the high technological value added in production (in economic terms) to compete with producers in the global market, have fairly well-paying prospects, but they live with the uncertainty of frequent workplace change, the need to constantly upgrade skills, or change in employment. The new electronic and information age has relatively few very highly paid jobs and many, many modest- or low-paying jobs which are constantly changing too.

3. Industrial organization relies less on a stable core of workers and more on contingent workers hired for short terms and with minimal benefits.

4. Gross and average economic indicators conceal this trend by averaging the incomes of the top 5 percent of wage earners (more than $200,000 annually) with those of the lowest earners. The resulting average looks fair, not bad, but it obscures the gross disparities between the number of income losses and the number of income gains. Average wages and 60 percent of family incomes, adjusted for inflation, have been dropping slowly for twenty years (*The New York Times*, April 17, 1995).

5. As technology raises productivity (more output with smaller or equal labor force), the gains are badly distributed. Almost all productivity gains in the economy (with slower than historic GNP growth) have gone to the top one-half of the income population at the same time that the lowest 25 percent have had real-dollar decline (Krugman 1994). Plans to cut public spending focus most attention on welfare benefits, about 10 percent of the fiscal problem, while over $265 billion of tax benefits to corporations are usually overlooked (*Economist* 1994), as are tax benefits accruing to middle-class and affluent families.

6. The loss of jobs with adequate wages, the shift to lower-paid work, the risk of repeated disemployment, and long-term unemployment threaten what has historically been the prime means for ensuring personal dignity and self-respect and creating a personal identity in a market economy. Adequate earned income is a prime means of maintaining the optimism upon which growth of the last decades has been based. Likewise, the perceived loss or decline in opportunity is threatening. Perhaps 20 percent of the adult population is redundant in the market

economy, including unemployed youth and early retirees. The putative base for individual and family security and for citizenship lies in jobs produced by the private economy. The growing loss of economic security is one factor, not the only one, contributing to families under stress, to disorganization, to alienation, and quite likely to minority youth resorting to withdrawal or violence (unemployment for this subpopulation is at nearly 40 percent). Compounding this situation is the fact that current economic tendencies have also eroded the consumption capacity of a large part of the population simultaneous with a general rise in social and consumer expectations. Reduced opportunities in an age of rising expectations and competition constitute a volatile mixture.

7. Both political parties accept the private marketplace as the main engine to produce jobs. The reported increase in new jobs has occurred mainly in low-paying service jobs or in highly competitive small enterprises where the failure rate is very high and work is either short term, part time, or contingent on temporary contracts between primary and secondary employers.

8. The failure of policy makers to hold the private sector responsible for this eroding economic base or for taking action to reverse recent trends presents the most serious dilemma. In all fairness, the growth in tax-financed employment (e.g., defense industries, larger numbers of police and firefighters, growth in public education and health care), an expanded social welfare system, and public-goods construction have obscured the weakening of the market economy during this period and its declining ability to produce sufficient well-paying jobs. This failure to lay the responsibility where it belongs leads to the charge that government is to blame followed by the urge to reduce government efforts and to privatize. Neither political party has found a way to see to it that adequate jobs are produced by the private sector. Vigorous efforts to this end appear to threaten other aspects of the network of interlocking interest groups upon which each party depends.

EVOLUTION OF THE CURRENT SYSTEM

The Great Depression Era

How did the present complex system, under so much scrutiny today, evolve? Was that evolution appropriate for its time, but now that the times have so changed fundamental rethinking is called for? It helps social welfare advocates to recall how radical the turnabout in government responsibility was that took place in the 1930s, during the first term of President Franklin D. Roosevelt. That turnabout was a complete reversal, shifting traditional responsibilities from the states and localities to Washington and the national government.

In the 1930s, the depression resulted not only in the financial insolvency of individuals and families but also of state and local governments as they tried to give economic relief to those who had lost jobs and were without any income. In addition, six thousand banks failed, wiping out the savings and other assets families and the elderly had set aside for emergencies and old age. Between 25 and 30 percent of the population was forced to subsist on public relief.

When President Roosevelt took office in 1933, his primary goal was to restore the economy and put people back to work. The strategy guiding his administration's policies and programs can be described as one of "relief, restoration, and reform"; however, at the core of all the New Deal programs was the desire to improve the economic conditions of the nation via employment-based policies. Toward that end, the federal government (1) distributed a billion dollars to states to help with the costs of emergency relief, (2) created a host of economic stimulation programs and farm subsidies, and (3) funded numerous public works and building projects to give employment to the able bodied for whom there was no other work available. For the longer term, the Roosevelt administration designed a contributory social insurance system designed to give basic protection to workers and their families against loss of income due to known hazards: (1) involuntary but temporary unemployment, (2) death of the wage earner, or (3) retirement.

The primary goal of the programs authorized by the Social Security Act of 1935—Unemployment Insurance (UI) and Old Age/Survivors Insurance (OASI)—was to protect wage earners (then mainly men) and their families. However, New Deal planners also recognized the necessity for the federal government of helping states to finance the costs of public relief programs for individuals and families not then eligible for, nor ever likely to become vested in, the social insurance programs. To accomplish this, the Social Security Act of 1935 authorized federal financial participation in a system of state-administered public welfare programs (i.e., Aid for the Aged, Aid for the Blind, and Aid for Dependent Children). The rationale for the federal government sharing with states the costs of public assistance for the aged, blind, disabled, and economically dependent children was the conviction that it would become a decreasing financial responsibility. It was widely believed that when the social insurance programs matured most retired or disabled workers and children living in families without a wage earner would be eligible for Old/Age/Disability/Survivors benefits and therefore not need public relief. There was no provision for federal financial assistance for poor relief or for social services (except for a modest crippled children's program). The basic principles of the changes signified by the Social Security Act of 1935 could serve as a starting point for both the defenders of the present system and proponents of welfare change were it not for the fact that in the ensuing years up to 1970 the scope of federal responsibility was expanded by rising expectations and a belief that the quality of life for everyone could be both raised and protected from economic risk.

The "Golden Years" of Exponential Growth: 1942–1980

By the common measure of dollars expended, the growth experienced during the period from 1942 to 1980 was impressive. Between 1950 and 1980, total public (and especially federal) expenditures for all forms of social welfare increased from $23 billion to $493 billion in *constant dollars*, or nearly twenty-one-fold (2,100 percent). Per capita spending in constant dollars increased 340 percent. Public spending for social welfare as a per-cent of gross domestic product (GDP), i.e., all goods and services produced, grew from 8.9 percent in 1950 to 18.7 percent in 1980. The federal share nearly tripled from 4 percent to 11.5 percent, and local tax-spending share increased from 4.9 percent to 7.2 percent. Such percentage increases were influenced by other shifts in public budgets, such as the relative decline in military spending after the Korean and Vietnam Wars, but the dollar in-creases remain impressive. Between 1965 and 1974 the *annual rate* of in-crease in federal-only spending on welfare ranged from a high of 18 percent in 1965 to 15 percent in 1970, a low of 5 percent in 1973, and 8 percent in 1974—all higher than the increase in GNP or cost-of-living indices for the period.

During the Cold War, and at least until the Vietnam War, it was feasible for government to pay for both guns and butter without adding new federal taxes. This arrangement was possible because, since 1913, the federal gov-ernment has relied on revenues from a progressive income tax (Hansan 1982). Under this progressive revenue structure, tax payments rose faster than the taxpayer's income, and a rapidly growing economy produced more than sufficient revenues with which to underwrite an exponential increase in the social welfare system with many constantly proliferating branches. These actions reinforced our national sense that America's resources were boundless, that progress in improving conditions of life for all had few limitations due to our science and vigor and an abundance of natural re-sources.

Following World War II, the GI Bill of Rights brought thousands of working poor and minorities into the higher education system and laid the basis for a greatly expanded middle class. Federal funds supported the building of a system of interstate highways; the expansion of defense in-dustries, often located in the hitherto impoverished South and West; new construction of hospitals in all parts of the nation to improve health care; and a national system for health research and technological research in the Pentagon. Collectively these initiatives injected billions of construction dol-lars for jobs and science dollars for technological change. During the 1960s, federal funds were also allocated to provide health care for retired and disabled workers and to help states finance the costs of better health care for the poor. Tax expenditures were allocated, too, for agricultural subsi-dies, the military and defense industries, and higher education programs for students of all income levels, along with a variety of housing subsidies and building programs. National tax dollars pumped a trillion and more dollars into the economy. And federal funds also contributed to job creation, if not goods production, by expanding the number of public employees in, for instance, police and fire departments, road construction and water supply, prisons, and so on.

The entire population benefitted directly or indirectly from this infusion of federal funds for corporate welfare, expanded social benefits, and assorted public goods. The period has come to be seen as a kind of "Golden Age" during which a middle-class welfare state of sorts developed. Levels of well-being increased for the majority of the population. Increasing productivity and GNP growth combined with limited increases in taxes and, later, more borrowing, tempered any pain due to the costs. The situation was not unique to America. Eric Hobsbaum's new history of the era, *The Age of Extremes*, uses the same term to describe conditions in most of the industrial world.

Creation of a Middle-Class Welfare State

Continuing for almost four decades, this environment imperceptibly led advocates to believe that the nation was committed to an almost unlimited reservoir of both public backing and financial resources to support continuous increase in social welfare programming—increasing the value of benefits, the number and type of benefits, and the entitled populations. Periodic efforts to limit social welfare spending were usually seen as temporary aberrations from the long-term growth trend. Confidence in the growth in social welfare was part of the broader national conviction that the nation's survival, its well-being and its strength, lay both in continuous growth which could be assured by continuous innovation from science and technology—the social investment concept—and in wider inclusion of all citizens in the benefits of this growth. Such growth and expansion became the expected norm of life.

By the 1990s, the economic position of almost everyone, and of every major economic institution and voluntary organization, was improved as a result of the receipt of some public funds via contracts, grants, subsidies, loans, benefits, employment, or direct tax benefits. The evidence is clear that at least half the adult population (excluding dependents) receive some or all of their income from these public sources. There are 3 million federal employees and over 2 million military personnel (despite real reductions in their numbers in recent years). There are over 2 million police and related employees plus other state and local uniformed employees and teachers (increased about 30 percent in the past ten years). There are about 700,000 postal employees and 6 to 7 million people employed in education, not all in a public system.

In industry, 123 billion tax dollars annually almost completely support military procurement and research. Other industries depend in part on this procurement. About $9 billion subsidize farm production. There are countless smaller subsidies and purchases coming out of tax funds that flow into large and small business and manufacturing for various good, and less good, economic reasons.

In 1994, over 42 million social security beneficiaries collected an estimated $300 billion in benefits, averaging $600 a month. Three million temporarily unemployed workers received benefits averaging $174 a month. Four million state and local civil employees depend in part on their state tax benefits. Three million retired federal civil servants have their own publicly financed social security system, which yields an average pension of $1,500 a month. Elected public officials, legislators, and retired military personnel have more-generous-than-average pensions, often enhanced by additional pensions (i.e., double and triple dipping). None of this income is perceived as welfare, although it is entirely based on taxes.

Health care is a major American industry which receives, overall, about 40 percent of its revenue from taxes via Medicare and Medicaid. Some portion of this revenue ends up in the paychecks of the 13 million health care employees. Tax benefits in the form of deductions for home purchase or mortgage guarantees amount to at least $5 billion a year to private home owners. Finally, means-tested public assistance or "relief": 10 to 11 million beneficiaries of Aid for Families with Dependent Children (AFDC) and Supplemental Security Income (SSI, formerly Aid to the Blind, Aid to the Disabled, and Aid to the Aged) receive benefits averaging between $358 and $381 a month. In addition, $1,378,000,000 in food stamps went to some 27 million recipients in 1992 as a supplement to inadequate or unavailable relief from other sources. In sum, the system of social welfare has become an important component in the economic well-being of perhaps 80 percent of the population and for significant private economic organizations via cash or credits from tax sources. Compare this with the approximately 10 percent of the population receiving means-tested public assistance or relief.

The "Free Ride" Ends

The so-called golden era is both of recent origin and built on a fragile foundation. Basic American beliefs about welfare, the limited role of government, and maximum individual responsibility were integral components of the founding of the nation. About 150 years elapsed before the growth took off, during which there was painfully slow development of any federal responsibility for welfare. Welfare before 1935 was built on the English Poor Law system and usually administered by state and local governments. From the Civil War to 1935, the federal government's welfare role was limited to health care for veterans and seamen, distributing public lands to open up the West (as a kind of income distribution), and operating the U.S. Children's Bureau.

Beginning in about 1972, underlying economic difficulties began to take hold. The economy slowed down as did GNP growth. Old social problems of poverty increased despite publicly financed antipoverty efforts. A score of new social concerns were added: Anxiety about jobs and security for the future increased among the newly enlarged middle class—at least for those living in newly achieved but tenuous comfort. Taxes at all levels of government began to be more visible as a substantial share of take-home pay. Inflation made the services called for by higher expectations—medical care and health insurance, child care, education, home ownership or rental—more costly. Two-wage-earner incomes became a necessity, while changed social mores produced more single-parent and one-wage-earner families with marginal incomes. Those who felt secure indulged in many more luxuries—a vacation home, cars for each family member, and the like. Racial tensions and discrimination did not subside rapidly enough, and street and household crime increased, as did substance abuse. A scary epidemic of AIDS, with all its human and economic costs, went along with growing moral discomfort about sexual freedoms and unwed teenage mothers. At the same time, concepts of individual freedom and choice continued to expand, leading to demands for public action to defend them. The gap between current national income and spending grew, increasing public and private debt, the interest on which further increased the strain on national and personal budgeting. And the gap between the worse- and better-off populations widened until it became the largest in the industrial world.

Over the course of twenty years, public dissatisfaction grew with what political parties and government programs were producing in relation to the sums spent on them. It is now no longer just too much spending, but spending seen as supporting improper, undesirable, antisocial, or immoral behaviors. Many factors contributed to the expansion of the public sector and to the growing gap between the better and worse off. However, the public has not focused on the complex web of causes but has, instead, opted to blame perceived failures on ill-defined government policies. Thus we come to the post–golden age, when disillusion and discontent foster a powerful civic demand for change—but with few answers to the question, change to what?

WHAT IS TO BE DONE?

The underlying social and economic changes of the past fifty years (only a few of which have been touched upon here) raise the prospect that the complex partnership principles and aims which have characterized the social welfare programs of the United States since 1935 are in need of review.

After fifty years of development in one direction it is not unreasonable, although it is very painful, to reexamine doctrines long accepted as immutable. At the present time, the most discussed solution is that of cutting social programs, taxes, and tax spending, and devolving many responsibilities (with or without federal fiscal backing) to either the private sector or to state and local governments. Implicitly this would involve a dismantling of some of the nation's safeguards against disruptions sometimes caused by social and economic conditions.

Supporters of the current system have thus far responded by documenting who will be injured by any proposed dismantling or devolution while arguing for more federal funding, without as yet proposing any structural changes in the way currently appropriated funds are being used. The real issue is that the proposals for radical change do not make it clear that if they are carried out, a wholly new system will have to be created to replace the national/local safety-net programs now in place—one presumably based in whole or in large part on either private enterprise or state and local government. There is no logical reason why such an approach should not be tried, except for the evidence that the present set of arrangements grew out of dissatisfactions in the 1930s when there were no federally supported safety-net programs. The difficulty is that almost all interest groups already are significant beneficiaries of the status quo. How much will they want to give up for an uncertain new regime. If changes are undertaken with the recognition that rebuilding a new support structure of any publicly acceptable shape will take time and may not save money (it may be more costly), then it can be done. On the other hand, if it is assumed that economic dependency should be treated more harshly or that somehow the private economy will magically reverse itself and boom again, and continue to boom (in the unbalanced form it has taken over the past twenty years?), then the nature of the transition will be more divisive and contentious than ever.

Modifying, Not Dissolving, Government Responsibilities for Social Welfare

The first step for believers in national responsibility for any form of a social welfare system is to confront rather than deny the fact that changed conditions require some change in the ideas which have governed the current system's evolution over the past sixty years. Advocates can accept that all is not well but that many elements of the past have too great a value for society to jettison without careful thought about alternatives. We suggest a few large but practical tasks which advocates can undertake now to create their own agenda for the next era, an agenda which lies between denial (or defense of the past) and hasty dismantling.

1. Which core functions should be retained as part of a national responsibility in both administration and funding of a social welfare system and which others might be devolved in whole or in part to states or the private sector?

2. For those functions fully retained as a core, do they need to be improved by restructuring, and how? For example, as a starting point, the initial premises of the 1935 Social Security Act might be used along with the national government's obligation to protect its citizens, not only in war, but as an employer of last resort. For the present, this last suggestion assumes that the primary, preferred source of income for achieving individual and national well-being continues to be based upon employment at an adequate wage in the private sector. A first function is thus, not providing income, but seeing to it that jobs with adequate pay are available and accessible for all who are able to work.

3. Which of the *add-on* functions that accrued over the past five decades might be drastically modified or devolved to others within the historic and current triad of national, state/local, and private sectors? For example, even if some social welfare functions are assumed by others, the national government retains a responsibility for last-resort monitoring and potential emergency action. The national government's ability to act to protect citizens when particular groups are grossly neglected or abused, or in cases of disasters beyond the capacity of other levels of government, is an essential part of nationhood. How will advocates choose to define this national ability and structure it into an altered paradigm of modified and reduced national authority which political, and especially economic, circumstances seem to require?

4. Review those major federal programs that most agree do not perform well enough but could be reformed in order to regain public approval. What structural changes can be proposed within present constraints?

5. There is a need for fresh thinking about how devolved responsibilities, wherever that may happen, can best be carried out in states or in the private sector. Is there a middle-road template for guidance as responsibilities are shifted to other levels of government or to new organizations? Or will advocates recast their next efforts, emphasizing working in a decentralized manner with numerous state entities and newly formed citizen groups currently outside the national advocacy constituency, all of which may be working at rebuilding a new social support system?

Groping to Redefine the Scope of Federal Government Responsibilities

Proposals for redefining the scope of the federal government's responsibilities begin to cluster in groups representing priority preferences of various analysts, but none of the priority clusters clearly preclude any of the others.

1. The federal government has a core obligation to secure and enhance the economy of the nation. Since most economic activity is in the private sector, the

clearest function for the national government is assurance that work is available for the able bodied at adequate wages. GNP growth can yield increased income for the social needs of those agreed upon as properly dependent due to illness, age, or other incapacity without onerous taxation or inflation if effectively managed. This function is central to any others which may be added. It conforms to the historic value of personal independence, which is only possible in an industrial society when one has an adequate earned income to sustain a family. If all able-bodied citizens are at work they also maintain the consumer demand necessary for the GNP to reflect healthy growth. Working adults are in a position to pay for some or all needed social and health services, giving them more choice and less dependence on others or public taxes. Those whose income is insufficient to cover essential needs can still act as full partners in deciding where public action or provision is necessary, for whom, and with what degree of sharing. This, if achieved, lays a solid foundation for public policy in many other contentious areas.

2. More technically, the federal government is essential for developing and maintaining national databases on which the daily functioning of most private sector and state and local government activities depend. No single state can develop the national data essential for insurance, economic development, investment, and public health as well as for use by industry and commerce. Essential databases have been developed by the government and require continuous upgrading as conditions change. Some of these are threatened by less thoughtful efforts to reduce public spending simply in order to cut costs without measuring the damage. In a related area, some scientific research can only be conducted by funding and collaboration across state boundaries, which require some central decision mechanism for efficient choice making. The national databases are also essential for research centers in industry, universities, and independent research organizations as well as for independent researchers. All the above is necessary nationally regardless of the scope of devolved power or management from national government to the state or private sectors.

3. Federal monitoring of the nation's well-being may remain a core function. The expansion of federal responsibilities has been accompanied by complex data reporting and regulation to secure equity or uniformity or accountability in the use of public funds. With extensive devolution, the function of data may change from control to monitoring. If there is to be a recognizable nation, then some supraordinate authority needs to be available for help in cases of great, unpredictable catastrophes. In a vast continent where resources are unevenly distributed, state capacities vary, and this can lead to extreme neglect or abuse of some populations, to the neglect of basic public health, or to malnutrition, any of which can threaten the national economy, security, or stability. A change in responsibility can mean that a national authority needs either a basis or mandate to intervene when necessary. Information about serious flaws and defects is a basis for responsible citizen decision making to authorize action.

From the very beginning of the nation, as seen in the *Federalist Papers*, the Constitution, and the Bill of Rights, a distinction was made between the powers of each state and the needs of all the people. The national government is the primary mechanism, as built into the founding documents of our country, to safeguard the well-being of all citizens, rather than depending solely on what separate states do or fail to do for their residents. There may lie ahead a major shift from the extensive reliance on Washington that has evolved in recent decades, but the shift must include a national safety-net mechanism for those times when crises overwhelm local or private capacities. A monitoring mechanism is essential for such a reserve or fallback function. The major difference would be abandoning the conviction that the uniformity of some kind of national minimum should be imposed or developed everywhere.

We believe the minimum core for national responsibility consists of (1) the economy, especially work and adequate wages for all able-bodied residents; (2) monitoring and its attendant mechanisms of building and maintaining national databases. Other core functions may be added and have been advanced by others. Scocpol (1995), for example, notes, in urging that the well-being of families and children be considered a national responsibility, that national policy is strongest when it reaches across many class, population, economic, and ethnic groupings to meet needs perceived by most citizens. The protection of public health, as distinct from financing access to doctors and hospitals, is another core responsibility often mentioned, as is personal physical security for all citizens. The latter ranges from a military force to protect the physical integrity of the nation to reduction of crimes against persons or property. There are differences about the scale and form of national involvement, but sovereignty requires some such functional responsibility. What may develop are national policies and programs to address the needs of broad populations—large majorities which represent shared interests of differing economic, social, and ethnic groups.

The foregoing is not yet a platform. The following is a list of various other program areas also being debated. Out of these areas a middle path might be crafted to redefine the scope and roles of the federal government in an era of political and fiscal constraints and the fundamental challenge to change.

1. The maze of national programs which address, piecemeal, work needs, mainly of the poor, the disabled, the aged, and various minorities. Alongside these are numerous subsidies and programs targeted to industry and agriculture which often are intended to produce employment or encourage research in technologies designed to improve productivity. This complex of programs and subsidies does not constitute a policy to encourage the development of work opportunities and decent pay levels so much as it responds to diverse special-interest concerns with diverse motives such as disincentives to public dependency and incentives to retire early from the labor force via pensions.

2. Income provision for those in need, ranging from AFDC, SSI, and food stamps

to those receiving unemployment insurance, disability insurance, and workers' compensation insurance.

3. Social Security, mainly the retirement program. Although exempted from current debate, this program will soon have to be discussed. It faces dramatically changed conditions since it was initiated: demographic changes, changes in longevity, changes in the nature of family structures, the new place of women in the workforce, and so on.

4. Health insurance. Recently debated intensively, this is still an issue about which no acceptable consensus has been reached on coverage of the uninsured, the escalating costs of health provision, and the extent of personal responsibility.

5. Education. Although not a major national responsibility, the education system is in serious trouble in major cities at least and, more broadly, in the equipping of a workforce with the tools suitable for global competition or for entry into better-paying jobs that become available.

6. Numerous small social service programs, often staffed by social and mental health workers, which address serious social problems such as child neglect and abuse, juvenile delinquency, crime, and personal care of the chronically disabled and handicapped. These often are folded into larger programs, such as health care, where they perform case-management functions to link numerous overlapping programs. To date, their results have been disappointing.

CONCLUSION

This excursion into the complexity of the current temper of the voting public and of well-organized political forces has considered proposals to sharply reduce the role of the national government in social welfare and to sharply reduce the cost of all public services beginning with public welfare. Discussion has concentrated on the challenge to, or opportunity for, advocates of social welfare to design a middle path between dismantling our national system and defending it as is. The challenge comes from the belief that the current dismantling effort is a crude way to respond to public wishes for change in the way national and local communities handle serious social problems. That effort has thus far avoided confronting the probable basis for much of the distress. Work and the responsibility of the private sector are major tasks for welfare advocates to confront, and these have not been at the center of their activity so far. Beyond that, there is an opportunity, after fifty years on one path of national growth, to redefine the essential core of national responsibilities that cannot be devolved or abandoned in order to better meet current conditions in the nation.

This middle road could be developed. It may involve paying attention to what it would take to rebuild a less centralized system of social supports fit for the unpredictable changes flooding into society that is also acceptable to voters and reasonably matches rising expectations and limited means. Social welfare advocates may not yet be ready for this, but something like it will have to be tackled if the current national social support system, on which so much of the population and so many private economic institutions now depend, is to be altered partially or dismantled either to make it more effective or to change the control mechanism for the allocation and distribution of national resources.

REFERENCES

Bureau of Labor Statistics. 1993. *Yearly wages of men and women, 1979–1992.* Washington, D.C.: U.S. Labor Department.

Chen, Y. P. 1993. A three-legged stool: A new way to fund long-term care. In *Care in the long term,* 54–70. Washington, D.C.: Institute of Medicine, National Academy Press.

Drucker, Peter. 1994. The age of social transformation. *Atlantic Monthly,* November, 53–80.

———. 1995. Really re-inventing government. *Atlantic Monthly,* February, 49–61.

Economist. 1994. Inequality: For richer, for poorer. November 5, 19–21.

———. 1995. The slippery slope. July 30, 19–22.

———. 1995. Voters, blame thyselves. October 29, 18.

Goudzwaard, Bob. 1994. *Who cares? Poverty and the dynamics of responsibility: An outsider's contribution to the American debate on poverty and welfare.* Washington, D.C.: The Center for Public Justice. 16 February.

Hansan, John E. 1982. The role of government in American social welfare. In *Human services on a limited budget,* edited by Robert Agranoff. Practical Management Series. Washington, D.C.: International City Management Association.

Hobsbaum, Eric. 1994. *The age of extremes.* New York: Pantheon Books.

Kilborn, Peter. 1995. Up from welfare: It's harder and harder. *The New York Times,* 16 April, E1–2.

Krugman, Paul. 1994. *The age of diminished expectations.* Cambridge, Mass.: Harvard University Press.

National Committee for Employment Policy. 1994. More men in prime not working. *The New York Times,* 1 December, D15.

The New York Times. 1994. Taxpayers are angry. They're expensive too. Citing data from Congressional Budget Office, Internal Revenue Service, Office of Management and Budget, Employment Benefit Research Institute. 20 November, E5.

Scocpol, Theda. 1995. *Social policy in the U.S.* Princeton, N.J.: Princeton University Press.

Shapiro, Robert. 1995. *Cut and invest to compete and win.* Washington, D.C.: Progressive Policy Institute.

Silverstone, Barbara, and Robert Binstock, eds. 1994. Reconsidering public policies on aging. *The Gerontologist* 34, no. 6:734–741.

Statistical abstract of the United States. 1994. Washington, D.C.: U.S. Government Printing Office.

Wolff, Edward N. 1995. *Top heavy: A study of increasing inequality of wealth in America.* New York: Twentieth Century Fund.

Chapter 2

Employment Challenges

S. M. Miller

After the dropping of the atomic bomb on Japan, Albert Einstein reportedly said that everything had changed in the world except our way of thinking about it. In a less dramatic vein, one could say that the same thing is happening in the employment and welfare arenas today. Should we embrace the changes, attempt to moderate them, oppose them, protect past achievements, push for the consideration of long-standing unrealized proposals, leapfrog to the innovational? Even if the answer is all of the above, questions remain: Which changes merit which responses and to what extent? Should we work within current political limitations or advocate solutions that now appear politically taboo? I do not offer answers to these questions in this chapter; I merely have them in mind.

My approach is to study broad employment issues but, to a major extent, from the particular perspective of those in means-tested programs, like the recently deceased federal Aid for Families with Dependent Children (AFDC) program, that now mainly reside at the state level. The two parts of this dual outlook are not consistently examined separately because I assume that the conditions and prospects of those receiving means-tested assistance are tied to the situation of the general labor force.

WHY EMPLOYMENT?

One does not have to be a Freudian, a Marxist, a political conservative, or a union leader to believe that work is a major anchor of people's lives. As Dostoyevsky would have said today, to destroy a person one need only destroy the meaning of his or her work. That statement does not specify the character of the "work" that is a personal and social anchor. Unpaid work for the household or community can be work-as-anchor, but questions about work issues today are mainly about paid labor.

I assume that paid employment is a crucial component of social policy. Indeed, I have long argued that *the most important social policy is national economic policy*. It determines the level of unemployment and wages (and thereby the number in need and the level of transfers because of the never relinquished principle of less eligibility: those that work should have higher incomes than those that receive public assistance). National economic policy also affects the tax revenues which could be used to help those in need. Further, high unemployment rates and/or economic insecurity affect people's willingness to help others. (In the 1992 presidential election, voters reported that they were more affected by what they perceived as general economic conditions than they were by their own immediate economic conditions.)

What are the arguments against emphasizing employment policies when attempting to reform social policy? Prominent are three critiques: (a) antimaterialism, (b) low prospects of achieving full employment, and (c) the punitive threats to those receiving public assistance.

The antimaterialist argument is associated with Claus Offe and some of the German Greens as well as their American counterparts. Stressing the importance of work maintains, perhaps intensifies, the desire for goods and services, leading to overwork, environmental destruction, commercialism, and antihuman values rather than to a more decent and sustainable way of life. (The extreme attack on the importance of work is Bertrand Russell's 1935 essay "In Praise of Idleness," which contends that "there is far too much work done in the world [and] immense harm is caused by the belief that work is virtuous" [*Economist* 1996].) This perspective is especially pertinent in the United States, which consumes a vastly disproportionate share of the world's irreplaceable resources thereby threatening the long-term possibilities for advancing the standard of living in countries whose people now live at very low levels.

Also involved in this view is a redefinition of what is deemed desirable in a standard (the expectations) and plane (the actual level) of living. This perspective demands reconceptualizing standard economic indicators like gross domestic product or the household command over resources as well. For instance, in this day of many two-earner and moonlighting households, economic well-being should be related to the time involved in attaining a certain household income. Time is a resource even, or especially, for people in public assistance programs, who have to manage visits to a variety of governmental offices as well as deal with the daily struggles resulting from inadequate resources.

Adopting this antimaterialist and environmentalist outlook would require convincing the American public that it would be happier and more content without cars, VCRs, word processors, or baggies and detergents. In any case, the antimaterialist proposal is a long-term conversion job, though it could be argued that it is important to strike a blow for it now.

A second issue faces those who call for a cultural change but do not hold an antimaterialist view. Reducing, say, aggregate hours of work without a compensating decline in the plane of living requires increasing either employers' labor costs or governmental transfers in order to maintain current levels of consumption. (Reducing taxes to increase after-tax income leads to fewer public resources for those in distress.) Some advocate a basic income guarantee for all as a human right. Not only would such a guarantee require an economy operating at a level that could provide a decent minimum for all, but it also assumes the unlikely political acceptance of higher taxes and large transfers (especially unlikely if African-Americans were perceived as major beneficiaries). Income guarantee programs receive much less political support than do programs that promote employment (Oliver and Shapiro 1995). Today, a guaranteed income is not on the political map (except in the guise of a low-level earned-income tax credit for the working poor).

The second critique is that an employment policy is unachievable, that we face a "jobless future" (in the words of the title of a book by Stanley Aronowitz and William D. Fazio) or, at least, a far-from-full-employment economy. (More than a few economists finesse the issue by defining a non-inflationary rate of employment—perhaps a 6 or 7 percent rate of unemployment—as full employment or, even better for public relations, as the "natural" rate of unemployment. The Clinton–Federal Reserve record of low inflation combined with an unemployment rate of below 6 percent challenges the Friedmanite normalization of high unemployment levels.) This political doubting Thomas skepticism about the supply of jobs has much going for it. Certainly it will prevail if there is no insistent demand to improve the employment situation. Employment levels and conditions (wages, security, fringes) are not simple technological distillates; they are the products of worker and governmental actions. Failure to advocate the improvement of employment levels and working conditions will insure their deterioration as even high-profit firms reduce their labor forces, moderate wages, and contract fringe benefits.

The third critique revolves around public assistance programs. An employment-oriented approach, as in the 1996 dismantling of AFDC, is going to be punitive, requiring states to have most of those in means-tested cash programs working after a limited stint in such programs. The outcomes will be onerous: more difficulty in getting needed assistance and requirements to "work off" grants, frequently in meaningless tasks that burden already heavily burdened mothers, pushing them into low-paying, low-fringe-benefit jobs without the social support (e.g., child care, medical benefits) needed to facilitate working for a sustainable income.

The assault on welfare and the pressure to force adult recipients (principally mothers) into just any kind of employment are now welfare law and lore. Those who would defend the interests of current and potential recipients of means-tested benefits have to deal with employment issues. Ignoring them and simply resisting all work requirements will not be effective today. A counterprogram has to be proposed and fought for.

The situation of low-income households should be considered as part of general employment questions rather than isolated and stigmatized as a "welfare problem." *An employment-centered policy should not focus on public assistance recipients but on the general issue of improving employment levels and work conditions for all.*

The challenge will be to make employment and employment conditions prime issues without denigrating welfare and its recipients. Even if one discounts the trendiness of much of the postmodernist discourse on discourse, it is important to understand that the language used will be very significant. A high degree of consciousness about the framing of employment and welfare issues will be critical (Fraser and Gordon 1994).

THE ECONOMIC-POLITICAL APPROACH

Advocates' broad orientation should be to present the issue of employment of those on means-tested programs as part of the wider question of the fate of the working poor, lower-paid workers, less attractive workers, contingent workers, part-time workers, the economically insecure—in short, the growing majority of the labor force which is in bad economic shape or threatened.

Political and economic segregation or isolation of those receiving means-tested benefits stigmatizes them, lowers the quality of the programs in which they are enrolled, and contracts the time in which results are expected to become evident. Their employment prospects are tied in with those who are economically endangered but not receiving "welfare" (or whatever states will call their AFDC programs).

An insistence on decreasing the overall unemployment rate is, by itself, an inadequate platform. Work arrangements have changed dramatically with the growth of contingent and part-time work, contracted-out operations, low-wage and low-fringed jobs, and general employment insecurity. The quality of jobs is a prime concern.

The policy goal should be to promote employment generally and improve the quality of low-pay/low-fringed jobs in particular. Other issues that would need to be addressed in a broad attempt to improve the situation of the bottom half of the labor force include discrimination, the regularization of work, and job security.

GENERAL ECONOMIC POLICIES

General or macroeconomic policies are of great importance for what happens to employment and wages. It was once said that the United States needed a good five-cent cigar. Today, it needs a new economic paradigm. Currently, the Keynesian model is only partially adequate.

Great economic and political shifts undermine Keynesian possibilities: "fine-tuning the economy" was a glittering '60s metaphor with a short life (although Federal Reserve Board chair Alan Greenspan is currently treated as Walter Heller incarnate, at least until the next crisis). A new American economy has appeared, transformed by the heightened rapidity of movements in capital and labor (for example, automobiles are now an international product, involving labor and parts from factories in a variety of countries). At the policy level, concern about inflation is high for it affects international competitiveness; national economic and employment growth are regarded as threats to long-term prospects and the bond market. The results are the limited growth of good jobs during economic expansion, increasing income inequities among employees, enormous growth and concentration of paper wealth, the decline of some bellwether industries and firms and the emergence or merger of others, the loss of the political flexibility to use federal fiscal and transfer policy to smooth the economy or promote growth, and the swelling of the importance of finance. (Progressive banker Robert Zevin makes a compelling case that the so-called nominal economy of interest rates, exchange rates, stock markets, and so on is more dominant in the overall economic situation than the so-called real economy of production and consumption.) These changes demand a radical rethinking of many Keynesian-type perspectives, at least in the American liberal versions.

The Keynesian outlook is not sufficient for today's situations, even if many elements of it are crucial. Implied in today's Keynesianism are the promotion of domestic demand (e.g., higher minimum wage, promotion of unionization, the earned income tax credit), low interest rates, perhaps a curb on imports and an increased tax progressivity, and a limit to the reductions in social programs for the working class, the middle class, and the poor. (I do not partake of the lumping together of everybody who is not labeled poor into the middle class [Miller and Ferroggiaro 1995].) The mantras of "revenue neutral" and zero deficits mean that fiscal policy cannot be used to expand or deflate the economy. Monetary policy, a broad brush, then becomes the main way of dampening inflationary forces or promoting growth. And that policy card is held by the Federal Reserve, pervious to the financial community and resistant to its congressional mandate to concern itself with employment levels as well as inflation rates.

States will be increasingly important in affecting consumption and investment. With the swing toward devolution to the states of many programs, their decisions will play a greater role in the governmental capacity to influence the economy's course. The federal role in affecting economic policies and outcomes will be diminished relative to that of the states. (By the late '40s, Harvey Perloff, influenced by the American Keynesian Alvin Hansen, was already stressing the affect of state and local expenditures on demand and on smoothing the business cycle.) Coordinating individual states' policies with those of the national government will be a major challenge. New approaches are in short supply.

Industrial and Regional Policies

One interesting suggestion would vary Federal Reserve interest-rate policies by region. These policies are affected by the national unemployment rate, which results from averaging the rates of high-unemployment states with those with low-unemployment states. A relatively low national unemployment rate would lead to Federal Reserve policies that did not benefit high-unemployment states. It is increasingly important to recognize that "Each state is in a unique economic situation and what would be correct for one is wrong for others." One way of doing that is for the Federal Reserve to have the power to lend money at low rates to those states which have high unemployment. The general point is that "our economic policies are still crude and undeveloped," especially for the economic and political conditions currently unfolding (Stoneman 1995).

Earlier in the post–World War II period, overall economic growth produced full-time jobs, rising wages and narrowed wage differentials. Today, that is not the case. Consequently, policy makers need to shift from being primarily or solely concerned with the overall rate of economic growth as measured by gross domestic product (GDP) to paying attention to the *content or composition of economic growth*. This new concern for the content of GDP would lead to the promotion of developing or expanding particular industries and regions. A variety of considerations would then enter into economic choices: employment prospects, wage levels, attributes of employees (e.g., skill level, gender, race), survivability, and the like.

Yes, this is an advocacy of instituting industrial policies, an idea which was "disappeared" from political and economic discourse in the Mondale campaign of 1984. In the current political scene, overt action to affect the composition of output is unlikely to be supported. Covertly, policies constantly affect the growth of particular industries (and political favoritism benefits particular corporations). For example, the business consultant supremo Peter Drucker (1993) opposes efforts at fine-tuning the economy, but if a depression occurs he favors an infrastructural expansion. Indeed, that is what the Eisenhower administration did in the so-called Defense Highway program, its Arthur F. Burns–inspired spur to economic growth and stability. Certainly military, space, health, education, public works, and other expenditures benefit particular industrial sectors and regions.

We do not regard these programs and expenditures as sectoral or regional policies because motivations and labels overshadow consequences. More generally, economic and social structures and policies inevitably have distributive consequences: their benefits and costs are not evenly spread over the population. (For example, anti-inflationary policies harm the last to be hired and those in low-wage jobs whose wages would improve in a high-expansion period. Those with fixed incomes, however, benefit from the policies.)

Since second- and third-order effects are the bread and butter of economic analysis, the opposition of many economists to industrial and regional policies must rest, at least in part, on the belief that (somewhat) unintended effects or unstated objectives are always more desirable than intentional efforts. This counterargument states that planned efforts usually fail and often are counterproductive. A classical reply to this view is that the negative consequences—such as waste, corruption, or misuse—of some industrial and regional policies are not an argument, as Aristotle taught, against their appropriate use. Unless, of course, one believes that American democracy leads to incorrigible recidivism.

Spending policies, tax breaks, and cash and noncash transfers do not distribute goods evenly over the economic landscape. Particular sectors or regions benefit or are neglected, perhaps even harmed. Such decisions are industrial, sectoral, or regional policies, whatever political rationale they are assigned or other purposes they may have. Industrial and regional policies could stimulate industries that are more likely to employ lower-skilled workers and discriminated-against groups or that lower the cost of living for the bottom quintile or third of the population.

I am not advocating a turning away from the promotion of general economic growth, but an effort to accompany general growth measures with more specific efforts to secure an expansion that does not neglect the interests of lower-income groups.

As states' spending grows relative to federal, they too will have to become even more concerned about who benefits from their activities. Indeed, states and localities have long been involved in some form of industrial policy, broadly defined. They offer tax breaks and various incentives, such as training subsidies, to encourage firms to locate plants in their area, and provide inducements to construct an office building or move a sports team into the region. The payment of bounties to develop a hi-tech industrial concentration is not unknown. The question that has been raised is, who benefits from the second-order effects of such subsidies and who loses? (Remember urban renewal as "Negro removal"?)

Obviously, most politicians (except when it benefits their constituents) and mainstream economists oppose overt industrial policies. Perhaps a new name is needed to relegitimate paying attention to the employment and distributive consequences of expenditures. ("*Relegitimate*" because in the last seventy years the United States has had, among many other similar endeavors, the Reconstruction Finance Corporation and the Tennessee Valley Authority.) At the present time, this shift may be more achievable in some states than at the federal level, though federally as well as locally enacted, big-city enterprise zones are small-scale regional (in both the geographic and financial sense) policies. Shakespeare was wrong to doubt the value in a name.

The general point is that those concerned with social policy not only have to be concerned with macroeconomic policies, but also with industrial and regional policies, whatever names provide cover for them.

Other Meso-Policies

A variety of middle-level policies are constantly available as a way of improving employment and wages, including raising the minimum wage, which is particularly important for low-wage workers; increasing employment by reducing hours of work; improving the earned income tax credit; protecting employees by expanding workers' rights to pensions, job security, and other employment benefits; enlarging targeted government employment programs as the government becomes "the employer of last resort" for some; promoting unionization, especially in low-wage sectors, which requires new approaches to organizing and to the structuring of labor organizations. This array of options strongly suggests that much can be done to improve the employment situation.

Social Policies and Employment

National policies providing basic security to all are needed, especially with the growth of contingent, part-time employment and contracted-out work relationships. In an effort to regularize work situations, some activities could be required of firms, others would require government funding and, sometimes, action. Improved job conditions would mesh the employment situation of those receiving or having recently received means-tested benefits with that of other workers. It is politically difficult to demand particular services for the former when many other employees do not have access to them.

Some form of health insurance (or a national health service) that guarantees adequate care for all is the main priority. Without such protection, the attraction of employment diminishes for those who have received means-tested medical benefits. Child care is another important service that requires government financing. Who runs the child-care service is less important than the government subsidies which make it available to all.

The availability of transportation is now a priority for social policy for it affects much of life, certainly including job possibilities. (The Poverty and Race Research Council is funding research which will be used in a Los Angeles case challenging that city's inadequate public transportation as an instance of racial discrimination. Could one also say class discrimination?) Improving accessibility would improve the job and everyday-life possibilities for many. Public subsidies to that end could make a significant difference.

With the decline in the percentage of the unemployed who receive unemployment insurance benefits, improving the unemployment insurance (UI) system should not be neglected. Those low in the employment queue and those in insecure jobs are subjected to regular bouts of unemployment and need UI benefits. Unfortunately, UI is likely to become a target of budget balancers and promoters of low-wage jobs.

With the diminution of the federal role that goes along with the devolution of social welfare, perhaps some states, counties, or cities will develop a decent level of basic benefits and services. They also might create new programs, as occurred in the 1920s and early 1930s when Wisconsin and New York State initiated programs that were later copied by other states and developed into national efforts during the New Deal.

Education has been increasingly termed an economic good, a contribution to the quality of human resources. Improving the educational development of those in families with low incomes and high stress would be an important economic step. It should also be a significant social step in providing for the beneficiaries a deeper understanding of the society in which they live. Unfortunately, education is increasingly vocationalized and narrowed, often to the end of attaining jobs which are not available.

MICROECONOMIC POLICIES

General, industrial, and regional policies will not be sufficient to expand the number of jobs available to low-skill workers. (Skill level is a relative and imprecise term subject to economic, technological, and organizational change as well as to tradition and public relations. The concept of "comparable worth" is a reaction to the perception that tasks at a similar level have been classified and recompensed differently, depending on the gender of the employee.) There is a great need to expand the number of jobs available to those unlikely to develop the capacity for high-skilled employment and to develop the capacities of the many who could advance.

I have already mentioned enterprise zones as one effort at employment creation. In the same family are community economic development efforts and Grameen Bank–type entrepreneurial loan programs. The Community Reinvestment Act presses banks to make loans in neglected localities, thereby supporting entrepreneurial activities and private investment in those areas. Targeting public works projects for low-income areas can also increase employment prospects. Offering inducements to private developers and companies to locate in low-income areas can have a similar effect.

Welfare-Employment Policies

The programs mentioned above are ways of increasing the supply of jobs in low-income areas. Another strategy is to make low-skill workers and those receiving means-tested benefits more attractive to employers by offering subsidies to those who hire them. My experience with Transitional Employment Enterprises (TEE) in Boston, the forerunner of America Works, is that a sizable amount of training and support is needed to make the program work. (A new Minneapolis program has an interesting twist: as the enterprise operating the program succeeds, it intends to provide stock in the enterprise to its graduates.)

Moving to decently paid employment from or with public assistance should be made easier, primarily by improving the social supports that come with that employment. Many in public assistance programs are not currently able to find jobs that provide sufficient income, health protection, and child care. The campaign for adequate jobs and social protection for all should be pushed. Then, the number of recipients volunteering for employment programs would probably be sufficient to reduce much of the political pressure for reducing the welfare rolls by indiscriminately forcing mothers into an unsympathetic and disadvantaged sector of the labor market. The 1996 welfare changes will force needy mothers to work. I support making it easier for low-income mothers to get and keep jobs which improve their plane of living. The difficulty—well-known to those willing to be informed—is that facilitating work in the general labor market by AFDC recipients will increase costs, at least in the short run.

Other Targeted Employment Policies

Other things that should be done to improve employment conditions include fighting discrimination; reducing credentialism that requires educational levels not actually necessary for a particular job; developing a much more effective training program than now exists—a really serious and coordinated system of job training and retraining; promoting the upgrading of employees. It is also important to improve the social situation in many inner-city areas. This may not have a clear connection to jobs (though Massey and Denton [1993] believe it does), but there is certainly some link between the two.

A RESEARCH ISSUE

A problem in policy deliberations is the uncertainty about the actual effects of programs and policies. On the basis of the enormous number of evaluation studies, would we have high confidence in recommending a series of programs? If the smallest doubt undermines confidence in the reliability of these voluminous reports, can it be that research efforts, as well as the process of policy development, need their own reevaluation? One area of neglect is the lack of attention paid to the quality of administration and leadership in conducting programs. The result of benefit-cost and other research approaches is to downplay or ignore administration, a common failing of policy innovators like Franklin D. Roosevelt and Lyndon Johnson that should not be continued by the model builders and evaluators of today.

CODA

In today's political and cultural climate, paid employment is an ascendant goal. We cannot divert our attention from it, at least not in the short run, while governmental spending is contracting and family budgets are strained. The political approach recommended here is to deal with the broad problems of employment and, in this context, to try to improve the situation of those in poor economic situations and with low job prospects. A variety of policies are available. The once-fond hope that "tight full employment" would solve all problems, including those of disadvantaged workers, is not realistic. Nor would such a goal solve all employment issues. What is needed is a mix of policies that avoids a mixup of policies.

REFERENCES

Drucker, Peter. 1993. *Post-capitalist society*. New York: Harper Business.

Economist. 1996. Why Jack is a dull boy. 5 January, 113.

Fraser, Nancy, and Linda Gordon. 1994. A genealogy of "dependency": Tracing a key word of the U.S. welfare state. *Signs* 19, no. 2: 309–35.

Massey, Douglas, and Nancy Denton. 1993. *American apartheid: Segregation and the making of the underclass*. Cambridge, Mass.: Harvard University Press.

Miller, S. M., and Karen Ferroggiaro. 1995. Class dismissed. *American Prospect* (spring).

Oliver, Melvin L., and Tom Shapiro, 1995. *Black wealth/white wealth*. New York: Routledge.

Stoneman, William E. 1995. Regional economics. *Boston Globe*, 25 December, 15.

Chapter 3

Policies to Improve Employment Outcomes for American Workers

Robert I. Lerman

WHAT IS THE PROBLEM?

In September 1994, *Fortune* magazine featured "The End of the Job" as its cover article and called the traditional job a social artifact. Meanwhile, in his new book, *The End of Work*, Jeremy Rifkin declares the end of jobs as we know them because technological change is eliminating jobs and bringing about the decline of the global labor force. Rifkin's thesis strikes a responsive chord for those who see the large and highly publicized corporate layoffs as portending a future with little real work for the masses.

These reports are completely at odds with the facts. Today, the proportion of working-age Americans holding jobs is reaching all-time highs. While concerns about the state of the U.S. job market are widespread, the reality is a record that is very strong on the creation of jobs, though weak on wage growth and wage equality. Unemployment rates in the United States have been low by world standards; job growth has outpaced the rest of the industrial world allowing the economy to absorb the vast influx of women and immigrants entering the workforce into jobs. In spite of large defense cutbacks, downsizing of major corporations, and an economic slowdown in other advanced economies, the U.S. economy now manages to generate employment for 126 million American workers. Without any government mandate or public jobs program, nearly all of these workers find employment that involves the creation of goods and services for the large and slowly expanding economy. As of August 1995, the unemployment rate (seasonally adjusted) was 5.1 percent, implying that nearly 95 percent of the 133 million people looking for work were able to find employment.

Although workers are generally able to find jobs, many work only at low wages. The United States may have achieved unemployment rates that are low by world standards, but the typical American worker has experienced little of the wage growth common to other advanced economies. In his 1995 Labor Day address, Secretary of Labor Robert Reich stated that the median wage for an American worker was $475 per week, an amount below the inflation-adjusted 1979 earnings of $498 per week. According to Barry Bluestone, "Since 1973, real average weekly earnings for the more than 80 percent of the workforce who are counted as production or non-supervisory workers have fallen by 19 percent." The decline in wages for those at the bottom is an unusual phenomenon. Those in the next to lowest decile of the weekly wage distribution (those in the 11th–20th percentiles) achieved wage gains of 31.5 percent over the 1940s, 27.8 percent in the 1950s, 19.2 percent in the 1960s, but then suffered declines of 1.5 percent over the 1970s and 16.9 percent in the 1980s. At the same time, weekly wage growth for all workers declined from 24 percent growth in the 1960s, to 5 percent growth in the 1970s, to a decline of nearly 8 percent in the 1980s.

The major factor dividing the wage-earning population is educational attainment. In 1979, mean annual earnings of college graduates were 64 percent higher than the earnings of high school graduates. By 1994, the mean earnings of college graduates was 84 percent higher than those earned by high school graduates (Bradbury 1996). Unfortunately, there are fewer winners than losers; nearly three-quarters of all workers and about 70 percent of new entrants to the job market have not graduated from college. As of 1995, only one in three twenty-five to thirty-four-year-olds year-olds had achieved a degree beyond the high school diploma.

Certainly, the rising wage gap between college-educated and high school–educated workers represents an unwelcome increase in inequality. But these trends also have an important positive side—they document a job market in which employers are increasingly demanding and willing to pay higher premiums for skilled and educated workers, for people who learn well in school and on the job. To reinforce the point, suppose we found—as scholars did find in the mid-1970s—that employers were reducing the premium they were willing to pay for skill. We would have to infer that employers have little use for extra skills, that adding educated workers to the labor market might create academic unemployment or frustrations when their jobs end up requiring little of the capabilities they worked so hard to achieve. Fortunately, in today's world, employers are increasingly demanding higher skills. From this perspective, if we can only raise education and skill levels, we will be able to turn the unskilled into well-educated workers. Recent evidence further documents the ability of the economy to create jobs at high occupational levels. In 1983, professional and managerial jobs accounted for about 21 percent of total wage and salary employment. Between 1983 and 1993, when the economy generated almost 20 million new jobs, one in three of these jobs were in the professional and managerial categories (Rosenthal 1995). Between April 1993 and April 1996, professional and managerial positions made up over half of the 7.2 million–job increase in employment.

Workers able to obtain one of these high-level jobs do face a higher possibility of layoff than in earlier years. Yet, the validity of the notion that jobs are becoming much more unstable for workers as a whole is unclear. A careful study by Henry Farber (1995) found little evidence of increasing job instability for workers as a whole, though other researchers do find rising instability. On the other hand, as the review article by Dave Marcotte (1995) makes clear, instability definitely increased for less-educated and minority workers.

Another exaggerated concern about the job market is the notion of the existence of a large body of contingent and temporary workers. A February 1995 Bureau of Labor Statistics survey found that, at most, about 2 to 5 percent of employed workers were in contingent jobs. If one includes all workers (including the self-employed and independent contractors) who expect their employment to last for an additional year or less and who had worked at their jobs for less than one year, the proportion of workers in this status amounts to only 2.8 percent of total employment. About one-third of these workers prefer this contingent arrangement.

If the overall availability of productive jobs, including those demanding skills and education, is not the problem, what is? In my view, the United States faces four fundamental difficulties.

1. *Wage stagnancy, low productivity, and earnings inequality.* The decline in wages for many groups of American workers is one of the nation's most serious problems. The problem results from two main sources: a) the low productivity growth since the early 1970s; and b) the demand shifts away from less-educated and other low-wage workers. The Council of Economic Advisors, in their 1995 *Economic Report of the President*, presents data on productivity showing the slowdown from nearly 3 percent per year between 1963 and 1972 to about 1 percent per year from 1973 to 1994. While some economists (Gordon 1996) have argued that the bias in the consumer price index has caused official figures to overstate the productivity slowdown, few dispute the reality of a slowdown in productivity growth.

   According to Gary Burtless, the inequality of male earnings has been rising since about 1950. Indeed, in his analysis, the largest increases in inequality took place during the 1950s. By any measure, the 1960s were a time in which the labor market tightness rebounded to the short-run benefit of low-wage workers. However, since 1970, wage inequality has been rising, with two-thirds of the increase due to increasing inequality within age-education groups and one-third due to rising inequality between groups.

2. *The continuing and serious job problems of minorities and the disadvantaged.* Unemployment rates for black youth remain at well over 30 percent. Even by age twenty-three, about one in four black men and women report having no earnings at all for over a full year. Inner-city disadvantaged groups face locational problems that limit their ability to find and keep jobs. These impersonal job statistics mask much more serious social problems, such as the decline of marriage and the rise of youth crime, that may be related to the poor career options of disadvantaged and minority youth. To Elijah Anderson (1994), the alienation associated with what he calls "endemic joblessness" has led to an oppositional street culture that can even engulf young people from "decent" homes. Unable to gain self-respect through solid performance at school or on the job, street youth (especially young men) prove their manhood by showing their peers that they can conquer women sexually and become a father and that they can steal something from another and flaunt it.

The racial dimension complicates the problem by creating a vicious circle. The history of blatant racial discrimination and salient examples of continuing discrimination add to the bitterness of many inner-city youth against the system and to their expectations that hard work in school will not pay off. Employers, sensing that a lack of basic skills and an unwillingness to work hard is a common trait among lower-class blacks, discriminate by attributing the average traits of blacks to individual black job applicants. Even employers in the neighborhood are unlikely to take a chance on youth who lack credible references.[1] The evidence of continuing discrimination reinforces the rejection by black, ghetto youth of the mainstream system and allows them to rationalize their lack of effort in school.[2]

The continuing inflow of immigrants and the renewed effort to move welfare recipients into jobs will add to the supply of workers in the low-wage labor market, thereby driving wages down further and making job opportunities scarce.

3. *Weakness in overall skill preparation and enhancement.* The poor links between schools and employers, especially for those not going on to a college degree, have contributed to the wage losses experienced by high school graduates. Partly because youth leaving high school lack necessary skills, employers are reluctant to hire them for demanding jobs or to invest in training.[3] About 60 percent of all twenty-five-year-olds obtained no training after high school; the figures are even higher for noncollege youth.[4] Paul Osterman (1995) reports that even by their early thirties, more than 35 percent of male high school graduates have failed to find stable employment. The informal U.S. system performs worst for low-income and minority youth since they lack the informal job contacts available to middle-class youth. Without the hope that their high school performance will lead directly to a rewarding career involving added training, too many students avoid the effort required to achieve high academic skills. Although there are other causes of the poor relative achievement of American students, today's weak connection between learning and post-school careers certainly contributes

to the problem. Training in the private sector is extensive, but not intensive, even for long-term employees.

4. *Uncertainty about jobs for heads of families.* Although overall unemployment rates are relatively low by the standards of European economies, there is still a large absolute number of families whose heads cannot find jobs and must resort to welfare assistance. Currently, it is difficult to determine whether a low-income head of a family simply cannot find any job (even a job paying only the minimum wage) or is reacting to the disincentives of welfare, housing, food, health, and other benefits in choosing government assistance over reported employment. Given the uncertainties about the availability of jobs, it is difficult to know the relative importance of each factor. But, even if job availability was a minor factor overall, it still is likely to be significant for a sizable absolute number of families.

WHAT PUBLIC POLICIES SHOULD BE UNDERTAKEN TO DEAL WITH THESE PROBLEMS?

I have five policy suggestions for dealing with these problems:

- increasing economic growth, partly by reducing the perceived and actual noninflationary unemployment rate;
- creating a system of youth apprenticeships and related training for non-college-bound individuals;
- developing a last-resort employment system that would help supplant public assistance;
- making the earned income tax credit more accessible on a weekly basis (but eliminating its marital dissolution incentives); and
- improving the nation's job-placement system.

Reducing the Perceived and Actual Noninflationary Unemployment Rate

Until recently, economists generally accepted 6 percent as the lowest unemployment rate achievable through macroeconomic policies that would avoid raising the rate of inflation. Despite the economy maintaining a combination of inflation rates of less than 3 percent and an unemployment rate of 5.5 percent, macroeconomists still believe that moving to lower unemployment rates will generate too much pressure on wages and ultimately prices and will begin increasing the inflation rate. Since these views are accepted at the Federal Reserve, there is a reluctance to lower interest rates even in the face of low inflation rates. The Federal Reserve is targeting no more than a 2.5 percent growth rate, a rate that is too low to reduce unemployment. Recently, business leaders have come out for raising the growth targets. Liberals should get behind this effort because it is the most important strategy for tightening the job market and encouraging employers to train workers, even the disadvantaged. It is also the best way to push up wages at the bottom of the distribution. Press reports indicate that employers in tight (very low unemployment) labor markets are raising entry-level wages to attract workers. Labor scarcities are most likely to lead to increased training efforts by employers as well as a willingness to hire disadvantaged workers. In Wisconsin, for example, where unemployment rates have reached 4 percent and below, welfare recipients outside Milwaukee have increased their employment rates substantially.

The effort to increase growth targets and lower unemployment targets may be able to attract bipartisan support. Richard Lugar and Steve Forbes, 1996 presidential candidates, touted the benefits of higher growth targets, which they would attempt to achieve through controversial changes in tax policy. They correctly pointed out that a higher growth rate can generate significant fiscal dividends for social programs. In California, where state revenues will unexpectedly rise because of the recent recovery, a Republican administration plans to expand educational funding substantially along with implementing a cut in taxes over three years.

Although I am calling for increased emphasis on lower unemployment targets and higher growth targets, we should not dismiss the threat of inflationary impacts. If inflation does increase, policy makers will no doubt tighten monetary policy, thereby reducing growth and increasing unemployment. Thus, all the efforts to expand growth should be undertaken within the context of avoiding inflationary impacts.

Creating a System of Youth Apprenticeships and Related Training

Elsewhere (Lerman 1996), I have presented the detailed arguments for developing a system of youth apprenticeships. For the purposes of this forum, I shall sketch the main points of the rationale for the policy and the next steps required to move beyond recent efforts to implement this strategy.

The rationale for building a youth apprenticeship strategy rests on the record of the past failures of U.S. programs, on realities facing non-college-bound youth, and on the success of a well-developed apprenticeship approach in other countries.

First, the primary set of federal job-training programs for youth has accomplished little. The results of the recent Job Training Partnership Act evaluation revealed no gains from training for youth. Even efforts to replicate the somewhat successful Job Corps have yielded no net benefits. The summer youth employment program did provide income support to youth, but apparently no lasting earnings gains. Even an entitlement program offering jobs to all poor youth in high school or who had dropped out of high school failed to make a dent in the problem of high unemployment and low wages. These programs, by their nature, are relatively small interventions in comparison to the experiences of youth going through the mainstream educational system.

Implementing a youth apprenticeship approach beginning in the late–high school years can have a number of important positive effects. Such a system would and (in some places already does) embody a contractual arrangement between employers, workers, and schools whereby a seventeen- or eighteen-year-old (a high school junior or senior) combines work-based and school-based learning over a two- to three-year period in order to achieve a certified competency in a career field along with a high school degree. The U.S. system would require an infrastructure to specify and test occupational competencies, to develop work-based and related school-based curricula, to provide occupational information to students at least by junior high school, to train workplace trainers, to provide extensive counseling to students and parents, and to monitor the quality of the learning experiences.

In describing the German apprenticeship system, the *Economist* (1992) sees that

Adolescents who were bored by school find their enthusiasm reignited, partly because they are treated more like adults and partly because they start to see the links between learning facts and earning a living. The cost of training is divided between the Lander, which provide the vocational schools, the employers, who pump 2% of their payroll costs into training, and apprentices themselves, who work for only a nominal salary. The transition between school and work, so traumatic elsewhere, is rendered almost painless. Above all, the system reinforces a culture in which training is cherished and skilled workers revered.

Were such a system implemented in the United States, the system would

1. *Raise incomes of noncollege youth by increasing productivity.*
2. *Provide clear pathways and incentives for youth.*
3. *Utilize learning in context extensively.*
4. *Improve the linkage between training and careers.* Because employers are unlikely to offer apprenticeships in areas where there are few jobs, mismatches are less likely. Evidence indicates that the information flow between employers and trainees does indeed lessen the mismatch between training choices and employer positions. Students are more likely to learn current practice rather than old approaches since competitive employers specify the competencies.
5. *Channel youth work into constructive settings.* High school students are often working as unskilled service workers to earn spending money. Youth apprenticeship channels this impulse by attempting to make workplaces into learning environments and linking work with training toward an attractive career.

6. *Influence the structure of employer demand as well as the quality of labor supplied.* The development of apprenticeships causes employers to rethink their use of skills, to upgrade jobs by raising their skill levels, and to find ways to increase the utilization of non-college-educated youth with skills. Youth apprenticeship is a universal strategy, but its main benefits would flow to the very noncollege workers who have suffered wage reductions over the last fifteen years. For these reasons, apprenticeship is especially promising for inner-city and minority youth.

7. *Improve the formal system of placement in training and jobs, thereby reducing the disadvantage of poor youth with respect to informal channels to jobs.* Apprenticeship provides a formal mechanism in which employers can have confidence and through which they can try out marginal workers.

8. *Reduce the negative influence of peers by exposing young people to constructive adult peer groups.* The peer pressure to become involved in crime and drugs and to father children outside marriage can be intense. Youth apprenticeship creates a natural mentoring process in which the mentor/trainer has a stake in the success of the apprentice, not only at the work site, but in academic studies as well.

9. *Improve incentives and help inner-city youth before they experience serious trouble by starting early.*

10. *Give employers the chance to watch young people as they learn critical skills.* Minorities and disadvantaged youth are most likely to suffer from group labels suggesting a lack of motivation and basic skills and questionable integrity. An apprenticeship gives the young minority worker a chance to demonstrate his or her individual strengths during a probationary period after which employers can make their long-term hiring decision. Indeed, employers may find school-to-work programs an especially appealing source of qualified minority workers (Osterman 1995).

The youth apprenticeship model is not an untested idea, but rather a successful and effective system operating in advanced economies, including Austria, Denmark, Germany, and Switzerland. Under the basic model, most seventeen- to nineteen-year-olds begin structured, two- to four-year programs of school-based and employer-based training culminating in a recognized occupational certification. On a largely voluntary basis, employers have generally provided enough apprenticeship places for all youth who wish to participate.[5] Patriotic and social concerns cannot be the primary motivators for employers since, despite the abundance of places, only about one in four German employers actually offer any apprenticeships. At the same time, German multinationals often find the apprenticeship approach so useful that they set up programs in other countries, where patriotic concerns are irrelevant.

We are beginning to see small but serious youth apprenticeship programs operating in some parts of this country (especially in Wisconsin, Maine, and Pennsylvania). The 1994 School to Work Opportunities Act (STWOA) gives states a chance to build the infrastructure and model programs. Unfortunately, to this point, the school-to-career movement has been too much of a school restructuring program, too oriented toward reaching all students with modest intensity rather than reaching a subgroup with major intensity, and too little an industry-led system taking place industry by industry. Unless the approach becomes more industry-oriented, we will not see the kinds of major investments necessary to make youth apprenticeship a reality. Skeptics argue that U.S. employers will never make the kinds of investments that those in other countries do. Now, it may well be true that we will not have nor require apprenticeships for 70 percent of a cohort. However, developing such systems for 20–30 percent of a cohort would make a major difference in expanding quality career options for young people.

To illustrate what can be done, consider the finance youth apprenticeship program in Wisconsin. With a combination of school-based and work-site training, apprentices move from teller-related functions to handling new accounts and performing lending functions, customer support, and accounting. At schools, students will take courses on the principles of depository institutions, marketing for depository institutions, business law, and operations. The state government, community colleges, and bankers collaborated to develop this impressive set of skill requirements. Wisconsin has already developed competency standards for fourteen separate industries and has over one thousand students in apprentice slots. To illustrate the interest of some employers, the Wisconsin Auto Dealers Association petitioned to have their industry included in the youth apprenticeship program.

To move the process along more quickly requires additional federal leadership, especially in the areas of skill standards, research and development, and diffusion of research results. Another way the federal government can take the lead is to establish youth apprenticehips within its own employment system.

Developing a Last-Resort Employment System for Heads of Families with Children

National polls consistently document the public's opposition to "guaranteed income" or "welfare" programs as well as the public's support for "guaranteed jobs" programs. Despite this long-term preference for job guarantees over income guarantees, politicians and policy analysts have generally avoided moving toward this policy in a significant way. An important exception was the 1977 welfare reform proposal of President Jimmy Carter to provide enough jobs so that every family head would have access to a job that, together with non-employment supplements, would bring the family's income above the poverty line. Unfortunately, opposition from both liberals and conservatives prevented the proposal from becoming law. The reasons for the opposition from liberals were first, that recipients should not be forced to work at low wages and second, that state and local governments might use recipients to substitute for existing, more highly paid public employees. Conservatives objected to the higher costs of jobs programs (requirements for overhead expenses) and to the make-work character of the jobs. More recently, conservatives have argued that low-wage jobs are plentiful.

Let me first deal with the conservative opposition. If, as they argue, low-wage, private-sector jobs are widely available, then a minimum-wage, last-resort program will not attract any takers and will cost little. This is especially true if the earnings on public jobs do not qualify for earned income tax credits while low-wage, private sector jobs do. The argument that jobs programs are generally make-work goes against the experience of recent work-relief programs, in which employers generally rate workers as reasonably productive. However, because of this concern about public jobs programs, the government should largely fund individual projects that can be monitored, audited, and provided with technical assistance. The jobs should go mostly to projects with visible output that can be readily displayed to the public.

The liberal opposition to last-resort employment at low wages has eroded for some time. Faced with the prospect that welfare mothers will have to leave cash assistance for good after five years, liberals are strongly arguing for at least providing some type of job floor. The welfare reform bill advanced by Senate Democrats favored providing, not only jobs, but also vouchers for placement and employer subsidies so that former recipients can find and keep jobs. William Julius Wilson (1996) advocates a Works Progress Administration (WPA)–style jobs program at subminimum wages. The concern about displacement of public employee union workers is also less significant today because of the depletion of the public sector. Still, while union opposition to New York City's workfare program has not prevented the program's expansion to over twenty-five thousand welfare recipients, organized labor's opposition to a broad-based, minimum-wage public jobs program could become more vigorous in the future.

One way for the jobs program to minimize displacement would be to channel a sizable share of the jobs to nonprofit agencies and to work on concrete public projects. The experience of Canada's Local Initiatives Program in the 1970s suggests that sponsoring small, concrete projects can be a fruitful way to create productive work, to monitor the programs, and to increase program accountability by making the threat of cancellation real.

Developing public support for replacing cash assistance with productive work could be difficult. The key is to insure cost-effective administration and sponsorship of sound projects that yield visible outputs. Programs not producing the promised outputs should be provided with technical assistance, but if they continue to fail, the job-creation authority should end their funding. Training should take place in the context of a job and a project instead of on a stand-alone basis. The jobs should be structured so that participating low-income workers can achieve enough to obtain a credible reference. However, the jobs should not pay more than the minimum wage in order to target the positions for those who cannot obtain other jobs and to limit the costs of the program.

Finally, the jobs should be available to all heads (primary earners) of families with children and should not be restricted to former welfare recipients. Last-resort employment will do less to discourage two-parent families because the second parent will be able to work without the family losing income. Requiring work will limit the ability of mothers in one-parent families to stay home with their children and receive cash assistance. To strengthen the attachment of fathers and lessen the increasing marginalization of low-income fathers, I recommend that even in single-mother families, fathers be allowed to take the public job in return for paying a substantial amount of his earnings for child support.

Improving the Earned Income Tax Credit (EITC)

The EITC has a great potential to raise the earnings and work incentives of low-wage parents. As of 1996, families with two children are able to receive a subsidy of 40 percent of approximately their first $9,000 in earnings. This means that a $5-per-hour job immediately becomes a $7-per-hour job. A worker earning $8 will, for over half the year, be earning at an $11.20-per-hour rate.

Unfortunately, at this point, few workers are fully aware of how the EITC influences their incomes. Another problem is that, over some ranges of earnings, the EITC can penalize marriage substantially. Consider a mother of two children earning $9,000 per year and a father earning $16,000 per year. If they live together outside marriage and each parent claims the EITC, they will be able to keep a full and a partial credit of over $5,000 as well as food stamps worth about $2,000. If they marry, they will lose virtually their entire $7,000+ benefit package.

I suggest two changes to improve the EITC. First, make the credit easier to understand and to access on a monthly or biweekly basis. This approach will allow workers to obtain the EITC on an ongoing basis and thereby raise their basic living standards. Second, provide a separate, more generous schedule for married couples. Otherwise, the large and growing number of disincentives to marry or to remain married will be criticized for having the same unintended consequences as our existing welfare system.

Improving the Job-Placement System Dramatically

The decline in the performance and importance of the U.S. Employment Service is a major concern. Certainly, we have a large number of effective private job-placement agencies. But disadvantaged and low-income workers often lack adequate access to these agencies. In discussions two decades ago about how to lower the full-employment unemployment rate, improving job placement was always a major topic because lowering the time between the appearance of a job vacancy and a hire should lower frictional unemployment without generating inflationary pressures. Yet, in recent years, the issue has attracted little attention among policy makers and, except in the case of John Bishop (1993), little research.

At this point, it is unclear what exactly will work best to upgrade job matches and job finding for workers. The federal government can take the leadership in examining a range of options, from the one-stop shopping centers pushed by the Clinton administration and some states to the vouchers for job finding advocated by the Progressive Policy Institute. In this instance, I have no single preferred policy option other than calling for shifting resources away from the traditional job service and toward a broader array of options.

CONCLUSIONS

Because the U.S. labor market faces serious problems, it is easy to forget its important strengths and flexibility compared to the job markets in other countries. In a January 18, 1996 *New York Times* article titled "Economic Weakness Stirs Gloom in Europe," Nathanial Nash points to a 10.6 percent European unemployment rate and little indication of a recovery significant enough to reduce unemployment substantially.

Before embarking on too many new initiatives, we should follow Senator Daniel Patrick Moynihan's advice to "do no harm" and to learn about the best policy options with as much rigor as possible. The most progress will take place by building on a solid knowledge base and on common values of Americans. I believe my suggestions can attract the support of a wide spectrum of the public. Expanding growth, creating a system of youth apprenticeships, providing jobs to heads of poor families, improving the EITC, and upgrading the job matching system are all initiatives that can make a dent in important labor-market problems as well as appeal to the values of the American people.

NOTES

1. In his study of the Red Hook neighborhood of Brooklyn, Philip Kasinitz (1993) found that employers discriminated against local residents because they as-

sociated them with crime and poor work attitudes. The discrimination was not entirely racial since members of other racial groups in the area besides blacks were also cast as undesirable and since employers did hire black West Indian immigrants. Employers relied on referrals from existing workers to determine which workers would be reliable and honest.

2. Based on his research on blacks and Mexican-Americans in Stockton, California, John Ogbu points out that, while parents encourage children to get a good education, their low-level jobs, unemployment, and problems with "the system" convey a different message. To quote Ogbu: "The result, inevitably, is that such children become increasingly disillusioned about their ability to succeed in adult life through the mainstream strategy of schooling" (p. 158). See Ogbu (1990).

3. As one example of the dissatisfaction with the capacities of workers, about half the small manufacturers responding to a National Association of Manufacturers survey reported that a lack of skilled labor and lack of basic education skills are two major problems. See U.S. Congress (1990).

4. Lynch, Lisa, "The Economics of Youth Training in the United States," *Economic Journal* 103 (September 1993): 1292–1302.

5. Germany did experience a shortfall of places during the years 1982–1986, but this was an exceptional period that combined a serious recession with a peak level of seventeen-year-olds. See Steedman (1993).

REFERENCES

Anderson, Elijah. 1993. Sex codes in the inner city. In *Young unwed fathers: Changing norms and emerging policies*, ed. Robert Lerman and Theodora Ooms. Philadelphia: Temple University Press.

Anderson, Elijah. 1994. The code of the streets. *Atlantic Monthly*, May.

Bishop, John. 1993. Improving job matches in the U.S. labor market. *Brookings papers on economic activity: Microeconomics* 1: 335–90.

Bluestone, Barry. 1995. *The polarization of American society: Victims, suspects, and mysteries to unravel.* New York: Twentieth Century Fund.

Bradbury, Kathy. 1996. The growing inequality of family incomes: Changing families and changing wages. *New England Economic Review* (July/August).

Economist. 1992. Education survey. 21 November, 11.

Farber, Henry. 1995. Are lifetime jobs disappearing? Job duration in the United States: 1973–1993. *Industrial Relations Section Working Paper No. 341.* Princeton University.

Gordon, Robert. 1996. Problems in the measurement and performance of service-sector productivity in the United States. *National Bureau of Economic Research Working Paper 5519* (March).

Holzer, Harry. 1992. Youth and the labor market of the nineties. In *Dilemmas in youth employment programming: Findings from the Youth Research and Technical Assistance Project.* Washington, D.C.: Employment and Training Administration, U.S. Department of Labor.

Juhn, Chinhui, and Kevin M. Murphy. 1995. Inequality in labor market outcomes. *Economic Policy Review* 1, no. 1 (January): 26–34.

Kasinitz, Philip. 1993. The real jobs problem. *Wall Street Journal*, 26 November, A18.

Lerman, Robert. 1996. Building hope, skills, and careers: Creating a youth apprenticeship system. In *Social policies for children*, ed. Irwin Garfinkel, Jennifer L. Hochschild, and Sara S. McLanahan. Washington, D.C.: Brookings Institution.

Marcotte, Dave. 1995. Declining job stability: What we know and what it means. *Journal of Policy Analysis and Management* 14, no. 4 (Fall): 590–598.

Ogbu, John. 1990. Minority status and literacy. *Daedalus* (Spring): 141–168.

Osterman, Paul. 1995. Is there a problem with the youth labor market and if so, how should we fix it? In *Poverty, inequality, and the future of social policy: Western states in the new world order*, ed. Katherine McFate, Roger Lawson, and William Julius Wilson. 387–414. New York: Russell Sage.

Reich, Robert. 1995. *Frayed-collar workers in gold-plated times: The state of the American workforce 1995*. Washington, D.C.: U.S. Department of Labor.

Rosenthal, Neil. 1995. The nature of occupational employment growth: 1983–1993. *Monthly Labor Review* (June): 45–54.

Steedman, Hillary. 1993. The economics of youth training in Germany. *Economic Journal* 103 (September): 1279–1291.

U.S. Congress. Office of Technology Assessment. 1990. *Worker training: Competing in the new international economy*, 166. Washington, D.C.: U.S. Government Printing Office.

Wilson, William Julius. 1996. *When work disappears: The world of the new urban poor*. New York: Alfred A. Knopf.

Chapter 4

Reviving an Affirmative Concept of Corporate Duty: The Public Corporation

Howard Schweber

One of the persistent themes in discussions of American industrial policy and future economic development is the role of corporations in the nation's economic life. America's political economy is built around a philosophy that identifies the private sector as the engine of prosperity, a conception that has taken serious hits in recent years as a result of evidence that corporations' search for profit at times contradicts the idea of playing a role in securing the nation's economic health. Emphasis on immediate profit, much heralded by shareholders and corporate raiders in the 1980s, has been blamed for American industry's failure to create an economic infrastructure capable of supporting long-term national growth. Particularly when compared with the Japanese or Western European patterns, it appears that American industry is driven by short-term thinking.

Unconstrained by guiding principles imposed under a national industrial policy and lacking an internal motivation for long-term planning, it seems that time and again in the last thirty years, American industry's aggressive pursuit of immediate profit has resulted in gypped consumers, unprotected workers, and local and even regional economies held hostage to the whims or speculations of twenty-five-year-old MBAs (Masters of Business Administration). There is a feeling of betrayal in the realization that the private sector, intended in the American myth to be the engine of progress, has instead become a source of uncertainty and economic peril. The degree of rage that this issue has aroused is most evident in the negative emotions that are focused on the class most blamed for the conduct of modern business: the much-despised Yuppies.

Regardless of the merits of the account presented above, it is worth noting that a notion lurking in the discussion is the idea that corporations *ought* to be bound by some particular sense of duty based on the special role that they play in our national economy. The most developed legal conception of corporate duty is the duty to the shareholders to maintain the highest possible value for publicly traded stock. The idea that a public industry's sole responsibility is to be profitable and efficient, however, is not an inherent element of corporate capitalism. Instead, this restricted notion of public corporate duties appears historically as the hypostatization of merely a single element of an earlier idea that the very existence of a corporation expressed its commitment to a range of duties *broader* than those imposed on other business entities. This is not an idea gleaned from isolated comments or moralizing editorialists; rather, the idea that corporate status imposes a broad range of public duties and the eventual dissolution of that ideal into a cramped demand for empirically determinable rates of return on investment both received their clearest articulations in the law of corporations. A review of the history of that law, in turn, suggests the need and the possibility for the revitalization of the affirmative notion of corporate duty.

THE HISTORICAL DEVELOPMENT OF THE CORPORATE ENTITY: THE DECLINE OF "PUBLIC PURPOSE"

Up to the middle of the 1800s corporations were public entities. The idea of an entity called a corporation is a very old one. In English law of the seventeenth and early eighteenth centuries, however, the idea of a "corporation" did not encompass a private moneymaking enterprise, only local governments and charities. By the late 1700s the idea of a business corporation was certainly recognized, but it remained a rarity. State legislatures, for example, had only conferred seven corporate charters on private businesses as of 1780. Once the idea was introduced, however, its utility for doing business was obvious, and 295 additional corporate charters were granted between 1790 and 1800.[1]

In the nineteenth century, business corporations became fairly common, but there was no clear distinction between private and public corporations. In antebellum America, the term *corporation* continued to refer primarily either to municipalities or to publicly chartered enterprises granted special privileges in return for their performance of a public service: running a banking system, constructing canals and turnpikes, and especially building the railroads. The formation of the corporation was justified in terms of the public goals that its existence would further. "With respect to acts of incorporation," wrote Judge Roane of the Virginia Supreme Court in 1809, "they ought never to be passed, but in consideration of services to be rendered to the public. . . . It may be often convenient for a set of associated individuals, to have the privileges of a corporation bestowed upon them; but if their object is merely *private* or selfish; if it is detrimental to, or not promotive of, the public good, they have no adequate claim upon the legislature."[2]

With public purpose came public powers and support from the public purse. State financing (largely through state bonds) and the grant of special powers, including eminent domain, made corporations the bête noire of Jacksonian Democratic-Republicans, who found the grant of special privileges inherently elitist. By the 1830s the idea of special privileges granted to particular industrial concerns in the name of the public interest was anathema to a rising class of political thinkers whose notions of political economy had been profoundly influenced by the writings of Ferguson, Smith, and other Scottish Common Sense writers. Thus William Leggett, quoting Dugald Stewart: "Little else is required to carry a state to the highest degree of opulence, but peace, easy taxes, and a tolerable administration of justice; all the rest being brought about by the natural course of things. All governments which thwart this natural course, which force things into another channel, or which endeavor to arrest the progress of society at a particular point, are unnatural, and to support themselves are obliged to be oppressive and tyrannical."[3]

Laissez-faire theories of political economy carried two crucial messages for corporations: the grant of particular privileges by their state charters were anathema, but the economic pursuits of private corporations were the natural course of the nation's development. "It would be a very strained and unwarrantable inference from any remarks we have made, to say that we are an enemy to churches, public libraries, or charitable associations, because we express hostility to special legislation. It would be an unwarranted inference to say that we are even opposed to the principal of incorporation; since it is only to the principle of *special incorporation* that we have expressed hostility."[4]

Leggett's nod to churches and libraries was, of course, the beginning of the idea of the nonprofit corporation. A general law of incorporation would permit purely private business associations to take advantage of the corporate form; in this context even laissez-faire-ists as extreme as Leggett recognized the desirability of preserving a special class of corporations given special treatment in recognition of the social utility of their services.

In the context of the early nineteenth century, then, to ask the range of a corporation's duties seems almost nonsensical: corporations existed for stated purposes for which they were granted very narrowly defined powers by their charters. This idea persisted well into the middle 1800s. Thus an 1843 treatise on the law of corporations could declare the "general and well settled principle, that a corporation had no other powers than such as are specifically granted; or, such as are necessary for the purpose of carrying into effect the powers expressly granted."[5] As late as 1886 the association of special corporate charters with limited powers remained prevalent, a theme exhibited in the rule that "all corporate acts which the legislature has not authorized remain prohibited."[6] "A doubtful charter does not exist," declared the chief justice Jeremiah Black of Pennsylvania in 1856, "because whatever is doubtful is decisively certain against the corporation."[7]

The counterpart to the idea of limited powers was the idea of legal liability for exceeding those powers, the *ultra vires* doctrine. As the century progressed, however, the idea of special corporations—the successor to the earlier idea of a corporation as a public entity—gave way to the notion of corporations as general business enterprises. "No longer was the business corporation a unique, ad hoc creation, vesting exclusive control over a public asset or natural resource in one group of favorites or investors. Rather, it was becoming a general form for organizing a business."[8] Not only were general incorporations more frequent, but courts took increasingly expansive views of the powers granted by legislatures under special charters. As the definitions of corporations' powers became more and more expansive, the question of corporations' duties began to emerge, particularly in the context of corporate liability.

The shift from special incorporation to the general incorporation of business enterprises meant a sharp decline in the power of the state to control the conduct of the corporation. In 1819, in the *Dartmouth College* case, the Supreme Court had ruled that a state could not revoke the charter of a private corporation by virtue of the Contracts Clause of the Constitution. As a result, the issue of distinguishing between public and private corporations became crucial. In 1833, Joseph Story, sitting alone, drastically constricted the category of public corporation, restricting it to those that "exist for public political purposes only, such as towns, cities, parishes, and counties," or those that were entirely owned by the government.[9] For example, Bowdoin College was held to be private despite the fact that it had been founded and initially funded by the state of Massachusetts, since later private funds had been added. The state endowment of the college, then, was a public subsidy to a private corporation and did not give the state power of control. *A fortiori*, corporations such as railroads and steel mills that received public subsidies remained private corporations as well, and hence their charters—once granted—were not subject to revocation or revision by the state legislature. The trend toward an ever narrower category of public corporation spread quickly, culminating perhaps in the peculiar reasoning by means of which the Indiana Supreme Court arrived at the conclusion that the Indiana State Board of Agriculture was a private corporation.[10]

Under the theory of public subsidy granted by the terms of a contract (the corporation's charter), there appeared to be no state authority to regulate the conduct of corporations at all. In 1848, the Supreme Court ruled that corporations were subject to the federal government's power of eminent domain; thirty years later, in a pair of cases, the Court ruled that corporations were subject to regulation under the government's general police powers.[11] The outcomes in these cases are much less interesting than the fact that these questions were raised at all. From a concept of the corporation as the creation of the legislature, American law had moved to the point where a ruling by the Supreme Court was required to affirm that corporations were not completely immune from the rule of law despite their special "contractual" relationship with the government.

The contract model was ultimately impossible to sustain. By the 1890s there were thousands of incorporations every year under general laws that covered broad categories of business activities. The fiction that each of these acts of incorporation represented a negotiated contract between the business and the legislature was simply too flimsy to accept. In 1886, in *Santa Clara v. Southern Pacific Railroad*, the Supreme Court—without citing precedent or basis—announced a new conception: the corporation as natural person with constitutionally guaranteed rights.[12]

It is not entirely clear what the Court meant by its extension of the Fourteenth Amendment to corporations. By the early decades of the twentieth century, however, *Santa Clara* was taken to stand for the idea that corporations were natural persons, entities possessed of "personality," and hence were politically guaranteed rights against interference from state legislatures.[13] Since the government's authority to regulate the economy was a well-recognized tradition, this move essentially had the peculiar consequence of declaring that corporations were only incidentally economic entities. By 1905, with the famous *Lochner* case, this notion was well entrenched.

One casualty of the conception of corporations as natural persons was the ultra vires doctrine mentioned earlier. If corporate charters were affirmative grants of specified authority to engage in enumerated kinds of conduct, then actions by a corporation that exceeded the mandate of the charter were clearly improper. The model of the corporation as a natural person, however, was part of the idea of the corporate charter as simply a device to conduct business in a convenient way; hence a corporation was authorized to act in any way that its members would be authorized to act. "The courts," wrote William W. Cook in an 1894 treatise, "have gradually enlarged the implied powers of ordinary corporations until now such corporations may do almost anything that an individual may do, provided the stockholders and creditors do not object."[14] By the end of the 1920s the ultra vires doctrine had eroded to the point of irrelevance.

The demise of the ultra vires principle represented the end of an affirmative conception of corporate duties. Instead, the duties of corporations, like those of other citizens, would be defined negatively. This meant that the special, public duties of corporations under the older conceptions would give way to two sources of obligation: the common-law duties that bound all "persons," and general regulations passed by the legislatures under their police powers. The issue of regulation has been the focal point of debates over the role of corporations in society and the role of government vis-à-vis corporations for the past one hundred years and is likely to remain so. During the period from the 1870s to the 1930s, however, legal doctrines and political attitudes combined to sharply limit the role of government regulation as a check on the equation of profit with social virtue.[15] With the decline of the limited charter, the private law of tort and contract became the primary mechanism for defining the duties of the corporation. It is worthwhile, then, to look briefly at the kinds of private duties that were imposed on corporations by the courts during the formative years of American corporations law.

PRIVATE CORPORATIONS AND THE IDEA OF PUBLIC DUTY

The emergence of corporations with broad powers to conduct business activities occurred during a period in which the idea of generally applicable duties was becoming the cornerstone of American private law. The most important expression of this idea was the emergence of a general theory of negligence that largely replaced complex and specific writs of trespass and nuisance. The emergence of a general tort of negligence was based on the idea that there exist nondelegable duties that all persons owe to all other persons at all times. This idea of a broadly defined "duty of care" came to replace earlier liability doctrines that depended on status relationships and formal descriptions of events to fit preconceived categories of legal action. Conversely, however, the new standards required courts not only to consider the defendant's conduct and its consequences, but also issues of standards of judgment applicable to *both* parties, to ensure that judgments would articulate community norms. These new standards did not arise in the context of corporations, but the attempt to apply the new laws to corporations—particularly railroads—became their most important testing ground.

Prior to the 1840s, corporations, like all other property owners, had been governed by a simple and ancient rule: every person had an obligation to use his own property in a fashion such as to avoid causing injury to another, a standard that closely approximates a general strict liability standard.[16] Under this scheme, corporations such as railroads had a peculiar advantage, being immune from liability for nuisance because of their charters. Nuisance, in fact, might have been a devastatingly effective legal tool against emerging industries, as it provided a remedy for injuries "indirect or remote, as distinguished from an immediate invasion by one man of another's property . . . the injury of nuisance is of a more comprehensive or miscellaneous character than any other; namely, that it relates to rights not in their nature specific, definable, or tangible."[17]

Regardless, the action for nuisance was quickly replaced as a significant element of tort law in the 1850s. Beginning, famously, with Lemuel Shaw's statement in *Brown v. Kendall*,[18] American tort law moved to embrace the emerging notion of negligence: liability should proceed from fault.[19] The formalism and restrictive pleading rules of earlier periods were replaced by factual pleading and universally applicable standards of conduct. Driven, perhaps, by the increasing degree of interaction between strangers in a modernizing society, the idea of duty thus moved from a statement of a traditional relationship of obligation, limited by ancient privileges and immunities, to an idealized articulation of societal norms which claimed universal application.

In precisely the period in which the idea of universal tort duties was evolving in the law, business corporations presented legislatures with the argument that their business was so speculative that only immunity from private lawsuits could guarantee their success. To be subject to liability for harms in the traditional manner would, so went the argument, strangle infant industry in its cradle. In 1873 Chief Justice Doe of New Hampshire, adopting the fault requirement, rejected the strict liability principle in evangelistic terms: such a rule, he wrote, would "impose a penalty upon efforts, made in a reasonable, skillful, and careful manner, to rise above a condition of barbarism. It is impossible that legal principle can throw so serious an obstacle in the way of progress and improvement."[20]

Thus from the beginning the idea of ensuring profitability was joined with the idea of restricting traditional duties of care. As a result, early negligence doctrines took forms that are usually described as inventions designed to shield corporations from the redistributive tendencies of juries in private suits, whose sympathies might be expected to be with the injured plaintiff. The requirement of fault was only one element of the new negligence doctrine. Contributory negligence, described as a "cunning trap" for plaintiffs, was a rule that denied recovery altogether in the event that the carelessness of the plaintiff contributed in any way to the occurrence of the injury. In addition, liability was limited to the "foreseeable" consequences of a defendant's conduct, a rule that extended immunity from nuisance claims to immunity from all claims based on "indirect or remote" injury.[21] Most extreme, perhaps, was the development of the "fellow servant" rule that prevented an employee from recovering anything from his employer in the event his injury was caused by the negligence of a fellow employee.[22]

Throughout the antebellum period, the issue of railroads' immunity from the kinds of private claims that had traditionally been paid by turnpike and canal companies acted as a focal point in the debate over the railroad corporations' claims of public benefit. In Michigan in the late 1840s the railroads' refusal to pay for injuries to farmers' stock provoked a "railroad war," in which rails were torn up, locomotives overturned, and the Detroit depot finally burned to the ground. In constitutional conventions held in 1850 and 1851 in Michigan and Ohio, respectively, delegates declared their insistence that railroads be held to their public purposes, under threat of revocation of their charters. The railroad charters had been granted under theories of "public purpose." The phrase "public good," in these debates, came to symbolize the position of Republicans like Rufus Ranney, later a justice of Ohio's supreme court: "Public good and public use are different terms. . . . If the exercise of corporate power promotes the public good, continue it: if it does not, take it away."[23] Populist legislators in Michigan established laws declaring that farmers must be paid compensation for damaged stock but that legislatures were not obliged to pay compensation for revoked corporate charters.

The national trend, however, was clearly to the contrary. After the Civil War, the national interest in an expanded rail system, and concomitantly in expanded visions of managerial centralization, was not open to question. As the experiences in Michigan and Ohio demonstrated, one of the necessary antecedents to recognizing the overwhelming national interest in the relentless march of industrial progress would be a reinterpretation of the duties of chartered corporations. The greater goal of industrial progress could not be trammeled by local duties to representative legislatures or liabilities to farmers and small-town residents who continued to display a distressing tendency to get themselves run over. Equally important, industrial corporations had to be shielded from an even larger category of potential liability, injuries to workmen.

In legal terms, the treatment of railroads—and, by later extension, other industrial corporations—represented a sharp deviation from long-established rules governing the liabilities of corporations. A nice illustration of this fact is found in a review of the first digest of tort law published in the United States, Francis Hilliard's *The Law of Torts or Private Wrongs* (1859). In his discussion of corporation liability, Hilliard relates numerous traditional cases involving turnpike companies, townships, and other pre-industrial entities. No special standards are announced for railroads beyond the general observation that "[t]he rights of the public will be protected against the municipal as well as the railroad corporation."[24] Similarly, in Freeman's 1856 *Illinois Digest*, one of the first state digests of tort law, there is only one case under the heading "railroads," involving a passenger who was injured in a train collision.

The situation was often different in the courts, however. For instance, in a series of cases,[25] the Illinois Supreme Court turned to the highly formalized differentiations between levels of duty owed by bailees to fashion a new and universally applicable set of standards for railroad cases. It is unquestionably true, of course, that there are a variety of settings—paid freight transport, passengers' luggage—in which a railroad acts as something like a bailee. The Illinois court, however, went much farther: narrow and formal standards of due care, ordinary care, and utmost care were imported whole cloth from a particularly arcane area of contracts law to become the governing standards for public corporations. This approach was not peculiar to Illinois; by the 1870s these standards of care were almost universally applied by American courts.

This was only one regional example of a larger phenomenon: the restriction of corporate liability to those toward whom there was a special "duty." In 1869, the first edition of Shearman and Redfield's *The Law of Negligence* contains no mention of *duty* in its table of contents.[26] The definition of "culpable negligence" makes it clear that the only issue is the conduct of the defendant: "Culpable negligence is the omission to do something which a reasonable, prudent and honest man would do, or the doing something which such a man would not do, under all the circumstances surrounding each particular case." In the fifth edition, published in 1898, the same treatise lists *duty* as an element in eight different topics in its table of contents. Instead of "culpable negligence," the key concept is defined as "actionable negligence": "The first element of our definition is a duty. If there is no duty, there can be no negligence. If the defendant owed a duty but did not owe it to the plaintiff, the action will not lie."

By the 1880s, issues of corporate duties to the public were closely tied up with issues of class politics. One of the most influential essays on the subject of railroads' tort liability was published by Francis Wharton in 1876.

We are accustomed to look with apathy at the ruin of great corporations, and to say, "well enough, they have no souls . . ." But no corporation can be ruined without bringing ruin to some of the noblest and most meritorious classes of the land. Those who first give the start to such corporations are men of bold and enterprising qualities, kindled, no doubt, in part by self-interest, but in part also by the delight which men of such type feel in generous schemes for the development of public resources, and the extension to new fields of the wealth and industry of the community.

As for those who invested in such enterprises, they too were deserving of protection: "professional men of small incomes, and widows and orphans whose support is dependent on the income they draw from the modest means left to them by their friends."

Nor were the benefits of industrial capitalism restricted to the bourgeois classes. The corporation itself may be soulless, and those investing in it may deserve little sympathy, but those whom it employs are the bone and sinew of the land . . . When the corporation's income ceases, then the labor is dismissed. We hear sometimes of the cruelty of the eviction of laborers from their cottages at a landlord's caprice. But there are no evictions which approach in vastness and bitterness those which are caused by the stoppage of railway improvements or of manufacturing corporations.[27]

Wharton's article was written to present arguments for why a railroad should not be liable for a fire, caused by the negligent conduct of the railroad's employees, that destroyed several houses.[28] There was no question that the fire was caused by carelessness; thus, under traditional causation rules the railroad would have been liable for all the damage.[29] Instead, the court tortured syntax and logic to limit the railroad's liability to the loss of the first burned house on the curious theory that the destruction of houses thereafter was not "caused" by the railroad employees' negligence.

New standards of liability evolved along distinct class lines. Immigrant workers and farmers were barred from recovery by broad applications of newly devised or imported concepts of contributory negligence, privity, and the dreaded fellow servant rule. Railroad passengers, however, were owed "the highest degree of care, diligence, vigilance and skill . . . with a view to the comfort, safety and transportation of passengers and their baggage; and they are liable for slight neglect or carelessness in any of these particulars, qualified, however, by the reciprocal duty of the passenger, that his want of ordinary care does not cause or contribute to produce the injury."[30] The "reciprocal duty" of the passenger was a final safeguard against the possibility that railroads would be subject to claims by nonrespectable persons.

These twin ideas—that railroads had different levels of duty to different segments of the public and that the public had reciprocal duties toward railroads—came to characterize the private liability of corporations. Shareholders can sue directors today under theories familiar in Hilliard's digest; consumers, following the law of bailments, are not owed more than the minimal possible degree of care (except where such a duty has been created by statute), nor are inhabitants of environments threatened by pollution, nor injured workers.[31] Strict liability doctrines reemerged over the twentieth century in the areas of products liability and expansive theories of interstate jurisdiction over corporate defendants, but the idea that the existence of a publicly issued corporate charter created privately enforceable duties toward members of the public *tout court* did not survive into this century.

Historians differ as to the actual effect that these doctrines had in limiting recoveries. By the end of the 1800s, moreover, contrary doctrines were beginning to develop. The "last clear chance" rule placed liability on whichever party had the last opportunity to prevent the injury from occurring, defeating the effect of contributory negligence in many cases. "Duty" was gradually interpreted more and more expansively to extend to all members of the public with whom a business came into contact. The old strict liability standard was revived for a limited class of cases involving "ultrahazardous" activities.[32]

In the twentieth century, courts pushed tort law toward a role as the great equalizer between industry and private citizens. Under the "sociological jurisprudence" approach inspired by Holmes and established by Pound, Frankfurter and, especially, Brandeis, industries were called upon to make their enterprises safe enough to accord with prevalent community understandings and standards. Part of this role involved the identification of new bases for damages claims. In 1902, for instance, Holmes upheld a verdict for fright damages, citing "a good deal of suffering of a hysterical nature" allegedly caused by a subway collision, despite the fact that claims of this type had been previously unheard of.[33] The incorporation of the science of probabilities into judicial thinking sounded the death knell for the foreseeability doctrine, which had limited the liability of industrial concerns to only the most immediately caused harms. As Justice Holmes famously remarked, "to those who understand probability anything is foreseeable." In the end, instead of a doctrine to reduce liability, foreseeability was reconfigured by Cardozo into the idea of a duty owed toward anyone in a "zone of danger," expanding the scope of potential plaintiffs.[34]

By the 1930s, the system of modern American tort law was in place. Particular details—liability to bystanders, for instance, or the law of implied warranties—remained to be worked out, and remain inconsistent among states today. However, as the brief discussion above attempted to outline, a major function of tort law in America since its inception in the 1850s has been to provide a remedy for the costs of industrial development, with particular emphasis on the use of the courts to define and enforce standards of safety, fair pricing, and commercial conduct.

One sharp exception from the pattern described here is the treatment of labor relations. The codification and tort formulation revolutions of the mid-nineteenth century had their least effect in altering the feudal era remnants in the law of "master and servant."[35] The fellow servant rule, in particular, aroused much revulsion and, as noted, was the subject of legislation in a number of states. Eventually, public reaction against the injustice of laws governing labor led to the enactment of workers' compensation. This removal of a large portion of all tort cases from the private law system was accompanied by a recognition that the alternative—making the standards of adjudication in employment cases the same as in other industrial injury cases—could ruin American business, so frequent were worker injuries at that time.

PUBLIC REGULATION OF PRIVATE CORPORATIONS: THE SEARCH FOR THE "PUBLIC GOOD"

As noted earlier, the debates over the scope of corporations' duties under tort law coincided with the development of new theories of industrial regulation, the public side of the principle of negative corporate duty. Modern regulation of corporations began in the Progressive Era, but like so much else in this account, its beginnings do not necessarily coincide with its modern-day form.

The most important development in the rise of corporate regulation in the Progressive Era was the redefinition of the idea of public purpose in terms of a duty toward a form of political economy rather than toward local interests, specific projects, or identifiable individual citizens. Chartered special corporations had been the bête noire of laissez-faire Democrats in the 1830s; in the 1890s the sides were reconfigured into arguments for and against the idea of regulation. Regulation, however, carried with it little of its traditional baggage of utopian social design. Government regulation of the local economy in order to promote civic virtue was a practice with ancient antecedents: the first American colonies had passed laws governing wages, prices, product quality, days and hours of business operation, and sumptuary laws that restricted public displays of wealth, all in the name of preserving Christian order.[36]

Regulation in the Progressive Era, however, was something quite different from these early forms of enforced communalism. Instead, the ideal that became dominant, developed under the early leadership of the Massachusetts Railway Commission and its head, Charles Francis Adams, was one which focused on efficiency.[37] The Massachusetts Railway Commission was quite different from a modern regulatory agency; most importantly, it had only advisory powers, a model of regulation by friendly persuasion that was Adams's hallmark. In the 1860s, Massachusetts had "the densest rail system in the world." In 1871, a terrible accident at Revere led to a "revolution in safety" in Massachusetts, as, for the first time, a regulatory commission armed only with advisory powers and the weight of public opinion was able to effectively dictate standards to a powerful industry.[38] This event empowered the commission, enabling it to put into effect regulations governing competition and early antitrust laws.

Massachusetts was not unique. The first wrongful death statute in America had been passed by New Hampshire in 1850; it applied solely to railroads.[39] Various states in the Midwest passed "Granger laws" regulating rates and safety conditions for railroads. These laws did not survive judicial scrutiny, on the grounds that they represented impermissible attempts by states to regulate interstate commerce. Therefore, in 1893 the Interstate Commerce Commission (ICC) (itself established in 1877) enacted the first federal safety statute, the Safety Appliance Act, 27 Stat. 531–32 (now 45 United States Code, sec. 7, 1964), which required interstate railroads to have safety equipment and declared that any employee injured by a train lacking such equipment would not "be deemed . . . to have assumed the risk thereby occasioned."[40] This was the beginning of what would eventually become the Occupational Safety and Health Administration. In 1908 railway employees were given special rights of recovery under the Federal Employers' Liability Act.

Adams and other Progressives who favored federal regulation of railroads stressed the public benefits of efficient, reliable operation. Regulation was to be an instrument of political and economic "science"; what we would now refer to as rationalization became the dominant norm for those who sought to legitimize the imposition of restrictions on the conduct of business entities. Despite Adams and his followers' emphasis on cooperative relations and efficiently operating markets, there remained a profound tension between the ideas of railroads as entities bound by the duty of delivering a public service and as private corporations. Was it proper for the government, for instance, in the name of public safety and service, to restrict the profitability of business entities in which thousands of private citizens invested their savings and entrepreneurial geniuses flowered?

No one was ultimately more influential in developing the modern justification for regulation than Brandeis. Against Darwinian claims that businesses naturally tend toward "bigness," Brandeis argued on empirical grounds that small businesses acting as a group would create a more efficient marketplace. This theme, the virtue of small business, has remained the standby of a certain class of political conservative to this day. Brandeis argued that small businesses should be encouraged to combine to compete against larger corporations on the grounds that small businesses were, ultimately, both more virtuous *and more profitable*. The ideal of efficiency as a public virtue folded seamlessly into the idea of profitability as an index of public virtue: "the business of America is business." This ethos of the political economy had direct consequences for the conception of corporate duties. Paradoxically, in his fight against the trusts, Brandeis established the modern conception of the corporation as something utterly differentiated from the older forms of business organization (partnerships, limited companies) that they replaced.

The epitome of the line in Brandeis's thinking came in a series of Interstate Commerce Commission hearings in 1910, *In the Matter of Proposed Advances in Freight Rates by Carriers*. Several major rail lines had requested permission to raise their rates, citing their declining profitability as evidence of business necessity. In response, Brandeis introduced the public to the idea of scientific management, not only as a panacea for industrial ills, but as a moral imperative. Brandeis presented expert testimony that by introducing efficient management practices the railroads could save $1 million a day. He persuaded the ICC to deny the railroads their requested rate increase on the grounds that if they would be able to become more profitable by merely increasing their efficiency, then they had a duty to do so. The factual claim turned out to be largely chimerical, but the phrase became a slogan for those who most eagerly embraced the idea of efficiency.

The idea that corporations had a duty to their shareholders to turn a profit was not a new one. The devastating losses suffered by state treasuries that issued securities to support railroad expansion in the 1830s had led in no small part to the depression of 1837 and fueled the drive toward restrictive charters and, later, toward regulatory reforms. What Brandeis added to the argument was a language of scientific rationalism that defined the corporation's duty as involving maintaining the *highest possible* rate of profit; in other words, the elevation of profit to, not merely one goal, but the preeminent raison d'etre of the corporate entity. This conception is markedly in tension with the idea of the corporation as a natural person incidentally engaged in economic activity; the tension between these two conceptions of the proper role of corporations continues to bedevil American policy making to this day.

Federal statute making would, of course, extend immensely beyond the railroads after the 1937 ratification of the expansive authority granted to the federal government under the Commerce Clause.[41] The process of development into the modern corporate ideal was conceptually complete, however, with the *Advanced Rate Case*. From publicly created entities devoted to a public purpose, to private entities bound by restrictive public charters, to "natural" business entities bound by broadly applicable private duties, to combinations bound by strictly delimited private duties in the name of public goals, and finally to private business entities regulated by public authority solely in the interest of promoting efficiency and profit— the engines of American capitalism.

THE EMERGENCE OF NEW CORPORATE FORMS: THE MODERN CORPORATION AND BEYOND

The development of new and different forms of interaction between government authority and business corporations was accompanied—and perhaps driven—by an equally profound change in the nature of the corporations themselves. In 1977, Alfred Chandler definitively characterized the "modern" business in his book *The Visible Hand: The Managerial Revolution in American Business*.[42] Chandler argued that the emergence of the modern business corporation was the result of developments that made "internalization" of market processes more profitable than competition between individual business units in an open market. These developments were centered in two areas: technology, especially the technology of information processing, and the development of new theories of managements.[43] Among the key features of modern businesses, which Chandler identifies as appearing in the 1850s and becoming dominant after World War II, are the existence of a hierarchy of salaried managers, ownership by capital separate from the operations of production, and internal specialization among the sub-units of a company. From a social perspective, the end result of this process was the creation of a new class of managers. This new class, in turn, played a crucial role in preserving the growth of the economy. "[I]n making administrative decisions, career managers preferred policies that favored the long-term stability and growth of their enterprises to those that maximized current profits."[44]

Along with the emergence of a new managerial class, at the beginning of the twentieth century the rise of the modern corporation resulted in a profound shift in control over business affairs from stockholders to directors. In 1896 the Supreme Court could declare "when the charter was silent, the ultimate determination of the management of the corporate affairs rests with its stock holders."[45] Thirty-five years later, a textbook on corporate management identified the new order of business management succinctly: "the powers of the board of directors . . . are identical with the powers of the corporation."[46] This philosophy fit neatly with the idea of the corporation as the engine of economic activity, with directors adopting the position of engineers (i.e., experts), an attitude that reached its own extreme point of development with the 1960s dictum that "a manager manages," a reference to universally applicable first principles of stewardship equally suitable for the affairs of a business, a national economy, or a war.

The development of the modern corporation, propelled by the advent of national stock exchanges and electronic communications (exemplified by stock tickers), also meant that corporations ceased to have any particular location. Theodore Roosevelt set up a Federal Bureau of Corporations; Presidents Roosevelt, Taft, and Wilson all proposed the creation of federal corporate charters. As Taft declared, corporations were "in fact federal because they are as wide as the country and are entirely unlimited in their business by state lines."[47] In part, calls for federalization of corporate charters reflect an understanding that in fundamental ways corporations had supplanted many of the policy-dictating functions that would otherwise be served by governments. Too big and too fluidly organized to be effectively controlled by the state governments that putatively created them, and with limited federal interference, corporations, by the 1930s, were the dominant economic and political actors, a role for which there was broad public support right up to the Great Depression.

The Depression and the New Deal recovery that followed resulted in the creation of a modern scheme of government capable of exercising regulatory authority over modern corporations. Both federal regulation and the director-controlled model for the modern corporation reached their apotheosis in the 1970s. By this time, corporations were not only natural persons, they were among the least-regulated citizens of any state. Corporate directors had for decades taken advantage of their geographical indeterminacy by shopping for the most favorable charter terms they could find. The state of Delaware, recognizing a source of revenue, enacted laws that were (and are) extraordinarily favorable to corporations in terms of tax and legal liability and specifically to management in terms of the degree of control over the corporation's affairs granted by the standard Delaware charter.

By the end of the 1970s, more than half of the five hundred biggest corporations in America resided in Delaware.

The description of corporate management and its relation to governmental regulation has changed in the past two decades. Since the 1970s we have seen the rise of what may be termed the "postmodern" corporation, fueled by the same transformative forces—technologies of information management, conceptualizations of business structures—that were at work in the middle of the 1800s. As a result of these changes, corporations no longer have the characteristics that were called upon to legitimate their role as the governors of our political economy. The claims of managerial expertise of an earlier generation of corporate directors appeared as hubris in the post-Vietnam era. The Reagan Revolution of the 1980s was not a return to the model of leadership by corporate elites but rather an articulation of Dugald Stewart's faith in a natural order of prosperity. Campaign-financing reforms of the 1970s had increased the importance of corporations in politics by curtailing the activities of wealthy individuals. Within corporations, the separation of ownership from control inherent in the modern corporation had reached a point where it generated widespread shareholder backlash. Fueled and guided by speculative investors who recognized the existence of huge potential short-term profits and, in junk bonds, the perfect lever with which to get at them, shareholder resentment of often high-handed directorial control led to an explosion of hostile takeovers, leveraged buyouts, and boardroom coups.

In this environment, a profound shift in the nature of corporate control occurred, resulting in the emergence of what I will call the "postmodern" corporation. The postmodern corporation is one in which capital, in the form of stockholders, is diffuse on the one hand, but actively involved in the determination of corporate policy on the other. This has been driven, in part, by the emergence of institutional investors as dominant forces in the market. Ownership of investment funds is diffuse, but practical control is held by fund managers, a departure from older systems of capital accumulation and control as radical as the creation of the in-house counsel in the 1890s. In addition, improvements in communications technology have enabled investors to act with incredible speed and to engage in trading by algorithm, pushing the imperative of short-term profit to calculations of ever-decreasing units of time. The desire for short-term increases in stock value—rather than for simple corporate "profit"—is imposed as an imperative by shareholder-dominated boards of directors on managers who might be supposed, in an older system, to have been the repositories of long-term visions.[48]

The existence of a class of management-oriented institutional investors in fact exacerbates the separation of control from ownership by further separating control from operation, a process akin to the development of absentee ownership. The result is to diminish yet again the connection between the interests of shareholders and those of the corporation, this time by the intercession of a category of capital, rather than managerial, elites: institutional investors, corporate raiders, and the threat of bond-financed takeover. Similarly, the integrity of the business entity is no longer a significant aspect of corporate valuation. A process of internalization of specialized functions into processes controlled by managerial elites is thus replaced by the acquisition of specialized functions by the combination with other corporate entities, which combinations are themselves controlled by capital elites.

One problematic characteristic of the postmodern corporation is that it cannot be relied upon as the source for a private-sector system of welfare capitalism. Consider the availability of technologies that permit the reductions in workforces, for instance. While such technological advances are likely to result in sectoral dislocations under any circumstances, traditionally, managerial elites were concerned to retool and reinvigorate the subunits of the corporate entity to incorporate the new elements into a process of production. This is of little cheer to the laid-off worker, of course, but it is of some comfort to economists, who can point to the emergence of new job opportunities as the corporation continues its growth.

By contrast, a postmodern corporation's response to technological advance has been almost completely destructive of the corporate entities themselves. The maximization of stock values is often best achieved by reducing the workforce *regardless* of the effects of such cost-cutting measures on the internal processes of production. In the long run, of course, such strategies may prove detrimental to the health of the enterprise, but that is precisely the distinction between modern and postmodern corporate rationalization. Other socially undesirable aspects of stock value maximization—movement of jobs overseas, short-term production and inventory schedules—can similarly be traced at least in part to a displacement of managerial imperatives by shareholder imperatives. Put another way, the yardstick of "value" has moved from capital assets to share price.

It will be protested, at this point, that this analysis gives short shrift to the hard-won power of investors—whether as individuals or pooled into pension funds, mutual funds, and the like—to exercise controls over the management of the companies whose efforts they underwrite. To the extent that this posits an opposition between the interests of individual shareholders and the claims of public policy, it is precisely the issue that this essay is *not* designed to discuss. Wharton had defended corporate privileges by identifying entrepreneurial capitalists, not only as the flag bearers for the march of civilization, but also as the guarantors of the general welfare. The point of this essay is precisely that the postmodern corporation does not play the socially desirable roles to which Wharton alluded one hundred years ago. At the same time, government's purchase over corporate actions by regulation has been further degraded by the devolution of management authority. Thus neither affirmative nor negative conceptions of corporate duty presently exercise a significant counterweight to the structural imperative to maximize immediate gain.

REVIVING THE PUBLIC CORPORATION

What, then—to borrow a phrase—is to be done? As noted at the outset of this essay, observers of American business practices frequently criticize the absence of externally enforceable duties for corporations beyond those specified in particularistic regulations and the pressure of an internalist conception of duty that elevates immediate profit to the level of a norm. The account presented above attempts to suggest the historical context in which this state of affairs came to predominate. In thinking about possible responses to a situation that is widely agreed to be undesirable, it is important to tailor the discussion to terms that have the potential for real effect. For example, it seems highly unlikely that any government of the United States will move to take significant control over our national economy in the foreseeable future.

Similarly, an expansion of the government's powers of negative sanction appears at present to be impracticable. Like any other politically driven (and bureaucratically controlled) process, the generation of government regulation reached the point of excess and has generated its own backlash. Undoubtedly, many of the regulations that Vice President Gore's task force and a variety of Republican-dominated committees in Congress have identified as superfluous are, indeed, deserving of their fate. As a matter of political reality, however, this atmosphere also makes it unlikely that initiatives for new regulatory schemes will be successful, regardless of the merits of the regulations in question.

For those who wish to contemplate ways to encourage progress in the development of national economic policies, then, a potentially fruitful alternative focus is the revival of the idea of affirmative corporate duties. A return to the days of special incorporations and a strong ultra vires doctrine is implausible, but there are a great number of things that both state and federal governments might undertake to try to influence corporate decision making.

In modern corporations, specific decisions are, at the end of the day, irreducibly a matter of the biographical forces governing the thinking and actions of a handful of individuals. In postmodern corporations, the same reduction leads to the outcomes of a process of preference optimization driven by data, with more or less interaction with human judgment depending on the design of the fund in question. The law, however, establishes the structural constraints within which both of these decision-making processes take place, the liabilities to which the corporation (and its officers, directors, and shareholders) are liable, and the power of government agencies at a variety of levels to intervene in the interests of local economies and national well-being. In the final analysis, the role of laws in the conduct of corporations is to define their public duties; therefore, our first point of focus should be the near total absence of any such duties in the assumption of the corporate form by business entities today.

In the next section of this paper I will outline some possible avenues for the creation of meaningful affirmative corporate duties—although the proposals may fit that concept only imperfectly—in the present political environment. I wish to propose the renewal of the idea of the "public corporation" and suggest three kinds of legal developments that could be used to accomplish this goal: (1) the creation of differing grades of corporate charter, carrying different legal duties and subject to different levels of public regulation and private liability; (2) a system of tax incentives designed to foster desirable corporate behavior; and (3) both incentives and sanctions on the process of business mergers and relocations designed to foster development of the private economy. These ideas resonate with other proposals that have been heard recently, particularly from Robert Reich and from a Senate task force headed by Senator Jeff Bingaman (D-N.M.).[49]

It should be pointed out that the emphasis in the discussion that follows is on the role of government in creating the environment in which corporations are created and act. At the risk of repetition, the political feasibility of a proposal is likely to vary inversely with the degree to which direct intervention in the command-and-control systems of corporate governance are called for. For this reason, I have not included proposals to use the law to decree the recognition of new classes of stakeholder, despite the very good economic arguments in favor of such a reconceptualization.[50] In addition, my focus is on the ways in which government might go about implementing policy preferences; as a result, the discussion of the actual goals to be pursued is deliberately general. Scholars and experts of all kinds have much to say on this question, of course, and will undoubtedly play a crucial role in the formulation of any final legislation, but in the end, that process is a political one, which will not be initiated unless and until there is sufficient support for the *idea* of the effort. As David Vogel has put it, "[t]he social performance of a large corporation comprises three dimensions: corporate philanthropy, corporate responsibility, and corporate policy."[51] The proposals that follow touch on the latter two of these elements, with an eye toward four specific areas of corporate conduct: interactions with consumers, interactions with employees, interactions with the local physical and social environment, and conduct in the national market for corporate securities.

The analysis above suggests that the postmodern corporation is subject to inadequate incentives to act in a socially desirable way. While it would be unreasonable to suggest that the idea of the business corporation as the basic unit of the American political economy should be replaced outright, there is no reason why that model of organization might not be supplemented by the creation of additional models. An example might be the creation of a new class of federally incorporated "P" (for "public") corporations. A "P" corporation would be subject to a restrictive charter that would commit it to perform desired business activities. Employment, operation, and reinvestment practices might all be required to fall within specified guidelines.

To make this proposal sensible, both negative sanctions for breach of the charter and positive incentives to justify organization under such restrictive terms would be required. As a negative sanction, there should be a procedure for the revocation of the corporation's charter in an extreme case. As positive incentives, I propose that "P" corporations be rewarded for their compliance with the terms of their charters in three ways: by preferences in the awarding of public contracts; by the availability of public financing, including the use of specific, government-guaranteed bond issues; and by the relaxation of regulatory strict liability standards based on activities by prior property owners.

The use of preference in the awarding of public contracts is both well established and controversial. From a legal and constitutional perspective, however, the kinds of objections to racially based set-asides that motivated the *Adarand* decision of last summer are entirely absent where the justification for the preference is directly related to the corporation's public obligations. Even the most well-intentioned racial preference program runs the risk of causing damage from political backlash that equals or outweighs its benefits to specific recipients. Aside from a certain—potent—generalized objection to "government," however, there is no plausible basis for political resentments of benefits given to corporations that assure continuing local employment, high base salaries with caps for executives, or continued local ownership and management and a "no-merger" policy.

The same politically attractive qualities appear even more strongly in the case of public funding, with the obvious comparative case of sports teams. A large part of the frustration expressed by residents of cities whose professional sports teams have left for better contractual arrangements derives from the sense of wasted investment. The National Football League (NFL), to take one example, is unable to prevent such moves by virtue of the fact that it lacks an antitrust exemption—a problem that obviously does not apply to governments.

Finally, the relaxation of strict liability standards based on prior use involves the explicit weighing of one public-policy initiative against another. To take the best-known example, the Superfund law was originally written in 1980 to finance the cleanup of polluted sites by moneys collected from guilty parties. When it became obvious that those funds would be drastically insufficient to pay for the Superfund program, the law was modified in 1984 to give us the present tangled system of crosscutting strict liabilities. This decision was made on the calculation that the alternatives—to give up Superfund entirely or to spread out the costs of the program by raising taxes—would be politically unpalatable. Well, if the imposition of the often extremely heavy burden of the Comprehensive Environmental Response, Compensation and Liability Act of 1980 (CERCLA) compliance can be imposed as a financing measure, then surely it can be as readily relaxed to encourage the revival of regional economies battered by waves of layoffs, corporate disappearances, and brutally escalating salary differentials.

Taxes, too, are means by which "P" corporations could be encouraged. The present corporate tax structure is sufficiently complex to provide continuing employment to a great number of law firms. This essay is not the place (nor am I the author) to engage in an extended review of the tax code. This is arguably appropriate, however, as it appears quite likely that some simplification of that code will be undertaken in the next few years. This next proposal outlines a general approach toward using revision of the tax code as an opportunity to exert pressure on corporate conduct.

A crucial recognition at the outset of this discussion is that under our current tax code private corporations are granted generous public subsidies, in the form of tax breaks, in a variety of areas, particularly in allowances for depreciation in the value of resources and equipment and industry-specific exemptions. The theory behind these tax benefits has always been that they were necessary to ensure the continued profitability of the businesses in question, which would in turn be of benefit to the public at large. Under this reasoning, "P" corporations should be entitled to receive benefits above and beyond those granted to other corporations. Conversely, existing tax benefits should be scaled back for corporations that are not bound by public duties.

The political feasibility of this proposal is unclear at the present time. Certainly there is resistance to the exercise of government authority through modification of the tax code other than the lowering of individual taxes. Conversely, however, popular resentment of corporate benefits and the republican vocabulary of duties argue powerfully for a more tailored relationship between tax benefits and the creation of a public good.

Another area worth exploring is the investment side of the capital equation. The fact that it is unfashionable to call for an increase in governmental regulation of business does nothing to disparage the recognition by many careful observers that in many areas American businesses are comparatively *under*regulated rather than the reverse. The rules of the Securities and Exchange Commission, however, define much of the environment in which the postmodern corporation creates its profits. In the final analysis, movement on this score cannot be characterized as anything other than what it is: coercive regulation of a segment of the economy in the interest of public welfare. As recent experiences with efforts to gut environmental protections demonstrate, however, Americans are not necessarily averse to the existence of reasonable, beneficial regulations. Like the tax code—which is intimately involved in this process as well as in the more direct process of subsidy through deduction—current securities laws are so dizzyingly complex that pressure for their simplification in the near future seems likely. Such a process would create an opportunity to legislate notions of corporate duty by restricting the most egregiously postmodern corporate actions in the contexts of relocations and mergers. There are a number of ways in which the destructive tendencies of shareholder-driven reorganizations might be curtailed: existing recognition of the distinction between short-term and long-term security investment might be strengthened, or limitations might be placed on the permissible debt-to-equity ratio in a buyout situation.

The elements of the "P" corporation charter mentioned above all emphasize the relations between the corporation and government. Government can also play a role at the moment of the corporation's creation, however, in encouraging socially desirable forms of internal corporate organization. Employee representation on the board of directors would be one example, as would a requirement of broad dissemination of information within the corporation, particularly in the context of negotiations over terms and conditions of employment. In addition, the position of the directors might be strengthened against the demands of institutional shareholders by a rule that distinguished between strategic and immediate policy decisions and limited shareholder input on the latter. "P" corporations might be required to reserve a portion of their voting shares for employees in situations involving the purchase or sale of a company in recognition of the fact that the sale of an entire company involves noncapital stakeholders to a degree unmatched in the day-to-day management of business affairs. Alternatively, the voting system for shareholders could be modified to limit the influence that a single investing institution could exercise over the conduct of the corporation's affairs. It is true, of course, that in the final analysis the stockholders are the owners of the company,[52] but the structures of communication and decision making within the corporate system have a great deal to do with dictating the connection between ownership, operation, and control.

It is important to recognize that "P" corporations might present less-tempting investment targets for those concerned with maximizing their profits. On the other hand, the financial and legal benefits that this proposal provides to the bottom line of a "P" corporation's books would—in the long or medium term—be more than sufficient to make such an entity a profitable investment. If short-term securities speculators are discouraged from participation in this class of business enterprise, those seeking secure investments might find these corporations highly attractive. In this way, "P" corporations, unlike nonprofit corporations, have the potential to become a significant segment of the market, and hence to play an important role in delivering capitalism's social goods. For this to happen, however, it is crucial that policy makers recognize the necessity for making socially positive corporate conduct attractive to capital.

The idea of a "P" corporation makes the most sense in the traditional contexts of public corporations: transportation services, banking, managed health care organizations (MCOs),[53] communications, public works, and education. The public-works category is likely to become much more important in the coming decades, as privatization of government services runs up against a gigantic backlog of demand for social welfare, "workfare," and infrastructure projects. In this context, it is worth noting that a federally issued corporate charter has the benefit of preventing corporations from bidding states off against one another to get the most beneficial deal, thus weakening the public purposes of the proposal.

The proposals presented above are vestigial, of course. They are presented to suggest directions for the development of further ideas. Certainly there is a profound tension between our national commitment to reliance on the private business sector as the engine of our collective prosperity and trends in corporate management. The restoration of the idea of affirmative corporate duties is one potentially promising route to address this tension. The idea of "duty" is quite different from the obligations imposed by punitive regulations governing product or environmental liability. Rather than external restraints imposed on existing institutions, affirmative corporate duties must be made intrinsic to the construction of the corporation itself. Business corporations are an essential element of our economy, but the mere fact of existence does not warrant special treatment. By contrast, a category of corporation developed around, and dependent upon, the performance of public duties should reasonably expect to be fostered and supported in its efforts. This distinction is the essence of the idea of a private sector that acts as the vehicle for public progress.

NOTES

1. These figures are taken from Morton J. Horwitz, *The Transformation of American Law: The Crisis of Legal Orthodoxy*, vol. 1 (New York: Oxford University Press, 1992).

2. Roane's comments are quoted in the context of a lengthy and excellent treatment of the history of American corporate law in Horwitz, *Transformation of American Law*, vol. 1, p. 112.

3. *Cleveland Plain Dealer*, 17 December, 1836. Reprinted in Lawrence H. White, ed., *Democratick Editorials: Essays in Jacksonian Political Economy* by William Leggett (Indianapolis: Liberty Press 1984), p. 37.

4. *Cleveland Plain Dealer*, 24 December 1836, p. 339.

5. Joseph K. Angell and Samuel Ames, *A Treatise on the Law of Private Corporations Aggregate*, 2d ed. (1843), p. 66, quoted in Lawrence M. Friedman, *A History of American Law*, 2d ed. (New York: Simon & Schuster, 1985), p. 198.

6. Victor Morawetz, *A Treatise on the Law of Private Corporations*, 2d ed. (1886), p. 617, col. 2, quoted in Friedman, *History of American Law*, p. 518.

7. *Commonwealth v. Erie and No. East Rr. Co.*, 27 Pa. 339, 351 (1856).

8. Friedman, *History of American Law*, p. 191.

9. *Allen v. McKean*, 1 F. Cas. 489, C.C.D. Me. (1833).

10. *Downing v. Indiana State Board of Agriculture* 129 Ind. 443, 28 N.E 123 (1891).

11. In *Fertilizing Co. v. Hyde Park*, 97 U.S. 659 (1878), the Court held that the police had authority to regulate transportation of offal through a village; in *Stone v. Mississippi*, 101 U.S. 814 (1880), the Court ruled that a state could repeal a corporate charter that permitted operation of a lottery under the general antigambling law.

12. "The court does not wish to hear argument on the question whether the provision in the Fourteenth Amendment to the Constitution, which forbids a State to deny to any person within its jurisdiction the equal protection of the laws, applies to these corporations. We are all of opinion that it does." *Santa Clara v. Southern Pacific Railroad*, 118 US 394, 396 (1886).

13. Horwitz, *Transformation of American Law*, vol. 2, p. 75.

14. Horwitz, *Transformation of American Law*, vol. 2, p. 78.

15. On this point see Eric Foner, *Free Soil, Free Labor, Free Men: The Ideology of the Republican Party Before the Civil War* (New York: Oxford University Press, 1995).

16. See Samuel J. M. Donnelly, "The Fault Principle: A Sketch of Its Development in Tort Law During the Nineteenth Century," *Syracuse University Law Review* 18, (summer 1967): 728–50.

17. Francis Hilliard, *The Law of Torts or Private Wrongs* (Boston: Little, Brown & Co., 1859), p. 66.

18. *Brown v. Kendall*, 6 Cush. 297, 60 Mass. 292 (1850).

19. There is considerable debate among legal historians as to whether the fault element was something new in American tort law. Friedman, along with (notably) Horwitz, Wex S. Malone, and G. Edward White, working from a variety of perspectives, argues that the introduction of the fault principle represented something new and that its main effect was to limit traditional bases for corporate liability. From this perspective the introduction of the idea of duty in tort law represented a further restriction of liability; only those to whom one owed a duty of care would be entitled to demand the exercise of any particular degree of foresight. A contrary historical thesis holds that fault was an element of liability in all but a very narrow range of cases (involving animals, migrating water, and other *ferae naturae*). From this perspective it is the universal applicability of the emergent duties of care that is the most notable feature. Authors who fall into this latter camp include Gary Schwartz and Richard Rabin. Regardless of which of these historical accounts is found to be most persuasive, an examination of the form that the concept of duty took in the latter nineteenth century, and its consequences for the public and legal conceptions of the role of corporations, is an important subject for study.

20. *Brown*, 53 N.H. 448.

21. *Ryan v. New York Central Rr. Co.*, 35 N.Y. 210 (1866).

22. *Farwell v. Boston & Worcester Rail Road*, 45 Mass. 49 (1842).

23. Alan Jones, "Republicanism, Railroads, and Nineteenth-Century Midwest-

ern Constitutionalism," in Ellen Franklin Paul and Howard Dickman, eds., *Liberty, Property and Government: Constitutional Interpretation Before the New Deal* (Albany, N.Y.: State University of New York Press, 1989), p. 249.

24. Hilliard, *The Law of Torts*, p. 508.

25. Commencing with *Central Military Tract R.R. Co. v. Rockafellow*, 17 Ill. Reports 541 (1856).

26. 1st ed. (Boston: n.p., 1869), pp. 5–6.

27. Horwitz, *Transformation of American Law*, vol. 2, p. 58.

28. *Ryan v. New York Central Rr. Co.*, 35 N.Y. 210 (1866).

29. The issue of an employer's vicarious liability for the negligence of its employees was also the subject of a great deal of litigation and doctrinal angst in this period. The upshot, however, was essentially a restatement of traditional master-servant rules, under which an employer is liable for acts of its employees that occur in the course of employment.

30. *Galena & Chi. Union R.R. Co. v. Fay*, 16 Ill. Reports 558, 570 (1855).

31. The role of workers' compensation is not mentioned here for want of space. It is noteworthy that workers' compensation statutes removed the largest single class of claims against industry from the jurisdiction of private law liability at just the time that industrial corporations were most successful at arguing that their duty to succeed superceded any other, more traditional, duties to avoid inflicting injury on their neighbors and employees.

32. *Bradford Glycerine Co. v. St. Marys Woolen Mfg. Co.*, 60 Ohio 560, 54 N.E. 528 (1899), involving the storage of nitroglycerine.

33. *Homans v. Boston Elevated Railway*, 180 Mass. 456, 62 N.E. 737 (1902).

34. *Palsgraf v. Long Island Railroad*, 248 N.Y. 339, 162 N.E. 99 (1928).

35. On this point, see especially Karen Orren, *Belated Feudalism* (Cambridge: Cambridge University Press, 1991). Orren's instrumentalist interpretation of the development of labor law as a remnant of feudal relations has been challenged by both legal historians and labor historians. See, for instance, Christopher L. Tomlins, *Law, Labor and Ideology in the Early American Republic* (Cambridge: Cambridge University Press, 1993) (arguing that labor law developed along with the rest of American common law in response to a change in the "mode of rule," a concept that will be discussed more than once in this essay) and David Montgomery, *The Fall of the House of Labor: The Workplace, the State, and American Labor Activism, 1865–1925* (Cambridge: Cambridge University Press, 1991) (arguing, inter alia, that craft-based labor organizations asserted premodern legal categories in resistance to attempts by managers to implement innovations in work relations, rather than the reverse). A persistent question for political scientists has been to explain the absence of labor socialism in America, and the concomitant paucity in social welfare programs, in comparison with other industrialized Western countries. For an excellent review of this topic, with emphasis on the interactions between labor organizations and the courts in the nineteenth and early twentieth centuries, see William E. Forbath, *Law and the Shaping of the American Labor Movement* (Cambridge, Mass.: Harvard University Press, 1991).

36. There are a number of good discussions of economic regulation in the colonial period. See, for instance, Christopher L. Tomlins, *Law, Labor and Ideology in the Early American Republic*, Cambridge: Cambridge University Press, 1993.

37. See Thomas K. McGraw, *Prophets of Regulation* (Cambridge, Mass.: Har-

vard University Press, Belknap Press, 1984), p. 5, citing Alfred D. Chandler, *The Railroads: The Nations' First Big Business* (New York: Harcourt, Brace & World, 1965), pp. 3–18.

38. McGraw, *Prophets of Regulation*, pp. 25–29.

39. Gary T. Schwartz, "Tort Law and the Economy in Nineteenth-Century America: A Reinterpretation," *Yale Law Journal* 90, no. 8 (July 1981): 1756.

40. Lawrence Friedman and Jack Ladinsky, "Social Change and the Law of Industrial Accidents," *Columbia Law Review* 67 (January 1967): 64.

41. *NLRB v. Jones & Laughlin*, 301 U.S. 1, 48 (1937).

42. Alfred Chandler, *The Visible Hand: The Managerial Revolution in American Business* (Cambridge, Mass.: Harvard University Press, Belknap Press, 1977).

43. Chandler, *The Visible Hand*, p. 7.

44. Chandler, *The Visible Hand*, p. 10.

45. *Union Pacific Ry. v. Chicago R.I & P. Ry.* 163 US 564, 596 (1896).

46. H. Spellman, *A Treatise on the Principles of Law Governing Corporate Directors* (Englewood Cliffs, N.J.: Prentice Hall, 1931), p. 237, quoted in Horwitz, *Transformation of American Law*, vol. 2, p. 98.

47. Quoted in Johnathan Rowe, "Reinventing the Coporation," *Washington Monthly*, April 1996.

48. For a case in point, see the *New York Times*'s account of the change in corporate culture at Chase Manhattan Bank that accompanied the arrival of mutual-fund manager Michael F. Price as chief shareholder. "The Company as One Happy Family, No More," *New York Times*, 4 March 1996, A12.

49. The task force called for the creation of a status of "Business Allied with America's Working Families," or an "A-Corp." That proposal, as excerpted in *Harper's Magazine*, May 1996, p. 45, was as follows:

Qualifications

"In order to qualify as an A-Corp, a business would have to:

1. Contribute an amount equal to at least 3 percent of payroll to a pension plan;

2. Devote an amount equal to at least 2 percent of payroll to employee training or education;

3. Offer to all U.S. employees, and pay at least half the cost of, a healthcare plan;

4. Operate for its U.S. workers a profit-sharing or gain-sharing or stock plan in which 50 percent or more of employees participate;

5. Ensure that the total compensation of the highest-paid employee is no greater than fifty times the compensation of the lowest-paid, full-time employee;

6. Ensure that at least 50 percent of all new investment in R&D occurs in the United States, and that at least 90 percent of all new investment in plant, equipment, and employment used to produce goods consumed in the United States is directed here;

7. Maintain above-average occupational safety and environmental compliance records."

Benefits

"We would modify the tax code to provide an enormous incentive for businesses to become allied with America's working families. Two different tax rates would be applied to businesses. A significantly higher rate (for example, 18 percent) would apply to the tax base of all businesses that had not qualified for A-Corp status. Businesses that qualify as A-Corps would pay a significantly lower rate (for example, 11 percent). This rate differential would finally provide American businesses with the kind of incentive that other countries routinely provide to businesses for corporate decisions they want to encourage.

As a qualified A-Corp, a business would also be entitled (1) to speedier federal-agency review and decision making, (2) to participate in voluntary compliance programs, and (3) to take advantage of newly created "safe-harbor" exemptions from certain regulatory requirements.

Qualified A-Corps would also be entitled to a strong preference (10 percent cost advantage, set-asides, and the like) when competing for U.S. government procurement contracts."

The task force also recommended implementation of a "less-than-one-and-a-half-percent" tax on the sale of securities within two years of purchase, in order to discourage short-term trading.

50. To cite only a few examples, in the 1980s Ralph Nader and George Lodge were associated with different conceptions of expanded representation of noncapital stakeholders on corporate boards. More recently, many economists have worked to reconceptualize the notion of "capital" inherent in the identification of stakeholder. See Margaret Blair, *Ownership and Control: Rethinking Corporate Governance for the Twenty-First Century* (Washington, D.C.: Brookings, 1995).

51. Thornton Bradshaw and David Vogel, eds., *Corporations and Their Critics* (New York: McGraw-Hill, 1981), p. viii.

52. But see discussion, Blair, *Ownership and Control.*

53. It should be noted that one effect of this proposal would, in all likelihood, be the displacement of nonprofit corporations from their present position of dominance in the health care industry. This particular topic is too complex to go into here, but in general it is noteworthy that many critics have questioned the appropriateness of the nonprofit form in big business (as which health care certainly qualifies!). See Robert Charles Clark, "Does the Nonprofit Form Fit the Hospital Industry?" *Harvard Law Review* 93 (1980): 1416; for a treatment of the development of nonprofit corporations generally, see Bruce A. Campbell, "Social Federalism: The Constitutional Position of Nonprofit Corporations in Nineteenth-Century America," *Law and History Review* 8, no. 2 (fall 1990): 149. In some senses, this proposal seeks to create an environment in which a great number—even, eventually, a preponderance—of corporations will choose to act in socially beneficial ways, a role that is presently imposed only on nonprofit corporations.

Chapter 5

Thinking About Social Security

Alvin L. Schorr

U.S. SOCIETY, SIXTY YEARS AFTER

As we address the current policy/political situation, we face both immediate and long-term issues. Many people are in trouble, and steps that are being taken on the national scene will both deepen and spread the trouble. We find ourselves urgently seeking immediate solutions, compromises, inventions that may ease the problem. We have to do this or, anyway, somebody has to do this; people eat and are sheltered in the short term.

At the same time, the structure of our welfare state—what I call here the social compact—is shifting under our feet. Nor is it to be reinstated as it was. The way people perceive the long-term goals in this area is important both for the success of the long-term struggle and because it may affect the acceptability of short-term solutions that we devise.

In this brief chapter, I address long-term goals, in part to make it clear that, with or without the conservative tide that has come upon us, the social compact was going to have to change. Indeed, although the move to deconstruct the welfare state is usually phrased in ideological or money-saving terms (deficit reduction, tax cutting), underlying social and economic changes demand a revised social compact.

Windup

As used here, the social compact is the set of assumptions about what citizens and the government owe to each other. This encompasses a vast range of commitments, of course, such as national and personal safety and the guarantees incorporated in the Bill of Rights and, on the other hand, commitments to be law abiding and pay various taxes. Here, I will deal only with the reciprocal responsibilities bearing on Social Security.

Current ideas about the social compact are directly traceable to a report of Franklin Roosevelt's Committee on Economic Security, which was developed in the context of the Great Depression and drew ideas from reformist movements earlier in the century and from European experiences. The further development of these ideas was soon influenced by Britain's Beveridge Report[1] and the sense, arising from World War II, that a new and better world was owed to populations that had made great sacrifices. The promise was articulated at a famous mid-Atlantic meeting of Roosevelt and Winston Churchill: freedom from want, freedom from fear, freedom of speech, and freedom of religion.

Not entirely consciously, the architects of "freedom from want and . . . from fear" held these eight assumptions:

1. Family support is provided, in general, by full-time work for men, who follow a traditional career pattern.

2. Men earn a so-called family wage.

3. Women are assured income, if not from their husbands, then through benefits to which men's work has entitled them.

4. Two parents and a child or children constitute a normal family. (Some families have a single parent, to be sure, mainly because of the death of a husband. They are protected as described in (3) above.)

5. The population includes many children and declining numbers of adults in successive age groups, which is to say, a relatively small percentage of aged people.

6. Society feels a preponderant sense of communal responsibility for those who are in trouble, possibly arising out of the Great Depression (when Adam Smith and Social Darwinism became equally hard to defend) and probably strengthened by World War II (WWII).

7. Related to (6), both here and in Britain, is the explicit idea that this responsibility rests with individuals as well as government. This concept was expressed in the United States by the insistence, particularly by labor unions, on a deduction from wages as the mechanism for earning and financing entitlement to Social Security.

8. The steady march to affluence and unexpectedly high revenues for government from year to year, which were fortunate facts as governments moved to implement the social compact, would continue.

In the United States, the fundamental structures that developed over the years (Social Security, which included old age, survivors', and disability insurance; unemployment insurance; workers' compensation; Medicare) were built around the principle of *social insurance*, with equal weight on both words. That is, citizens would insure themselves against economic risks such as retirement and unemployment. At the same time, coverage and benefit formulas would favor low-income people disproportionately, thus ameliorating poverty. For those for whom such protections were not adequate, there would be a safety net—i.e., means-tested programs (welfare, food stamps, public housing, Medicaid).

Fundamental Changes and What They Mean

The validity of each of the assumptions listed above has changed in fundamental ways, of course. Following the same listing and without going into detail, these changes are evident:

1. More than half of all women work outside of the home, including women with children and those with or without husbands. Moreover, full-time work is giving way in some large measure to part-time and occasional work. As of 1990, only 70 percent of employed women worked full time and only 64 percent worked fifty weeks or more a year. Careers are widely interrupted by unemployment or other reasons for leaving the market.

   This change means that, as the generations of women who were not expected to work outside the home pass from the scene, it will become less and less clear why spouses should receive benefits they have not earned themselves. Part-time, occasional, and interrupted work patterns mean that current rules about social security, unemployment insurance, and private benefits will, for many people, protect them at lower levels or not at all.

2. Offering a family wage is no longer the objective of most employers. Moreover, the job market is splitting between well-paying jobs and low-paying (unskilled, service-sector) jobs. The minimum wage, earned for a whole year, once provided enough income to support a family of *four* above the poverty level. Now, it just about does this for *two* people.

   Taken together with (1), above, *this means that* the portion of the population with low-paying, occasional, or part-time employment will not be able to save money or accumulate equity in a home or otherwise. That is, they will be very vulnerable economically and will need *more* protection than such people, say, twenty years ago. Based on their contributions, however, they will, in general, be *less* well protected.

3. Women are increasingly seen to be responsible for their own incomes. This along with the fact that their husbands' incomes, from which their benefits may currently be calculated, are debased means that spouses' benefits are likely to erode. The higher-income portion of the population is not likely to be concerned about this, as they are able to protect themselves with individual retirement accounts (IRAs) and other tax-free options. That is, the coalition of economic interests that has supported the social compact, as it has so far been formulated, may splinter.

4. Almost one-quarter of families with children are headed by a single parent. One-quarter (an overlapping figure) of women who have never married have had a

child. These proportions are not likely to decline and, indeed, appear to be rising. Single parents typically have the lowest household incomes in the population.

This means that social insurance provides the weakest protection for families with children. For them, retirement insurance is not an imminent problem, to be sure, but weaker disability, unemployment, and survivors' insurance are and will be serious problems.

5. The number of people over age sixty-five, that is, those who, in general, need to be supported to some degree, was 10 per 100 working-age people in 1930 and is expected to rise to 30 by the year 2025. On the other hand, the number of children, who also need to be supported by the working-age population, declined sharply from 1960 to 1990, mitigating the overall support problem.

   A *combined* dependency ration, 68 per 100 in 1990, is expected to go to 78 in 2025. To be sure, this is far short of the combined ratio of 95 in 1965, when baby boomers were young, which the nation seemed to manage without undue difficulty.

   Still, *this means that* as the years go by, the working population may expect to bear a heavier burden than in recent years. If, as now, anxiety about the government budget is high, there may be more severe difficulties in financing social security.

6. and 7. The preponderant sense of communal responsibility has faded in recent years. Individual responsibility is being asserted as if it were a new element in the social compact, focusing on employment and plainly expressing a deep sense of public frustration. These feelings have taken shape at the same time as severe cutbacks in safety-net programs, welfare in particular.

   This means that safety-net programs are likely to become gossamer thin as the years pass. The drive to induce or force applicants to work will persist and income-support levels will decline, especially if the wage levels with which they are compared remain low.

8. What is there to say about the relationship between anticipated government revenues and the demands placed on them that is not already well understood?

   This means that prospects for liberalizing programs, as they are now conceived, are dim.

A schema of these assumptions and changes appears in table 5.1.

WHAT MAY OR SHOULD BE DONE?

Reviewing social security trends across the world, Dalmer Hoskins, secretary general of the International Social Security Association, sees two alternative approaches to dealing with the role of social security in the changing world. "At the extreme end of the spectrum are those who would simply dismantle social security systems and opt for private solutions, with the responsibility for making prudent planning to meet the vicissitudes of life resting primarily with the individual." The "second and more subtle

Table 5.1
Assumptions and Current Realities of the U.S. Social Compact

Assumptions	Fundamental changes	Meaning
1. Support for families is provided normally by men working full time following traditional career paths.	More than half of all women -- with or without children or husbands -- work outside the home. Opportunity for full-time work is being replaced by part-time and occasional work.	It is becoming less and less clear why spouses should receive benefits they haven't earned themselves. Current rules about social security, unemployment insurance, and private benefits will provide lower or no benefits for many people.
2. Men earn a so-called family wage.	Most employers no longer intend to pay a family wage. The job market is splitting between well-paying jobs and low-paying service sector jobs. Full-time, year-round work at the minimum wage formerly brought a family of four above poverty. Now the wage is sufficient only for a family of two.	Low-paid, occasional, or part-time workers will be economically vulnerable, unable to save money or to accumulate equity in a home, in need of protection, but less protected based on their earnings.
3. Women are assured income, if not from their husbands, through benefits to which men's work has entitled them.	Women increasingly are seen responsible for their own incomes.	Benefits based on spouses' earnings are likely to erode. Higher income persons, unconcerned because they can protect themselves with IRAs and other tax benefits, will no longer support the compact.
4. A normal family consists of two parents and a child or children. Single-parent families arise largely because of the death of a husband and are assured income through the deceased husband's work-related entitlement.	Family composition has changed dramatically. Almost 1/4 of families with children are headed by a single parent. 1/4 of never-married women have had a child. Single parent families typically have lowest incomes of all families.	Social insurance programs provide the weakest protection for families with children. Reduced disability, unemployment, and survivors insurance benefits are an increasingly serious problem.
5. The population includes many children and declining numbers of adults in successive age groups, ... a relatively small percentage of aged people.	The number of people over 65, i.e., those needing some degree of social supports, has increased from 10 per 100 working people in 1930, to 20 per 100 in 1990, and will go to 30 per 100 by 2025. This trend is partially offset by decreasing numbers of dependent children per worker.	Working age people will bear heavier tax burdens. If tax burden is defined as an issue of intergenerational equity severe difficulties in financing social security may result.
6. The shared experiences of the Great Depression and WWII have generated a preponderant sense of communal responsibility for those who are in trouble.	Preponderant sense of communal responsibility has faded in recent years.	Safety net programs are likely to become increasingly inadequate, especially if wage levels with which they are compared remain low.
7. Individuals and governments share responsibility for social welfare and human well-being.	Individual responsibility is being asserted as if it were a new element in the social contract, focusing mainly on work and representing a deep sense of public frustration.	The drive to induce or force applicants to work will persist.
8. Increasing affluence and government revenues permit implementation of the social compact.	For two decades, real incomes have declined for between 25 and 50 % of the working population. This has generated pressure for caps on taxation and government spending, and for balanced governmental budgets.	Prospects for liberalizing social welfare programs, as now conceived, are limited.

Source: Alvin L. Schorr, "Thinking About Social Security," in *Social Welfare in Today's World* ed. Ronald C. Federico. Copyright © 1990 by McGraw-Hill. Reproduced with permission of The McGraw-Hill Companies.

approach" that he sees is to reduce the role of social insurance overall and rely on safety-net programs to relieve genuine distress. Unfortunately, Hoskins notes, historically such programs have turned out badly.[2]

Nevertheless, there are many permutations of the second alternative, including uses of the income-tax system to provide income to needy people (for example, the earned income tax credit or the exemption of Social Security income from taxation up to a prescribed level of total income). With respect to means testing, it may be useful to try to distinguish services that should be means tested from those that should not. (Writing about Britain, Howard Glennerster argues that housing and social care, which in practice were never universal anyway, should be means tested, while education and health care should not).[3]

Also, it is possible to think of more striking departures from current concepts. For example, if work is to be our core value in these matters, perhaps the opportunity to work should be assured, either by a deliberate policy of work sharing or by public work as a fall-back option. (The market has, in effect, moved broadly into work sharing but without the wage levels and fringe benefits that are assumed by proponents of work sharing.)

Or, if one assumes that present labor-market trends will continue and will progressively undermine the social compact, a different and striking departure would be to view some level of economic protection as a right of citizenship rather than as an earned benefit deriving from a work record. Indeed, President Clinton's proposed health plan was based on such a premise.

An examination of these issues and possible alternatives may raise very broad questions: To what extent, if at all, should the design of social insurance anticipate, and in a sense encourage, family arrangements which, though they may be the norm, are still not rhetorically acceptable? And, to what extent, if at all, should social insurance be used to achieve labor-market objectives, such as encouraging young elderly people to leave the labor market?

Short-Term Objectives

The financing problems of social security are not so serious or urgent as represented by people like the Concord Coalition. Social Security has been running a surplus year by year, which is expected to be $100 billion by 1999. The trust fund should reach nearly $3 *trillion* by 2020—several multiples of the $400 billion that has been regarded as a suitable contingency reserve. *After 2020*, and this is where the problem lies, it is estimated that the trust fund will be depleted every year until it is exhausted in the year 2030.

Reasons for this development include the increasing number of retirees, the steady slowing in the growth of employment, and stagnant real wages.

In other words, beneficiaries will increase while, relative to them, the number of contributors and the level at which they contribute will decline.

The problem will develop only after 2020 and is then not expected to be large. A payroll tax of 1 percent each for employers and employees starting in 2020 would deal with half of the shortfall. A variety of other measures are available: require coverage of the one-third of state and local employees not now covered, credit Social Security with the proceeds from the 1993 tax increase on Social Security benefits, compute benefits over thirty-eight years instead of thirty-five years.[4]

There has lately been some controversy about the technical accuracy of the calculation for the cost-of-living adjustment. If the method of calculation is truly in error and this is not merely a rationale for reducing real benefits, a corrected formula would produce substantial savings.

Finally (and I have not seen this proposed anywhere), in paying benefits, the system should *not* disregard substantial wage income of working beneficiaries as it now does. Such provisions mainly benefit the well-to-do elderly. Most of them enjoy work and would work anyway. To the extent that taking this income into account would lead some to give up work, it would be making room for younger people who need the jobs. (This is my answer to the question of whether social security may be used to achieve labor-market objectives.)

In 1983, the bipartisan National Commission on Social Security Reform, facing financing problems similar to today's, proposed a series of changes that Congress enacted. These represented course corrections, and they have served us well. The same strategy is open to us now, and there is plenty of time to pursue it. A thoughtful selection among the ideas noted above, as well as others that may be presented, will assure financial stability for the seventy-five years that is the horizon of Social Security planners.

Long-Term Objectives

The kinds of short-term measures I have listed would not alter the basic principles of Social Security. For the long run as well, I believe that we should maintain the universalist principle of Social Security. Indeed, Social Security is the central American program to which this should apply.

The reasons for this principle are well understood: means testing would lead to demands by many beneficiaries to opt out of the system, eventually turning what remains into a system very like welfare. Means testing and dealing with the loophole of assets transfer would escalate administrative cost. Means testing would fragment the political coalition that keeps the program strong.[5] One could find no better illustration of this than the fate of the sixty-year-old Aid for Families with Dependent Children Program.

I do not want to dwell on these arguments, but rather to direct attention to the difference between British and French reactions to economic downturn and declining government revenue. British policy changes have focused on efficiency, incentive, and means testing, as they have in this country. The French have focused on ways to be more efficient while maintaining "solidarity," as they say, and avoiding the creation of "excluded" categories of people. Martin Evans, Serge Paugam, and Joseph Prelis have just published a straightforward and thoughtful study of these policy differences and their effects, entitled *Chunnel Vision: Poverty, Social Exclusion and the Debate on Social Welfare in France and Britain*, from which I draw my comments here.[6] I invite you to look at it and see how much more decency and vision—without embracing bankruptcy—the French approach represents.

By the way, I do not mean to say that there is no place at all for means testing. Both countries have moved toward means testing, the British more substantially than the French. Finally, one can say that the policy differences between Britain and France represent differences in culture—of course they do—and regard the differences fatalistically, but I look at the matter the other way around: I believe that as we change our programs we change our culture.

The argument I have just made—that is, to stand by a sixty-year-old principle—is essentially conservative. On the other hand, I believe that we need to make a substantial shift in the way benefits are allocated, though we may embark on it gradually.

It is impossible to review the eight assumptions and subsequent social changes listed above without beginning to see that the increasing divisions represented in our society will be accentuated within the beneficiary population. The gap between the benefits of the well-to-do elderly and those of the poor elderly will enlarge. Entitled women and children will be worse off than they are now, both relatively and in terms of real income. The survival of the Social Security system in the United States will be threatened by dramatically inadequate benefits, as it is in Great Britain today.[7]

One way to deal with the problem is to move slowly toward a two-tiered system, that is, a social security system combining a basic pension for the elderly, widowed, orphaned, and disabled populations with an additional benefit related to wage levels for those who had made a payroll contribution over a specified level. It would be appropriate to pay at least part of the cost of the lower tier, or basic benefit, out of general revenues since it would be replacing the cost that would otherwise be incurred for supplemental security income (SSI) and whatever other welfare program we are to have. To the best of my knowledge, a two-tiered system for the United States was first envisioned almost twenty years ago by Martha Ozawa.[8]

Benefits in such a system would be skewed more than they are now to those who had the lowest earnings. A first step might well be to reintroduce a moderate minimum benefit, once provided as part of the American Social Security System, but phased out by legislation in 1977. A variety of technical changes—for example, reducing the adverse impact of the maximum family benefit for families with more than one child—might enhance improvements for beneficiary low-income families.

A number of European countries have two-tiered systems. Some started with a basic pension and added a wage-related benefit; others started with a wage-related benefit and inserted a basic pension. As this may imply, a move towards a two-tiered system would not be noticeable to the naked or untrained eye. Nor is it important that such a system should be named, only that it should be understood. The effect of this change would be to reorder benefits to the advantage of people with low and moderate incomes.

Even with such a change, we would not have raised a finger to ameliorate the desperate plight of women and children who are not covered by Social Security. There has been no lack of ideas over the years about how to correct this situation, but the current political climate is entirely inhospitable to such ideas and is likely to continue to be so for some little while. The best of the politically feasible ideas—although I regard it as far from ideal—may be the retention, not to say improvement, of the earned income tax credit, particularly if it can be made refundable.[9]

CODA

Instituting such changes may seem to be a great deal to set out to do; such a process may represent a longer look into the future than officials and voters are accustomed to entertaining; and the proposed system may be more communitarian that those who mourn the loss of community are likely to grasp.

Now consider this: The rate of savings has collapsed in the last ten years or so, dropping to less than 5 percent of national income from about 9 percent during the previous three decades. According to Gary Burtless, "the great bulk of the decline was due to changes in the savings patterns of people . . . who are 55 or older today."[10] Studying the same set of problems, James Smith of the Rand Corporation warns that, unless they change their ways, most of the people now in their thirties and forties "won't be able to retire."[11]

This situation has presumably resulted from the high rate of consumption in America—which resists restraint—combined with stable or falling real wages for many. These are not habits or conditions that will yield easily to hectoring and homilies, and they will mean that the majority of currently middle-aged people will come to retirement age *more* dependent on Social Security than their parents are now.

If the lower benefit levels of Social Security are not made more robust, it will represent a problem not only to the elderly in the third millennium but to their grown children as well, who, in accordance with established American habit, have tended to spend money on *their* children and hardly any at all on their parents. If these elderly parents should urgently need financial help, it will be bad news for their middle-aged children and their grandchildren.

The Social Security Board of Trustees looks seventy-five years ahead in planning financing. If we look even ten years ahead in the context of the current condition of our society, it should be evident that we urgently need such principles and changes, small and large, as have been indicated here.

NOTES

1. Beveridge, Sir William, *Social Insurance and Allied Services*, Macmillan Company, 1942.

2. Dalmer D. Hoskins, "Developments and Trends in Social Security, 1990–1992," *Social Security Bulletin* 55, no. 4 (winter 1992): 38, 39.

3. Howard Glennerster, *Paying for Welfare: Issues for the Nineties*, STICERD discussion paper, no. WSP/82, London School of Economics, December 1992.

4. These proposals are drawn from a letter from Robert M. Ball dated 10 January 1995.

5. These arguments are drawn from a letter circulated and signed by a number of social security experts, beginning with Henry J. Aaron, Robert M. Ball, Robert J. Meyers, and C. Eugene Steuerle, dated 24 May 1994. See also Alvin L. Schorr, *Common Decency: Domestic Policies after Reagan*, Yale University Press, 1986, pp. 28–34.

6. STICERD discussion paper, no. WSP/115, London School of Economics, October 1995.

7. Glennerster, *Paying for Welfare* p. 14.

8. Martha N. Ozawa, "Social Insurance and Redistribution," in Alvin L. Schorr, ed., *Jubilee for Our Times*, Columbia University Press, 1977, pp. 162–67. See also Robert M. Ball, *Social Security—Today and Tomorrow*, Columbia University Press, 1978, in which the author writes about a "double-decker" system.

9. For a detailed description and analysis of a children's refundable tax credit, see Schorr, *Common Decency*, pp. 87–95 and 109–13.

10. Quoted in "Older Americans Cited in Studies of National Savings Rate Slump," *New York Times*, 21 February 1995.

11. Quoted in "Why Baby Boomers Won't Be Able to Retire," *Fortune*, 4 September 1995.

Chapter 6

Public and Private Approaches for Redesigning Social Security

Yung-Ping Chen

INTRODUCTION

The economics and demography of financing retirement transcend geography and ideology. In the United States, both the Republican-dominated Congress and the Democratic president advocate, though to different degrees, cuts in Medicare and Medicaid and the reform of welfare programs. Similar discussions are gaining prominence in Latin America, Eastern and Central Europe, the former Soviet Union, and countries of the Organisation for Economic Cooperation and Development. Even Scandinavia, the mecca of social programs for the elderly, is not immune. In 1994, Sweden's opposition Social Democratic Party ran in the national election on a platform of raising taxes and cutting both social and defense spending in order to reduce the country's bulging budget deficits and massive national debt. This center-left political party, which had been responsible for building one of the world's most advanced welfare states, managed to win on that platform. Almost everywhere, in industrialized and developing countries alike, the same demanding question is being asked: Which offers better ways to provide for the older population now and in the future—public or private approaches?

In this chapter, I will summarize the World Bank's recent criticisms of social security programs and its proposal for a multipillar system of welfare payments and savings. I will then address the important issues of privatization and the major reasons for the financial problems of social security programs. Finally, I will illustrate how an existing social security plan may be redesigned into a self-sustaining and financially stable program.

SOCIAL SECURITY CRITICIZED

Existing systems of social security are being scrutinized and criticized in most parts of the world. A leading example is a 1994 World Bank report that has generated both interest and controversy. After reviewing old-age income security systems in more than a hundred countries, the report concluded that the problems with most publicly funded, pay-as-you-go pension systems (the World Bank's term for social security) are

1. high payroll-tax rates (payroll-tax rates for pensions are already over 25 percent in Egypt, Hungary, Russia, Brazil, and Italy);
2. tax evasion and labor-market distortions (in many Latin American countries, more than 40 percent of the labor force works in the informal sector);
3. early retirement (in Hungary the average retirement age is 54, and in Turkey many people retire before age 50 or even age 40);
4. misallocation of public resources (in 1990, Austria, Italy, and Uruguay spent more than one-third of their public budgets on pensions);
5. lost opportunities to increase savings (analysts of many countries believe that they have inadequate savings rates and that this hampers growth);
6. perverse redistributions to upper-income groups (in the early years of public plans, high-income groups have benefitted the most); and
7. positive lifetime transfers to early cohorts and lower returns to later cohorts.

These seven factors, argues the World Bank, have put many old-age income security systems in serious financial trouble.

PRIVATIZATION PROPOSED

The conclusion that the existing publicly funded, pay-as-you-go systems have performed poorly (with some nearing bankruptcy) led the World Bank to suggest implementation of multipillar systems with separate administrative and financing mechanisms for redistribution (welfare) and savings. The report proposes that governments use three instruments—or pillars—to provide income security for older people. First, instead of the traditional social security system, a publicly managed, tax-financed pillar would have the primary goal of reducing poverty among the elderly through means-tested payments. Second, a mandatory, but privately managed, individually funded pillar would have the primary responsibility for investing the savings of individuals. The third pillar would consist of voluntary savings-annuity plans for people who wish to save even more for additional income in retirement.

This proposed system of three pillars differs radically from a more familiar approach found in the United States. Here, the "three-legged stool" consists of Social Security complemented by occupational pensions and individual savings. Additionally, public assistance or welfare in the form of Supplemental Security Income (SSI) is available as a safety net. The first pillar in the World Bank proposal would perform the function that SSI now does (welfare), while the second and third pillars would facilitate savings. Basically, the multipillar proposal is an ambitious plan for privatizing social security.

A privatized system of individual saving and investment has a number of attractive features to recommend itself, but it also carries with it potential problems. Certain key issues would need to be addressed before privatization could be seriously considered.

Privatizing social security means that the primary responsibility for retirement income would shift from the taxpayers and government to workers, who would be required to save and to invest their savings in the private sector. Are individuals in general able and eager to manage their own investments? What opportunity cost will be incurred if they must do so? If, instead, money managers do it for them, how much will such services cost? What should the role of society be in cases of investment failure?[1]

The privatization debate essentially revolves around the advantages and disadvantages of defined-benefit plans with pay-as-you-go financing as compared to defined-contribution plans. In general, Social Security is a defined-benefit plan; it guarantees a benefit based on a predetermined formula. Privatized plans are defined-contribution plans; they do not guarantee a specified level of retirement income. Under defined-contribution plans, the worker, alone or with his or her employer, accumulates savings over time. The level of income during retirement depends on the amount saved and the preretirement investment earnings, taking into account actuarial and financial circumstances at retirement when the total accumulation is converted into a legal contract for income payments. This issue is obviously important because it concerns the adequacy of retirement income.

Most advocates of privatizing Social Security assume that the interest rates earned by the investable funds will be high. However, the financial market, like all other markets, has two sides—supply and demand. Increasing savings will increase the supply of investable funds. Unless the demand for investable funds increases commensurately, market forces will lower the rate of interest. While rates of investment return may be high for some periods of time in a country where privatization is implemented, it cannot be assumed that the rates of return will be consistently high over the long run.

Social Security generally provides retirement, survivorship, and disability benefits in a single package. No private insurance carrier offers an equivalent policy. Typically, advocates of privatization point to higher retirement benefits, which they contend could be offered by private investments. They are generally silent, however, about the benefits for survivors and for the disabled. Some proponents of privatization do try to provide for survivorship and disability benefits with a life insurance policy and a disability income policy. But they frequently illustrate the costs for providing these benefits by quoting the premiums private insurance carriers charge for such policies, which are lower due to their underwriting requirements. Moreover, not all occupations are insurable for disability by private insurance, and among those that are insurable, premiums for the same benefits can differ considerably by occupational category.

In addition, when part or all of the taxes that go into Social Security are converted into private investments, privatization's effects on income redistribution must be recognized. The feature of social adequacy that exists under Social Security (that is, the transfer to low-income earners) will be reduced or eliminated. Unless society can tolerate some of its citizens living in squalor or destitution, the cost of welfare for people who have not been able to save enough or who have failed in their investments must be paid. This income redistribution will come principally from higher-income people through the first pillar (taxation), thus reducing the higher returns that the well-to-do are expected to receive through the second or third pillar.

Finally, a serious question about the transition remains. How do we move from the current system of Social Security to the world envisioned by the privatizers? Because Social Security is financed on an essentially pay-as-you-go basis under which current taxes are used to pay current benefits, how are benefits to be paid when some or all of the taxes are redirected to privatized accounts? The costs involved in the transition to the new system need to be covered. Are workers now and those in the foreseeable future expected to (1) help pay for the benefits promised to current beneficiaries and those in the transition period and (2) contribute to the privatized accounts for their own retirements?

While the World Bank report does not discuss these issues, it does allow that, in order for the system of three pillars to work, three caveats are essential: Countries must have at least rudimentary capital markets, considerable government regulation is essential to avoid investments that are overly risky or to weed out managers who commit fraud, and a public system or pillar is needed to provide a social safety net for people whose lifetime earnings are low or whose investments fail. The World Bank should be commended for issuing these warnings. Nevertheless, it is important to note that capital markets need to be more than just "rudimentary," and sound government regulation takes time to develop and is costly to maintain. Conditions conducive to privatized plans of saving and investment do not yet exist in many countries.

SOCIAL SECURITY'S INHERENT PROBLEMS?

On the other hand, there is nothing basically wrong with the approach of social insurance that undergirds social security. Most of the seven factors that, according to the World Bank, have threatened so many publicly funded, old-age security plans are attributable to plan designers and policy makers. They are not intrinsic to the social insurance model of social security. "High payroll-tax rates" are largely required for high promised benefit payments, but such promises are not preordained. "Evasion and labor-market distortions" come from ineffective enforcement of the law and poor plan design; they are not an inherent part of social security. While "early retirement" is available to workers at relatively young ages without a reduction in benefits under many systems, it is not a *sine qua non* of social security. If it is agreed that there is "misallocation of public resources," it could be corrected, and it is certainly not an essential aspect of social security. The issue of "lost opportunities to increase savings" is still controversial. "Perverse redistributions to upper-income groups" are certainly not a predestined outcome of social security. "Positive lifetime transfers to early cohorts and lower returns to later cohorts," again, result mostly from plan design or changing demographics and are not an innate feature of social insurance. In short, all these problems are not inseparable elements of social insurance.

Despite these disclaimers, it must be acknowledged that the costs of social security everywhere have been rising and, if allowed to persist, will rise to even greater heights and possibly to financially untenable levels.

Four major factors seem to be at work in this phenomenon. The first two—growth rates of the population and of the economy—relate to the workings of a traditional pay-as-you-go approach to social insurance programs, an intergenerational transfer model in which the working generation finances benefits for the retired generation. This system works well as long as the population and the economy are growing sufficiently so that, over the long run, the taxes paid by workers and their employers increase faster than, or at least keep pace with, benefits paid out. In many countries, however, social security has become a focus of intense criticism and debate because of sluggish economic growth coupled with population aging.

A third factor in social security's escalating costs is the eternal temptation for politicians to promise ever-increasing types and levels of benefits. Finally, there's the historical fact that many social programs, including social security, are begun when economic and/or demographic conditions are favorable without regard for the long run. Over time, as economic and demographic conditions change, an imbalance between the program's income and what it spends can develop. If the government fails to act or acts too slowly to correct the imbalance, the program deteriorates.

The way to rectify this situation is not to dismantle Social Security and replace it with a privatized plan, as some have proposed. There is nothing intrinsically wrong with the social insurance model. Practically all of its financial problems have resulted from poor plan design and unwise policy decisions in the face of a slowing economy and an aging population. A better policy choice would be to redesign Social Security, making it as self-adjusting and self-sustaining as possible. A sustainable policy is one that adapts automatically to changing conditions. By its very design, an adaptable program prevents hidden time bombs from developing in the first place.

REDESIGNING SOCIAL SECURITY

How may the U.S. Social Security program be redesigned to deal with the economic and demographic causes of its financial problems?

A Wage-Based System

A major economic cause of the program's financial instability arises from the fact that its income depends on the payroll tax, which is based on wages, and its outgo reflects prices of goods and services, which determine the cost-of-living adjustments. The difference between the annual rate of change in the average wage and the annual rate of change in the consumer price index (CPI) is known as the real-wage differential. Variations in this differential can have a major impact on costs of the social security system.

The benefit structure can be made more nearly self-sustaining if the law provides that the automatic benefit increases will be based on the increase in the nationwide average wage rate minus some fixed percentage point.[2] The fixed percentage point should be chosen according to what the real-wage differential is expected to be over the long run. This procedure will result in a benefit computation based solely on one element—wages—thereby eliminating the instability brought about by the wage level and the price level changing at rates that diverge from those assumed in the actuarial model.

Basing Social Security's income and its outgo on wages would substantially stabilize its financing position insofar as variations in economic conditions pertaining to wages and prices are concerned. Aside from providing financial stability, a wage-based system would improve the relative equity between workers and retirees. Thus, if economic conditions were very favorable, beneficiaries would see their benefits increase, reflecting some of the general increase in the standard of living based on wage increases, which would exceed the CPI growth. Conversely, if economic conditions were unfavorable, benefit increases would be less than rises in the CPI so that beneficiaries would share in the general misfortune of the working population.

This proposal would not solve any financial problems arising from other economic elements, such as the unemployment rate. Nonetheless, the real-wage differential is by far the most important economic element in the long-range financing of the Social Security program.[3]

A Formula-Based Normal Retirement Age

The demographic cause of Social Security's financial problems results from the demographic load, i.e., the ratio of beneficiaries to workers/tax-payers. The U.S. demographic load is projected to increase by 58 percent by the year 2030. Preventing Social Security costs as a percentage of taxable payroll from increasing significantly will require addressing the rapid growth in the number of beneficiaries relative to the number of workers. Raising the normal retirement age is one way to moderate the rise in total benefit payments.

One way to reset the normal retirement age is to keep constant the ratio between (*a*) retirement-life expectancy and (*b*) potential working life.[4] The former refers to the average expected years of life at the normal retirement age. The latter is defined by the number of years between age twenty and the normal retirement age. Suppose the ratio between (*a*) and (*b*) is 1 to 3 in year *x* (for example, 1940). Assume that the average retirement-life expectancy increases by one year by a future year *y* (for example, 1990). If the ratio between (*a*) and (*b*) is kept constant (the same in both years), then a one-year extension of life will result in an increase of roughly three months of retirement and roughly nine months of work in year *y*.

However, increasing the normal retirement age is a contentious issue, igniting spirited debate. To avoid the inaction that often comes with such controversy, it might be preferable to reset the normal retirement age periodically (say, once every ten years) on an automatic basis according to national statistics on average life expectancy at the current normal retirement age. If an automatic extension of the normal retirement age can be part of the law, then the cost of Social Security attributable to increasing longevity could be systematically controlled.

Gradual Retirement with Partial Pensions

A third element in the redesign of the program is the institution of a system of partial pensions for partial retirement, thus coordinating the policy on Social Security with the policy on older-worker employment. At present, workers who want to retire gradually with an interim period of part-time employment confront a number of obstacles. Occupational pension plans rarely allow a beneficiary to continue working for the same firm. Social Security lowers benefits for those beneficiaries who find employment and earn beyond an allowable amount—a considerable work disincentive.

People work for a variety of reasons, and these reasons change as workers grow older. Many say that they are willing and able to work longer than the current retirement age would indicate, especially on a part-time basis. At age sixty-three and over, for example, enjoying work is the most frequently cited reason for working, followed by feeling useful, being productive, seeing it as an obligation, and maintaining health insurance. Significantly, the need for income is mentioned least often.[5]

Slow economic growth and population aging have raised concerns about the ability of society to finance pensions (public and private) and health services for the elderly. In addition, projections of a slower growth in the working-age population have led to concerns about labor force shortages in the future. One way to mitigate these problems is to prolong the working life of older people. A postponement of the normal retirement age coupled with a desire on the part of older people to work part time (as expressed in practice and in opinion surveys in many countries) would seem to provide a recipe for gradual retirement. Partial pensions for partial retirement may be a practicable approach.

In order to implement gradual retirement with partial pensions, institutional and attitudinal changes are needed. If we assume the willingness of older workers to remain in the labor market, occupational pension and Social Security provisions that offer retirement incentives (or work disincentives) should be eliminated. For example, the delayed retirement credit under Social Security should be made actuarially fair immediately rather than waiting until the year 2009 as provided under current law.[6] In order to accommodate workers in general and older workers in particular, flexible work schedules and training/retraining programs should be more widely and systematically available. The types of jobs available are also important. If, indeed, part-time jobs are what are needed to implement partial pensions, then the willingness of employers to create such opportunities and the cooperation of full-time workers to support them will be necessary.

To promote gradual retirement by means of partial pensions would require a major change in Social Security and occupational pension programs. However, to implement gradual retirement in the United States through a system of part-time work with partial pensions will have many salubrious effects, including easing concerns over the extension of the normal retirement age.

CONCLUSION

The widespread problem of rising retirement costs has prompted the question of which offer better ways to provide for the older population—

public or private approaches. Public programs of social security are prevalent in many countries, but they are under intense criticism. Increasingly, a privatized Social Security program is proposed as a replacement. Although a privatized plan for individual saving and investment has attractive features, some key questions about privatization await satisfactory answers. Also, while there is no denying that many social security programs are facing mounting costs, the financial problems of such programs appear to result principally from faulty plan design and wrongheaded policy decisions, especially in an era of sluggish economies and aging populations. The design and policy maladies that undermine social security should and can be corrected. With its costs controlled by better plan designs and sensible policies, a redesigned social security program will become self-sustaining and financially stable. With a stable social security program as a foundation for a basic level of retirement income, other means of income support can then be used as supplements.

NOTES

1. House Comm. on Ways and Means, Subcomm. on Social Security, *Proposals for Alternative Investment of the Social Security Trust Fund Reserves: Hearing before the Subcomm. on Social Security*, 103rd Cong., 2d sess., ser. 103–106, at 98–108 (1995) (statement of Yung-Ping Chen on key issues of privatizing Social Security).

2. Staff memoranda nos. 16, 19, and 20 from Robert J. Myers of the Nat'l. Comm. on Soc. Sec. Reform (1982).

3. Staff memoranda nos. 16, 19, and 26 from Robert J. Myers of the Nat'l. Comm. on Soc. Sec. Reform (1982).

4. Yung-Ping Chen, "Making Assets out of Tomorrow's Elderly," *Gerontologist* 27 (1987): 410–16; F. R. Bayo and J. Faber, Soc. Sec. Admin., U.S. Dept. of Health and Human Services, pub. no. 11–11500.6, *Equivalent Retirement Ages: 1940–2050*, actuarial note no. 105 (1981).

5. U.S. Dept. of Labor, *Older Worker Task Force: Key Policy Issues for the Future* (1989).

6. The delayed retirement credit (DRC) is designed to compensate workers for not receiving benefits when they defer retirement. In other words, DRC increases their future benefits. The DRC rate, under existing law, is 4.5 percent for persons born in 1929 or 1930. This is scheduled to rise to 8 percent for those born in 1943 or later. When DRC is at the rate of 8 percent, the compensation will become actuarially fair, in the sense that what one does not receive today, one will receive tomorrow. However, for all those born before 1943, thus attaining the normal retirement age before the year 2009, the compensation is actuarially unfair because future increases in benefits are worth less in present value terms than the current reductions in benefits.

Chapter 7

Health Care: An American Report
Rashi Fein

INTRODUCTION

It is most important for the analysis and understanding of recent events in regard to health reform in the United States to recognize that we have a rich, eight-decade-long history of failed attempts at comprehensive reform. Last year's (1994) health insurance bill was not our first attempt (nor, as it turned out, will it be our last) to erect a system of universal coverage. Importantly, however, it was our first attempt to weave a universal financing proposal into a fabric that also stressed expenditure containment via major delivery-system reform. It would have been far simpler for us, in terms of the cost and complexity of health care, had we moved to universal insurance early in this century, as suggested by Presidents Franklin D. Roosevelt in the 1930s, Harry Truman in the late 1940s, or even later by Richard Nixon in the early 1970s.

I stress the importance of the historical perspective because I believe that it is a mistake simply to focus on what happened last year and thereby assume that the full explanation for failure lies in events, personalities, and processes unique to that particular effort. That kind of "instant analysis" encourages a shallow voyeurism and silly gossip. Even worse, it trivializes the problem.

Of course, events, personalities, and processes made a difference, but in my judgment, more basic factors were at work. Put simply, I do not believe that, within the constraints of our political system as they were perceived by most politicians and political pundits, different tactics would have yielded a substantially different outcome in 1994. Once various strategic decisions were made—for what, at the time, appeared to many (including the president) to be valid political reasons, though that is a matter on which reasonable people can and do differ—the short-term result was almost inevitable.

Indeed, I would argue that, given the fact that this was the first time we had debated universal health insurance in some twenty years, it would have been most surprising if Congress had enacted major reform. The regret and disappointment are real, and the more so because the discussion about major reform has been tabled for some time to come. Though there is no question that America will again take up the issue of reform, last year did not turn out to be the first year of a debate that would continue without interruption for the half decade or more it would take for reform to be enacted (as was the case with Medicare for those sixty-five and over, first proposed in 1957, finally adopted in 1965, and markedly expanded in 1972). The tragedy is not so much that major, comprehensive reform (as defined by the Clinton plan) was not enacted—that should have been expected—but that last year's debate did not serve to erect a foundation upon which future dialogue and discourse could be built. Comprehensive reform, in contrast with a number of incremental (and, perhaps, disjointed) steps, is not on either political party's agenda for the foreseeable future.

Before proceeding, I want to stress the importance of phrases such as "in my judgment" and "I do not believe" in the preceding sentences. In the analysis of culture, traditions, attitudes, and their influence on politics and social policy, different observers will place different weights on various forces and reach different conclusions. I shall emphasize ideology over personality and time-specific events. Yet mine is but one of a number of possible interpretations. None of us is so distant from what transpired, either in time or emotional involvement, as to assure that our views are appropriately dispassionate (whatever that really means). I would be derelict, indeed, if I did not refer you to the various health policy journals for discussions of alternative explanations.

THE EFFECT OF TRADITIONAL AMERICAN VALUES ABOUT GOVERNMENT ON THE LEGISLATIVE AND POLICY-MAKING PROCESSES

While many factors contributed to the failure to enact any health care reform legislation (let alone meaningful reform) in the first two years of the Clinton administration, the overriding problem, as I see it, stemmed from America's individualistic orientation and deep skepticism, edging into antipathy, toward government. The president structured the legislation he submitted in ways that attempted to respond to the public's attitude toward government. Regrettably, the resulting complexity of the proposal confused many Americans and, with the help of negative advertising, led them to fear the changes that would ensue. Agreement with the goals of the program did not translate into support of the proposal.

It is worthwhile to examine in some detail the way American attitudes toward government affected the development and disposition of the legislation. The elaborate structure of checks and balances that interconnects the three branches of the U.S. federal government (executive, legislative, and judicial) and the complex relationships that exist between our different levels of government, especially between the central (federal) government and the various state governments, comprise a system that was not designed to operate efficiently and effectively (if by that we mean to enact legislation that can be easily administered in ways that address serious problems). Their experience with British royalty led the founding fathers to design a system that would protect us from the exercise of arbitrary power. There is a dominant belief in this country that government is best that governs least. Not by accident, the United States takes action slowly, in a cumbersome fashion, and only as a last resort.

Furthermore, the United States has a legislature that is bicameral in practice, not simply in name. The rules, practices, procedures, and traditions of the two houses of Congress are quite different. Nevertheless, both houses share the characteristic of unwieldy, duplicative, and overlapping committee structure. This is especially the case in the health field, where jurisdictional issues abound, as, for example, between financing and tax-writing, labor, health care, and antitrust committees.

If legislation is to reach the floor of either house for debate it must, of course, be referred from committee. Thus, in our nonparliamentary system, legislative debate on President Clinton's plan could begin only after it was introduced and sponsored by one or more members of the Senate and of the House, referred to committees in each house, and then acted upon (including being amended) and sent to the floor of each house. That last step, in fact, did not take place in either branch of Congress. The Clinton plan did not have a decent burial. Neither it nor any other health care reform plan reached the floor to be debated or acted upon by the full House of Representatives or by the Senate. Universal health insurance was not voted down. No plan ever came up for formal debate.

I should note that governance problems do not disappear even when legislation is passed in both houses. It is then necessary to reconcile the versions of the legislation as enacted by the House and Senate. If this is accomplished, and the president signs the legislation into law, enactment is followed by an extended process involving consideration of regulations for the administration of new legislation. With frequent elections and a less-than-powerful civil service, it is always possible that regulations will be drafted and legislation implemented by people who had opposed enactment. That prospect is, of course, enhanced when we have a divided government. All this hardly makes for efficient, crisp, government action.

AMERICANS' PERCEPTION OF GOVERNMENT

Many of these characteristics are found in other nations (particularly, perhaps, when there are coalition governments), though they most often exist in attenuated form, and differences in degree do make for differences in kind. What may be unique is that the already severe problems in governance in the United States have been exacerbated by an assault on the utility of government itself and on the validity of almost any proposed government actions. For almost two decades we have witnessed election campaigns in which those seeking elective office (including the presidency) have attacked the institution called government and its role.

The attack goes beyond a desire to shrink the size of government. Candidates from both major parties have contended that government is inherently wasteful and riddled with corruption and graft; inevitably out of touch with the electorate; automatically arbitrary, invasive, and populated by unaccountable bureaucrats; and, as a matter of course, prepared to tax and spend as if it is wiser than the taxpayers about where their hard-earned dollars should flow.

The problems are defined as structural flaws, which can be addressed by altering, not only the size, but the scope and role of government as well. A significant part of the electorate and the political leadership believes that the phrase "good government" is an oxymoron. The United States is a large, heterogeneous, and diverse nation; individuals feel distant from Washington, D.C., and far removed from the sources of power, thus the attack on government has proven effective. It is shocking but not surprising that at the present time, three out of four Americans say that they distrust government, a ratio that is higher than it has been at any other time during the twenty years that people have been polled on this matter.

To understand the current social and political environment in America, it is helpful to recall three important developments that occurred in the 1980s. The first was the disappearance of the perceived Soviet threat as a framework for analysis of issues and the "glue," or shared concern, that helped reduce the level of societal fractionation. It is important to note as well that in the view of many citizens and their representatives the Soviet threat did not disappear because of some stroke of luck, but because our side "won," i.e., because capitalism and market competition proved superior to socialism/communism and government planning. The implications of this view are self-evident: to assure that we are not subverted from within we need to eschew government planning. Government, the "enemy of the people," wants to plan—that's what bureaucrats thirst for. It follows that the larger government is, the more pervasive its planning. Therefore, we must reduce the size and influence of government. Furthermore, in the United States we have adopted a set of definitions whereby Soviet planning is synonymous with totalitarianism and market capitalism with political freedom. Many Americans believe that we are in a zero-sum game, that we must choose either despotic government or market freedom, and history teaches us to choose the market.

A second important development was the rapid growth of the federal government's annual deficit and consequent expansion of the national debt as a result of the "unusual" fiscal policy of the Reagan administration in the 1980s. Economists can (and do) debate the implications of the growing debt and deficit, especially in the light of such matters as the absence of an annual capital or investment budget. Nevertheless, the American public's perception appears to be that the United States is an impoverished, virtually bankrupt nation that someday soon will be spending its national treasure (certainly all of its tax receipts) in debt service. We, today's profligate adults, are robbing our children's future. This idea has led to a cry that the government should be run the way a household is—with an annual balanced budget. This argument, of course, fits the agenda of those who would reduce the scope of government, since deficit control is predicated on reductions in expenditures, not on increases in tax revenues.

Inevitably, this climate of opinion, as expressed by legislation requiring that any increase in expenditures for a specific purpose (e.g., health care) be offset by reductions in expenditures for another designated program (e.g., environmental protection) or (politically unlikely) increases in specifically designated taxes, has made it more difficult to enact health reform. I cannot lay too much stress on the antitax mood that prevails. The president's proposal was molded by his feeling that he had to submit a health insurance program that would not require a tax increase for its financing but would also not increase the deficit. "Keeping it simple" gave way to those two imperatives. A universal tax-based program was viewed as out of bounds. The president simply was not prepared to argue for an increase in taxes to finance health reform.

I would also suggest that a third change has been the increased recognition of international economic competition and interdependence (even as America appears to grow more disengaged, perhaps isolationist, at the national political level). This development is important even beyond its economic implications because it contributes to a pervasive view that, not only individuals, but even governments are impotent, that in a real sense we are all controlled by disembodied economic forces, that the market is more powerful than people or their institutions. Thus, not only is it difficult to influence one's government, but even if one could it would do little good since even the strongest government or president cannot resist the power of international currency and bond markets, the source of real power. This strengthens the feeling of impotence on the part of the citizenry.

These developments have operated to reinforce longstanding attitudes toward government and its desire and ability to act purposefully and to "do good." If a person believes that most (if not all) government expenditures are wasteful, then his or her normal antipathy toward taxes is reinforced by the view that useful projects (if such exist) should be financed out of cuts in those (many) activities that are wasteful. Furthermore, the unhappiness voiced by many Americans surely is also related to the fact that over the last twenty years median family income (in constant 1993 dollars) has been stable, growing by less than 0.2 percent over the two decades from 1973 to 1993 (less than 0.01 percent per annum). At $36,959 in 1993 it was only $66 higher in real terms than it had been in 1973. And this during a period of economic expansion! Furthermore, the stability that has been achieved in family income has come as a consequence of the increase in labor-force participation by women: up from 46 percent in 1973 to 58 percent in 1993, a 26 percent increase. For many American families, two earners are needed to achieve what one earner was once able to attain. The disquietude is compounded by fear engendered by downsizing, by changing employer attitudes about the need for stable and long-term employee relationships, by employer willingness and ability to use replacement workers during and after a strike—in other words, fear about job security.

THE CLINTON HEALTH CARE REFORM INITIATIVE

Thus the Clinton health program came into being in a pessimistic, ill-tempered, and fractionated climate, one in which many individuals were hunkering down to protect what they had and saw redistribution as something that would take from a "hard-working" middle class and give to a large number of "undeserving" poor (a group that had grown from 23 million people in 1973 to 39 million in 1993, or from 11 to 15 percent of the population). There were few grounds for optimism about a program formulated and proposed by an administration whose leader had been elected by garnering 43 percent of the vote from among the 55 percent of the voting-age population that cast ballots (thus, he had been elected by less than one-quarter of the eligible electorate).

I dwell on these various matters because, if we are to understand the problems of the Clinton health program, we must understand the attitudes that were instrumental in forming it. I have already stressed the importance of avoiding new taxes. I should also take note of the administration's desire to avoid the charge that the president favored an expansion of the federal bureaucracy and a takeover of the private sector, particularly of private insurance companies. Scholars will debate the degree to which the president (and the first lady) shared these attitudes or felt that he had to respond to the "will of the electorate" as well as to the power of a united Republican and conservative Democratic opposition. On the one hand, President Clinton noted that a single-payer system (roughly speaking, a tax-supported social insurance program) "would have the least administrative cost" of all the options under consideration and that it would be less expensive in total dollars than the approach he had chosen. On the other hand, and in the same address, he stated that a single-payer system "would be significantly dislocating in the sense that overnight, in a nation this size, you'd have all the people who are in the insurance business out of it."

Interesting as it might be to speculate on which is the real Bill Clinton (on this as on other issues), the fact is that the president's plan reflected America's politics and a deep belief in market capitalism and individualism. This combination has yielded an ideology not tempered, as in a number of other countries, by the presence of a political party of the left or even of a progressive center that searches for areas where cooperation can substitute for competition and where a sense of community can substitute for individualism. Thus, though the president believes in an activist role for government, it is not surprising to find that his administration also believes that that role should be restricted: Government should be active in creating and strengthening competetive markets and assisting the most vulnerable among us to enter those markets, and then—insofar as is possible—it should step aside.

The majority of Republicans do differ in important ways from the majority of Democrats on the meaning of "vulnerable" and "insofar as possible." But at the present time, a large majority in both parties share the view that government's primary role is to help structure economic incentives that encourage individual behavior that is associated with desired outcomes. I have termed this view "government as landscape architect," the designer of level playing fields.

The administration's most basic decisions in formulating the health care proposal came early. The detailed microcharacteristics of the plan, indeed its very complexity (which contributed to its demise), were the logical consequences of the early macrodecisions not to sever the link between employment and insurance, not to redirect the billions of premium dollars now paid by business firms and individuals away from insurers and health care delivery organizations and toward government (or quasigovernment institutions). Premiums were not to be replaced by taxes. There would not be a government insurance program analogous to or extending Medicare.

If taxes, which could reflect ability to pay, were not an option, various consequences followed. First, it became clear that the administration would have to retain private insurance companies, since someone other than government would have to collect the requisite funds. In turn, this meant that the earlier vigorous attack on insurance companies—an attack which had resonated with the American public during the election campaign—now seemed confusing and contradictory.

Second, since the administration was committed to equity but was unable to finance increased access through tax revenues generated on the basis of ability to pay, it was forced to add more and more complexity to the plan to achieve the redistribution necessary to help individuals and firms who could not pay the required private non-income-related premiums on which the program was based.

Third, without new taxes, dollars for redistribution would have to be found in savings achieved elsewhere in the health field—but where? The difficulties were unavoidable. Once the system retained (indeed, expanded) the linkage between employment and private insurance companies as underwriters, the president lost badly needed potential administrative savings. But finding savings elsewhere troubled those (chiefly Medicare beneficiaries, that is, the aged and disabled already covered via a social insurance and general-revenue-supported program) who intersected with the programs where the savings would be sought.

The president recognized that a tax-based social insurance system that incorporated potential administrative savings would require taxes that were lower than the level of premiums needed under an expansion of our existing system. Indeed, the president said that a tax-based system would have to replace "over $500 billion in private insurance premiums with nearly that much [therefore less] in new taxes." Yet he felt he needed to respond to the fact that Americans seemed to prefer premiums (even if higher) to taxes (even if lower).

Nevertheless, the problem was not that the new construct would cost more than another alternative. Rather, the problem was that, since the administration was unable to use tax revenues generated on the basis of ability to pay, but was decent and committed to increased access, it was forced to add more and more complexity to achieve its equity goals. The program, after all, relied on requiring that all employers, including those who today do not provide health insurance for their employees, provide such insurance. In turn, since private-sector premiums do not vary with income, this necessitated developing a system of subsidies to assist low-wage employees and low-profit employers who would otherwise not be able to enter the market.

Aside from the mistrust felt by employers who feared that subsidies would be available only to meet adjustment problems and, therefore, would be temporary in nature, there was the complexity generated, the appearance of arbitrariness, all sorts of "notch" problems contributing to the difficulty of achieving vertical and horizontal equity, and, when all was said and done, the need for some mechanisms that would generate the necessary funds or provide the requisite savings with which to finance the subsidies for low-income workers and, as well, for the unemployed who were not disabled or elderly.

I skip over the administrative issues involved in defining and monitoring employment (including part-time and self-employment), worker income, and establishment profits. Instead, I move to what seems to me the inevitable outcome: in an effort to avoid or minimize new taxes even while providing subsidies that increased government expenditures, the administration was forced to emphasize savings that would be achieved through delivery-system reform. Thus, financing reform was comingled with delivery-system reform. While many factors contributed to the program's demise—including the strenuous opposition from members of the small-business community who would be required to provide a substantial part of the insurance premium—the issues of system reform proved complex, confusing, and threatening. They added to the public's skepticism and increased the program's vulnerability. I, therefore, want to examine this in more detail.

It should first be noted that, though relying on system reform for savings, the administration recognized that system reform could not be achieved rapidly. As a consequence, the program called for a long phase-in period as well as for savings in already existing federal health programs. The phase-in period, in turn, created its own political difficulties. Members of Congress were asked to take unpopular actions today (e.g., mandates requiring employers and employees to expand insurance coverage and expend dollars), whose beneficial effects (e.g., universal coverage) would not be visible (or useful in reelection campaigns) for years to come. In addition, a skeptical nation had reason to believe that the implementation date would slip: in early September of 1993 the (not yet fully articulated) Clinton plan was to be implemented by 1 January 1997; by late October, the effective date had slipped by a year to 1 January 1998.

On the one hand, the long timetable removed the sense of drama, crisis, and urgency. Yet on the other hand, though politically long, five years was undoubtedly too short a period in which to accomplish the necessary systemic changes. These included a revolutionary change in the proportion of primary-care physicians in the physician population; the restructuring of the number and type of residency training programs; the creation of new and the expansion of existing health maintenance organizations (HMOs); the development of measures of quality necessary to provide consumers with information about alternative provider/insurance units, thereby making possible and furthering the healthy competition that (presumably) would restrain premium increases; the utilization of research to produce the reliable risk-adjustment factors required to assure that insurers and HMOs not compete on risk selection; and the erection of new regional structures to rationalize institutional responsibilities.

Unlike the situations in earlier reform efforts, in 1993 the administration had to take into account delivery-system changes that had been gathering force for twenty years. The Clinton proposal placed a heavy emphasis on the expansion of so-called health maintenance organizations and the growth of managed care. A rich discussion of the different types of organizations that are defined as HMOs would take us far afield. For our purpose of understanding the administration's emphasis, it is sufficient to note that the HMO is based on the equivalent of a contractual relationship between the subscriber and the organization wherein for a fixed, periodic (usually monthly) charge the HMO agrees to provide health care as needed from a previously agreed-upon comprehensive set of ambulatory and hospital health care services.

While there are many variations in the way that individual providers— e.g., physicians—might be paid by the HMO (capitation, salary, fee-for-service), in the physical arrangements in which physicians practice (large clinics or already existing individual private offices), in the degree of "management" control and the the extent of HMO infrastructure (e.g., number of patient visits per hour, use of triage nurses and nurse practitioners), as in many other economic and health care arrangements, the critical matter is that the HMO and its associated providers are at risk. The sharp distinction between insurance companies and independent providers whose incomes rise as utilization increases disappears.

The United States has had organizations akin to today's HMOs for many decades. These, however, had been few in number, concentrated in a limited selection of geographic areas, and had involved self-selected physicians as well as (to a considerable extent) subscribers. Today's HMO growth effectively began in the early 1970s as a consequence of federal efforts to expand this departure from fee-for-service medicine and, thereby, provide a set of economic incentives that would help reduce medical care utilization (though, presumably, not too much)—most especially hospital days per 1,000—thus helping to contain medical care expenditures. Because the Clinton proposal needed strong cost-containment mechanisms and because market ideology precluded legislation that relied on price controls or effective central budgets, the comprehensive health reform proposal was designed to encourage a movement from fee-for-service indemnity insurance into capitated managed-care programs.

The Clinton plan required employers to offer individuals a choice from among three generic insurance programs: (1) a health maintenance organization requiring only modest copayments at the time that care was provided by an HMO panel of physicians (and providing no covered benefits if the patient stepped outside the HMO); (2) a preferred-provider organization with similar modest copayments if care was provided within the network of physicians but with deductibles ($200 per individual and $400 per family), coinsurance (20 percent of visit cost), and an out-of-pocket maximum ($1,500 per individual and $3,000 per family) for care received outside the network; (3) a traditional fee-for-service plan with similar deductibles, copayments, and maxima as under preferred-provider, outside-of-network care. Employer contributions to premiums would be the same regardless of the patient's choice (and would equal at least 80 percent of a "weighted" premium). Thus, the employee would pay more if he or she chose to enroll in a more expensive plan (type 1 would be the least expensive; type 3, the most).

This structure was difficult to explain and appeared threatening, especially to the vast majority of Americans who were not enrolled in or had not encountered HMOs. Furthermore, it raised important substantive questions: for example, Who would certify the various delivery systems? How would the weighted premium be calculated? Who would make the necessary risk adjustments? These and other issues were obvious problems. What was not obvious was that the public would view the program as restricting choice and imperiling patient choice of physician.

One might have assumed that there would have been an objection to the notion that the health plan a person would join (and the range of choice of provider subsequently available) would be linked to that individual's ability to pay a higher premium. That objection would surely have been raised in various other countries. While all national systems offer "escape valves" that allow a small minority of citizens to step outside the universally available plan, the Clinton program would surely have ended up with much more than 10–15 percent of the population in the two highest-cost plans. Nevertheless, the public's objection was not about a design that permitted persons who had more money to buy a different, more expensive (and presumably better) product than persons who were not as affluent.

Rather, the issue of choice in the program somehow (most probably because of the plan's inherent complexity and the confusion sown and fertilized by millions of dollars worth of extraordinarily well-conceived advertising opposing it) came to be viewed as a case of the government taking away an existing right. In reality, many employers who currently contribute to health insurance premiums select the single plan (and, perforce, the providers) available to employees. Furthermore, unlike the Clinton proposal, existing arrangements seldom permit the subscriber to change plans if her or his physician shifts from one HMO to another. We have employer rather than employee, subscriber, or patient choice. The Clinton plan would have *increased* choice for millions of Americans. I stress this because it may come as a surprise to many people: Americans have less choice under private insurance than do their aged and disabled neighbors who are covered by Medicare, than do many of their neighbors who fall below the poverty line (as well as meeting other criteria) and are part of the federal/state Medicaid program, or than do the vast majority of residents of other countries under universal systems even more dependent on government.

The Issue of Choice

I describe all this not only to provide some insight into the Clinton plan, but also because I believe that the debate about choice, a debate in which perception and reality were 180 degrees apart, is most instructive. It provides an insight into the strength of American ideology.

How could a program that offered many Americans more choice and (except under very unusual circumstances) no American less choice be seen as restricting choice? True, the advertising against the program was brilliant: Harry and Louise, an "average" American couple discussing the Clinton plan in a series of television commercials, supported the vaguely articulated goal of universal coverage but behaved as if they were just like the rest of us—a puzzled Louise kept making the point that she didn't understand the over-one-thousand-page proposal and that there must be a better way. What resonated with Americans was that "there must be a better way," the way it presumably used to be, a way that seemed less bureaucratic and involved less government.

Once the issue of choice was raised, Americans intuited that government would restrict, not enhance, choice. Isn't that what governments always do? That government might enhance choice simply boggled the mind; that it would restrict choice fit all our preconceptions. This deep-seated ideology and these preconceptions account for the remarkable inability of the Clintons to explain their program.

The Issue of Global Budgeting

So, too, with the discussion of the need for global budgeting (proposed only as a weak and complicated fall-back position if market competition did not exercise sufficient restraint on prices and expenditures). Americans are not enamored of price controls, believing that government is not competent to administer them and that, in spite of income inequalities, decisions rendered by the "market" are closer to optimal than budgets adopted— nay, imposed—by government. Whether Americans love the market or simply distrust it less than government may be unclear, but the operational consequences are similar. Thus, when the Clinton program was presented as an unnamed, "hypothetical" program and was described and fully explained, many Americans said they liked it. When the same people were asked whether they approved of the Clinton program, they said they didn't. Ideology provided the answers; it was unnecessary to listen or to think.

Though I place primary emphasis on ideology, many additional factors help explain the failure to enact health reform in the first two years of the Clinton administration. We should not overlook the negative impacts of such variables as (1) the minority political status of the administration and lack of both trust in Bill Clinton and confidence in his young and inexperienced staff; (2) the difficulty that some (many?) men and women had in coping with a strong and highly visible first lady who "had not been elected to office" and yet was the "health czar"; (3) the existence and secretive behavior of the task force, made up of more than five hundred unnamed individuals, that developed the proposal; (4) the delay in the submission of reform legislation and consequent compression of the legislative timetable, bringing into play the politics of the impending November 1994 election; (5) the fact that the program would have altered the way every American, including those who already had coverage, related to the medical insurance and, even more importantly to the medical delivery system; (6) the decline of the bipartisan moderate center and the difficulties the president had with congressional members of his own party who felt little loyalty to party or president, some of whom criticized the reform from the right (too large a role for bureaucrats, too small a role for the competitive market), and some of whom did so from the left (too large a role for employment-linked insurance and for private insurance companies, too small a role for taxes as a financing mechanism); (7) the skepticism and "it can't be true" attitude engendered by the president's description of the program as one under which "the vast majority of Americans . . . will pay the same or less for health coverage that will be the same or better than the coverage they have"; (8) the problems resulting from the fact that compromises were made so early in the legislative process so that (*a*) the public did not fully understand the reasoning behind various elements in the proposal, (*b*) the president, in defending an already compromised proposal, was less forceful and appeared less principled in his defense of the measure than might otherwise have been the case, and (*c*) the legislative leaders had less opportunity to do their own bargaining with opponents, whereby, as in all compromises, all parties would receive something they deem important.

It is also important to stress the negative role that large sums of private money play in American election campaigns, through lobbying and influencing of legislators, and, of course, through media advertising, especially expensive advertising designed to obfuscate and preclude reasoned debate. In the health care debate, the potential "losers" were more organized and better financed than the potential "winners," the general public.

Of course, a host of tactical errors were made. Given the underlying ideologic problem, there simply was no room for these tactical mistakes, especially since the battle was joined under unfavorable conditions.

Other Unfavorable Factors

These unfavorable factors, which were present in the past, will play roles in the future as well. They therefore need to be understood. The first, which I have alluded to previously, stems from the combination of our nonparliamentary system with our weak party structure: even our politics is individualistic—candidates often eschew the party label, raise their own funds, and behave as independent loci of power. It is not likely that this situation will change—although one must note that the "radical" behavior, cohesiveness, and discipline of House Republicans elected in 1994 may bring some restructuring, realignment, and renaissance to parties.

The second is that, given the complexity of the health care delivery and financing structures that have grown up, we must search for exceedingly cumbersome and complicated mechanisms to meet conflicting objectives within the ideologic constraints under which we operate: We try to induce private structures to undertake the redistribution tasks that could come naturally to a government tax and social insurance structure.

Furthermore, we prefer to undertake this endeavor in ways that hide what is really happening. This means that the structures that will achieve the purposes at hand are not easily understood by the general public. Moreover, they are criticized by some (generally liberals) because they do not go far enough and are needlessly complicated, even as they are criticized by others (generally conservatives) who, in spite of the attempted "cover-up," recognize what is being advocated and, as a consequence, reject the proposal. Inevitably the complexity is likely to lead to increases in "error and failure rates." When enacted, such a program's complexity assures that it will not be fully effective. Regrettably, mobilizing public and legislative support for enactment requires overselling. The inevitable consequent disappointment serves to undermine belief in one's representatives and in the ability of government to be effective. This undermining of faith, of course, makes it ever more difficult to enact legislation.

Given the first two difficulties, it takes a very long period of sustained effort to enact any piece of legislation. Each year we have to build on the effort of the previous year, educate the public about the nature of the proposal, get more people to feel that they are familiar with the proposal and know it as an old acquaintance, perhaps even a friend. Eight years were needed to enact Medicare, a much simpler and much less threatening proposal than the Clinton health care reform effort and one that dealt with a population in which a very high proportion lacked any insurance at all. How could we have imagined that the Clinton plan, so comprehensive and so new and affecting a population in which most people did have insurance, could be enacted in one year? The amazing thing is not that the program was not enacted in 1993–1994. The surprise is that so many otherwise sensible participants in and observers of the drama believed that it would be.

It is hard to imagine that if the administration had remembered its history and the lessons derived therefrom it would have structured its proposal as it did. If the president had believed that his task was to contribute to a process that would make it easier for his successor (perhaps for himself in the last years of his second four-year term) to succeed in enacting reform, he might well have submitted a very different proposal. For the tragedy is that the effort at health reform is not a battle in which we will build on last year's proposal, amplifying it here and moderating it there but always continuing the debate. Aspects of the Clinton program may reappear in the future—many of the changes taking place in the organization of the delivery system enhance some of the characteristics of the Clinton proposal—but there is little reason for optimism about universal coverage or about comprehensive reform in the near future. That debate was short lived; those parts of the agenda will have to wait. Unlike the Medicare debate, in which essentially the same program was debated year after year, the argument for health reform was not significantly advanced by the efforts of 1993–1994.

WHAT THE FUTURE HOLDS

Health reform remains an issue in spite of the fact that it has been ignored by the body politic, in spite of the fact that premium increases have moderated, and in spite of the decline in the U.S. unemployment rate (even so, the number of uninsured increases by about 1 million per annum). It seems clear that political leadership and/or the next recession, with its more rapid growth in the number of uninsured, will again move health reform to center stage. What is unclear is what the shape of a reform proposal that would garner strong congressional or presidential support will be.

On the one hand, there are those who are convinced that reform can—and, given the American political system and ideology, should—be undertaken in incremental steps. They would encourage market forces to continue to change the delivery system and would concern themselves with filling in some of the existing gaps in coverage and increasing consumer price consciousness (via cost sharing and changes in tax legislation). They would address issues of insurance reform and would try to help individuals who already have insurance. Among the matters that appear to have the highest priority for many "incrementalists" are the issues of coverage for otherwise uncovered preexisting conditions and insurance portability when changing employers.

On the other hand, there are those who believe that, while incremental reform is the usual American approach to major legislation, it is a deficient strategy in this case. For some, that view is based on a belief that unless there is a single program that enrolls everyone through the same insurance mechanism, the poor and others, such as the unemployed, will not receive adequate attention or needed assistance, especially over the longer run. Their argument is that in the United States the only thing that will protect the poor is a universal program in which the fate of middle-income Americans is intertwined with theirs. Extended further, this argument suggests that if incremental reform begins with issues affecting middle-class people with or seeking insurance (issues like that of preexisting conditions), the thrust for reform will evaporate before it reaches the poor and others without insurance.

Others who oppose incremental reform suggest that the Clintons were correct in arguing that reform has to address many issues at the same time if is not to come apart over time. Thus, for instance, unless insurance is made compulsory, community rating (in which all insurers have to charge the same rate with minor adjustments, if any, for the subscriber's age and gender) cannot be sustained since younger and healthier subscribers would disenroll.

Whatever the analytic merits of the argument for comprehensive reform of financing and insurance, it is difficult to imagine that, after the events of 1993–1994, congressional leaders or the president will soon return to that issue. Though delivery-system changes, in particular the continued growth of HMO enrollment, should help resolve the argument that comprehensive reform would restrict choice, American politicians would approach an in-depth universal health care reform debate with a singular lack of enthusiasm. Even with the reelection of President Clinton in 1996 there is no evidence that suggests a resurgence of liberalism of the kind that could deliver major reform involving redistribution rather than small and incremental change. It does not seem unreasonable to suggest that American politics may well be dominated by a belief in market solutions and in the downsizing of government for some time to come.

Thus, whatever the merits of the analytical arguments for comprehensive action, it is far more likely that if there is any movement at all, it will follow the route of incremental change with emphasis on insurance-market reform. In the short run the various measures (relating, for example, to portability and preexisting conditions) will be of value to middle-class Americans who have or can afford to purchase insurance. Such measures, however, are not likely to be sustainable over the longer run since insurance companies will seek ways to insulate themselves from subscribers who might prove costly. Nor will such measures help solve the financing problems of the uninsured or of their health providers. Sooner or later the debate about meaningful reform will resume.

Four potential developments may speed the resumption of that debate. I mention them as a reminder of how little we know about the way the story may unfold and, therefore, how inexact predictions of the future may be.

The first event that would move the debate forward would be a major recession entailing a much more rapid increase in the number of Americans moving from the ranks of the insured to the ranks of the uninsured. The second involves the experimentation going on in the various states. It is difficult for an individual state to go it alone in developing a universal insurance plan because existing federal law requires the granting of a federal waiver before a state can undertake comprehensive reform; individual states are constrained by existing federal programs, each with its own characteristics; and, finally, the ability of individual states to finance the subsidies that would be required and to impose the employer requirements for insurance provision and/or the necessary taxes is constrained by the behavior of other, economically competing states. Nevertheless, various states are trying to expand coverage. If these efforts succeed (and there is no assurance that they will), they may have an impact on the national body politic.

The third development that could affect the timing of our next great debate on health reform is the potential increase in discomfiture with the changes taking place in the organization of the American delivery system, specifically with the rapid shift to managed care, often with restrictions on the individual's choice of delivery plan (and, thus, of physician and hospital) and, increasingly, under for-profit aegis. Though Americans may opt for the market over the government, there is still a considerable distrust of large, for-profit corporations. Nowhere, perhaps, is that more evident than in the health care arena. That is the case because the expansion of for-profit entities is both relatively new and troubling to those who understand that physician behavior may be constrained by their employers. In the United States, government plays a much smaller role in health care financing than is the case in other nations. Nevertheless, physicians in the United States encounter more interference than do others in their exercise of clinical judgment because of private efforts to maximize profits (of the insurance, the employer, or the HMO) by constraining physician behavior.

American physicians and patients are so busy fighting government that they seem not to have noticed that their behavior is increasingly influenced by abstract market forces whose power cannot be limited by voting them out of office. Perhaps, however, conditions will lead people to rise above their ideologic preconceptions. If physicians and patients find their behavior and relationships so restricted, and if those restrictions lead to a view that quality of care is compromised, it is possible that calls will be heard for government regulation of for-profit entities and, perhaps, even more comprehensive action.

A fourth factor that may increase the speed with which we return to a comprehensive health care debate arises from the fact that the Hospital Trust Fund, part of the Medicare program, is underfunded and that the sums now available in the trust fund are projected to be exhausted in 2002. Clearly, there are numerous ways to address that problem (including having a somewhat higher Medicare tax). It is possible, though by no means certain, that the need to address the Medicare problem—a need that also arises from the fact that the Republican congressional majority has proposed significantly reducing Medicare expenditures for physicians as well as hospitals in order to achieve a balanced budget in seven years even while reducing government revenues substantially—will lead to more wide-ranging discussions about the health sector, its organization, and its financing.

Many conservatives support the privatization of Medicare, which would be achieved by offering individuals the actuarial value of their Medicare benefit and encouraging them to purchase their own insurance. Part of the approach would encourage the elderly to purchase insurance with high deductibles (say, $3,000 per person per annum) and open tax-free medical savings accounts of amounts up to the deductible. Sums that were not spent would accrue to the individual. They argue that this approach would help restrain utilization and, thereby, obviate the need for rationing. It is evident that a similar approach—high deductibles and medical savings accounts—could also be applied to the population at large. Clearly, it would not enable people without insurance to enter the market. Nevertheless, that deficiency might not impede the adoption of this ideologically driven proposal, whose objective is to preclude a larger role for government and to increase the reliance on voluntary markets. Given the wide disparity in risk and the resulting differences in utilization and costs, it is clear that such arrangements could lead to market segmentation and the breakdown of insurance. Thus, if such ideas are put forward and seriously debated, it is possible that they will be rejected and that we might decide to move to universal insurance more expeditiously.

Health care reform remains on the American political agenda. Yet fundamental reforms that address equity considerations and require a greater role for government may have to wait for the American ideology that exalts the market and individualism to shift in favor of a sense of community and the strengthening of social capital. But, of course, I have used the wrong verb when I write "wait" for ideology to shift. Social capital and a sense of community are not created by waiting, but by hard work. Again, the lessons of Medicare are important. They suggest that with sustained effort the American political system can rise above entrenched ideology.

Today, the American way of organizing and paying for health care reflects American values. If we are to change the former in fundamental ways, we shall have to be willing to depart from the latter.

Chapter 8

Thoughts on a New Government Role in Health Care
Robert L. Kane

INTRODUCTION

Some years ago, my wife and I set out a framework to describe the potential roles of government in providing health and social services in an alliterative format using the letter *P* (Kane and Kane 1981). These roles consisted of planning, providing, purchasing/paying, policing/protecting, preparing (training), promoting, and policy making. It seems appropriate to revisit this list today, more than a decade later, to see how government has responded to current social and economic conditions and what its options now appear to be.[1]

Recent political changes have challenged the central role of government in influencing the shape of health services. As government becomes a party of last resort instead of first resort, many things change. The initiative shifts to other sectors and the principles of accountability become more passive than active. This change in emphasis from government to business seems to be cyclical (Reich 1987). It seems to be based less on empirical observation than on philosophic preference. Its implications are profound.

PLANNING

Historically, government has played an active role in setting goals for health care and establishing strategies to meet them. Health statistics are monitored. More recently, the federal government has gone through an elaborate planning effort, Healthy People 2000 (U.S. Department of Health and Human Services, Public Health Service 1991). Health goals across a number of areas were established and progress toward them has been monitored. Government has played a role, usually in concert with professional societies, in determining the need for future practitioners. The last major forecast predicted an excess of physicians in almost every area, especially in the specialties (GMENAC 1981).

Planning seems like a natural role for government. It is one of the central functions of government identified by the Institute of Medicine's report on public health (Institute of Medicine 1988). A governmental role in planning assumes a complementary role in implementing. The strategy would be to use government resources to create incentives to achieve the goals set. Until now, federal and state funding have been a major source of support for health care. Government funds have been the backbone of preventive services.

A shift to a system that relies primarily on a corporate private sector working through managed-care organizations would imply that such organizations would undertake planning functions, or at least would dictate the terms for such planning. Personnel requirements would be determined by the type of practitioners being employed and the expected growth of the sector. As managed care emphasizes primary care over specialty care and aims to minimize the use of expensive technology, the demand for the devalued services will diminish through market effects. Likewise, hospital use will fall and consolidations will occur.

At best, corporate planning addresses the population currently enrolled or targeted for enrollment. Little concern is given to those who are unserved. Government retains a responsibility for those left uncovered. One option, of course, is simply to purchase coverage for them, thus including them within the sphere of corporate concern. To the extent that these public clients are marginally unprofitable, they may be unattractive to private corporations, or those organizations may seek ways to serve them minimally.

One of the great planning efforts to come out of the pro-government agenda of the 1960s was the formation of several comprehensive health planning agencies. These groups were expected to determine the need for various services and to authorize only those services that fit their determinations. Between the problems of co-optation and legal challenges and the serious problems inherent in establishing a credible planning methodology, these efforts fell out of favor. Efforts to require prior certificate of need to prevent the overzealous utilization of expensive technology that would then drive up the costs of care became embroiled in political and legal battles.

Rational planning is more likely to occur in a well-defined system that can create an economic incentive for regionalization of services. Any attempt to impose the regionalization concept on a series of structures that held no common bond and shared no central mission was doomed to fail.

PROVIDING

In truth, the government has not been a major health care provider. No one has seriously proposed a national health service for this country along the lines of that found in Britain. The U.S. government's role historically has been that of a residual provider, the source of last resort. This burden of assuming the ultimate responsibility for those whom other social mechanisms have shunned has led to some unfair and unfortunate comparisons that have provided critics with misleading ammunition about the inefficiency of government care. The two areas of direct provision of health services (not counting the Veterans Administration (VA) hospital system) are public hospitals and public health departments. The role of the former was dramatically changed by the passage of Medicaid and Medicare, which provided major income streams to these hospitals. Although they continued to serve indigent clients with no payment source, their burdens were dramatically relieved. Medicare funds were used to further subsidize public hospitals through an added payment for those that were treating a disproportionate share of indigent clients. If these hospitals were also teaching hospitals, they received additional Medicare payments.

The availability of these federal funds established a new relationship between the levels of government. Local government began selling services to federal and state governments. (Such arrangements have not always existed. The original Social Security legislation specifically prohibited payments to recipients in publicly funded homes for the aged in order to discourage such institutions and thereby create a private nursing-home sector.)

Medicare has become a vehicle for public projects other than the care of older persons. As I mentioned above, graduate medical education (GME) has been quietly subsidized under the Medicare program, which pays both a direct GME payment for all postgraduate medical trainees and another indirect payment for care delivered by teaching hospitals. It is important to recognize that as much as 6 percent of the total Medicare hospital bill has been going to subsidize the training of physicians, many of whom will not devote their professional careers to treating older persons. And again, hospital payments under Medicare have also included a special payment for hospitals that provide a "disproportionate share" of care to poor persons.

It is not necessary that Medicare be the mechanism by which to subsidize other worthwhile activities, such as care for the poor or graduate medical education. This step was politically expedient at the time. Removing such programs from the auspices of Medicare makes better use of trust fund moneys.

Local public hospitals and thus local governments have become dependent on federal and state support. As state budgets have become tighter, they have attempted to slough off responsibility for local health care to cities and counties. Moreover, with the influx of poor immigrants, it is no longer clear that particular locales near border areas or ports should be uniquely burdened with such care.

Public hospitals have not been displaced by private ones. Although there is some legal authority to require private hospitals that have received Hill-Burton funds to provide free care, when a public hospital is available, it will likely remain the primary resource for such care. Proprietary hospitals have been noted to provide only those types of care that are lucrative (that is, not emergency or obstetrical services) and to avoid admitting indigent patients whenever possible (Watt et al. 1986).

Public health departments were once the primary source of home health care, but Medicare made such care a lucrative business. The growth in home health care has occurred largely in the private sector. Both proprietary independent companies (including several large national chains) and proprietary and nonprofit hospitals have established home health agencies that cater to both Medicare and private clientele. Public health departments are now competing with these private agencies. Once again, the proprietary agencies are not likely to treat indigent clients, leaving that burden to the public and nonprofit agencies. As the number of home health agencies proliferate, even while some become highly specialized in more lucrative, high-technology care, the role for public agencies must diminish. It is not clear how many can effectively compete with the more aggressive private firms without sacrificing their mission. Even the private, nonprofit visiting nurse services are finding the going tough.

The situation for public hospitals and home health care agencies has been complicated by the growth in managed care. As government-funded programs contract with these organizations, public providers find themselves competing to become subcontractors under the businesses that their parent governments have selected.

PURCHASING

Government is more likely to buy care than to provide it. There has never been strong support for some form of national (or even state) health service. The closest we have come is the Veterans Administration and a small, shrinking cadre of public health service hospitals designed to serve special clienteles.

Government is a large purchaser of health care. The federal government has, in effect, thus become the largest health insurance carrier in the country. Unfortunately, its policies have not been brought up to date. The Medicare program is an anachronism. It was intended to help older persons who had been driven out of the private health insurance market by risk-based pricing find a safe haven that provided comparable coverage at affordable prices. Large components of the program are still based on the original, 1965 model of private health insurance. Thus, Medicare beneficiaries enjoy a level of insurance not experienced by many working adults.

Concerns about Medicare's rapidly escalating costs have prompted unfounded beliefs in the power of managed care to stem the tide. However, even managed care will not address the program's fundamental problems. As currently practiced, Medicare managed-care organizations operating under risk contracts receive a fixed sum per enrollee equal to 95 percent of an adjusted average per capita cost (AAPCC) for Medicare beneficiaries in that county. These AAPCCs, in effect, reflect the costs and intensity of practice in different areas and vary enormously from one location to another. Thus, managed care can, at best, trim only 5 percent from the cost of Medicare, and that only if the population enrolled matches the overall Medicare population in that area. The problem is then doubly confounded when managed-care organizations recruit healthier-than-average clients and receive average rates for them. Even with the 5 percent discount they provide, managed-care contractors are getting paid too much. Evaluations of Medicare risk products to date suggest that they enjoy a favorable selection and hence are overpaid for the groups they serve (Brown et al. 1993). Capitation (paying a fixed amount per enrollee) makes poor economic sense when the rate is calculated on the basis of the average cost of a beneficiary and healthier-than-average subscribers are actually enrolled.

A shift to managed care will not address the underlying problem of substantial variation in Medicare payment rates. Because the AAPCC is driven by the fee-for-service rates, a solution must involve those rates. There is a substantial opportunity to achieve savings in Medicare by addressing the large discrepancies in the level of current Medicare expenditures across the country. Why should Medicare be paying twice as much per enrollee in Washington, D.C., or Maryland as it does for an average enrollee in Minnesota, Oregon, or Hawaii? In 1992, the average Medicare expenditure per enrollee was $4,792 in Washington, D.C., and $4,430 in Maryland, whereas the rates were $2,391, $2,336, and $2,157 in Minnesota, Oregon, and Hawaii, respectively. These differences cannot be explained by differences in factors like age, gender, and health status.

As with most health insurance, Medicare benefits come in two parts. Part A covers hospital care, limited nursing-home care, and home health care. Part B pays for physician services and outpatient care. Part A represents about two-thirds (63 percent in 1992) of total Medicare spending. Most of that (82 percent) goes to hospitals, which are reimbursed on a uniform basis across the country under a program known as the Prospective Payment System (PPS). PPS pays a fixed amount per hospital discharge according to a patient's diagnosis. Although there are some minor adjustments for wage-rate differences and extent of care for needy persons, in effect, all hospitals in the country are paid about the same amount for a given type of care. Nonetheless, in 1992, Medicare paid out $2,533 per enrollee in Washington, D.C., and $2,450 in Maryland for hospital services as compared to $1,518, $1,243, and $1,193 for the same types of services in Minnesota, Oregon, and Hawaii, respectively.

The same basic pattern of variation is seen with regard to physician fees. Washington, D.C., and Maryland are displaced from the top of the list one notch by Florida, which has annual expenditures of $1,322 per enrollee whereas the other two have expenditures of $1,242 and $1,195, respectively. Once again, though, the discrepancy between those spending the most and the least is about 100 percent.

Substantial differences in Medicare spending remain even after differences in populations and wage rates are taken into account. The most expensive quintile of states spends about one-third again as much per beneficiary than does the lowest quintile. If the Medicare program could bring the high-expenditure states into line with the low-expenditure states, the fiscal solvency of the program would be established without having to inflict any undue burden on patients or providers. It is not immediately obvious that the cost of doing business is dramatically greater in the Washington, D.C., area than in Minneapolis. Nor is there compelling reason to believe that the Medicare beneficiaries treated in the more expensive places are any healthier as a result of the extra money spent on them.

The big question today is how to get sufficient control over the amounts paid to reduce the variance. Managed-care organizations (MCOs) could offer an opportunity for price competition if they could become the only providers for Medicare, but no organization will accept a price for capitated care that is substantially less than what they would receive if they continued to provide that care under the present fee-for-service arrangements. It is harder to control the costs when Medicare services are sold in small pieces in the fee-for-service marketplace, but it is not impossible. Heavier price controls could be targeted at those states with substantially higher adjusted levels of spending. The price paid for a given service could be combined with a volume discount to prevent purveyors of services from simply increasing volume to compensate for lower prices. It is feasible to use retroactive adjustments to control for case-mix differences across locations.

Contracting out to managed-care organizations saves the government very little. The profits go to the shareholders, not to the taxpayers. Rather than accepting a hypothetical 5-percent savings based on an inaccurate capitation rate, Medicare needs to adopt some of the strategies of managed care. Medicare could itself operate as a managed-care system if it were willing to revise some of its policies, most specifically those dealing with beneficiary choice of provider. Medicare could direct care and control costs better if it could exclude expensive providers, restricting beneficiary choices to those providers who offer the best arrangements. Medicare needs to be able to control who cares for the beneficiaries it covers. Physicians that abuse the system by ordering excessive tests should not be permitted to participate in the program. Patients should not be able to visit an infinite number of physicians in search of care. Case management should be used to help high-cost beneficiaries find the care they need more efficiently. Services that can prevent future complications should be offered. Rather than paying an average rate in a county or similar region for care, the program could stimulate competition.

Instead, both Medicare and Medicaid have opted to contract all care. The managed-care numbers do not add up. We would have to believe that managed-care organizations are incredibly efficient if they can charge 20 percent or more for administrative tasks (when Medicare charges less than 5 percent for the same work) or that they are not providing the same services. Medicaid, unconstrained by requisite beneficiary choice, behaves like any other payer and allows its beneficiaries to select from a defined pool of managed-care organizations, and if none is chosen it assigns one. At present, Medicare has no such authority, but it should.

Another important step in controlling Medicare costs would be to prohibit the use of Medigap policies that cover the Medicare copayments and deductibles. These payments were introduced as a means to discourage frivolous use of services. Over 80 percent of Medicare beneficiaries have purchased insurance to cover these costs (or had it purchased for them). Hence the disincentive to use care is eviscerated.

Historically, taxpayers have been loathe to grant public-service recipients greater benefits than they enjoy for themselves. Policies around welfare payments for mothers and children that used to favor keeping mothers at home with their young children changed when working mothers resented having their tax support helping someone else to achieve a lifestyle they could no longer afford for themselves. Similarly, working people will become increasingly unhappy when they are forced to submit to managed care while Medicare recipients are not. In the past, the older population has received preferential treatment. While wages were declining relative to inflation, Social Security recipients got cost-of-living adjustments. Recent political actions raise serious questions about whether this privileged status will endure.

Medicaid offers a rather different story. It has not developed in the way that its framers envisaged. A product of the economically positive 1960s, it may not be sustainable in a more pessimistic era. Originally, Medicaid was designed primarily for those who were receiving public assistance in a state, but it was later expanded to include the "medically needy." None of the designers anticipated that nursing homes would become the engines to fuel medical poverty for older clients.

Medicaid has emerged as two quite distinct programs with very different insurance components. Care for AFDC and other nonelderly public-assistance recipients is closely akin to ordinary health insurance. Most recipients need coverage for obstetrical services and well-child care thereafter. A small proportion (but larger than the rate for the rest of the population because of risk factors associated with poverty) need very expensive, high-technology care to support extremely ill newborns or to care for problems that emerge in the first few years of life. This situation lends itself fairly easily to becoming incorporated into traditional care systems. Some might argue that these high-risk populations need special attention because they face special obstacles in using primary care, but to the extent that such preventive care reduces the subsequent costs of expensive care, private corporations will be motivated to find better ways to deliver it.

The situation with long-term care is quite different. The distribution of costs across beneficiaries is much more even. Everyone is high cost, but some are higher than others. About half of those entering a nursing home leave within three months, and the rest may stay for many years. Unfortunately it is hard to predict who will fall into each half. Efforts to use noninstitutional community care have generally been disappointing as a cost-saving measure (Weissert 1986), but that has not diminished the enthusiasm for the idea. Indeed, there are some examples of states like Oregon that have dramatically changed the distribution of spending between community care and institutional care and achieved overall savings, but thus far they are the exceptions rather than the rule.

The so-called dually eligible population, those who receive support from both Medicare and Medicaid, present special problems. They must conform to the practices of both programs. Because Medicaid coverage is effectively shaped by that of Medicare, capitating the former is awkward without including the latter. But Medicare capitation can occur only with the beneficiaries' consent. Removing this requirement would make merging the services covered by these programs much easier.

Not all long-term care is provided to older persons. Younger disabled people have a very different agenda. Their goals are to achieve parity with the rest of society. They want control of the resources expended on their behalf. Many services cover some form of personal assistance that allows them to function in social situations, including work. In effect, these disabled persons are asking that society help to create a more level playing field by paying the costs associated with the compensatory services needed to conduct the basic affairs of daily life.

Three decades of welfare-rights advocacy have created the view that Medicaid services are an entitlement conferred by the unfortunate coincidence of poverty and illness or disability. Medicaid recipients must endure more restrictions than do Medicare beneficiaries (for example, choice of provider and type of plan), but the services available to them are defined by federal policy. Moving responsibility for providing Medicaid exclusively to states would de facto remove these guarantees and revert to a more individualized situation.

The underlying issue, beyond the obvious political trade of less money for fewer constraints, is whether a resident of the nation should receive different levels of care for the same problem on the basis of where she or he resides. Such a formulation implies that there is presently no variation from one part of the country to the next, an image that is quite misleading. Rather, under the present system, active steps should be taken to rectify this situation, whereas if Medicaid were left entirely to the states such variation might be celebrated.

Government has used its payment authority to change the way health care is reimbursed. In several instances, government systems have pioneered new approaches or revived older ones. Prospective payments for hospitals dramatically changed those institutions' incentives and, consequently, their behavior. With a fixed payment per discharge, revenues and costs were redefined. Efficient production of services was encouraged, but so, too, was cost shifting. What had once been hospital services were now taken outside to create new income streams. Indeed, the analogy of a balloon expanding in one place as it is compressed in another led to the press for the more inclusive approach offered by managed care.

Medicare also introduced a fee schedule for physicians designed to improve the balance of payments between specialists and generalists. It even anticipated the potential response of increasing volume to offset loss in price. Although only a modest effort in a needed direction, its limitations again pointed to the need for more comprehensive solutions.

PROTECTING

When public funds are used to purchase care from private agencies, especially proprietary ones, there is usually the expectation of careful scrutiny to assure that these funds are well spent. It is not surprising, then, that a number of regulatory systems were established as part of the Great Society legislation of the mid 1960s. Regulation is traditionally fostered both by a priori concerns and as reactions to catastrophes. For example, after a series of scandals that uncovered both shoddy care and financial exploitation (Mendelson 1974; Moss and Halamandaris 1977), severe nursing-home regulations were imposed.

The need for regulation and oversight may be greater in a managed-care environment. Because prepayment creates incentives for providing less care, more protections must be available to be sure that consumers are not underserved. The usual counterargument that consumers are protected in a managed-care situation by their ability to disenroll is misleading. Consumers who fail to receive the services that their medical conditions demand are not likely to be missed by the managed-care organization, especially if that organization is not paid a higher premium for such high-risk cases.

Most of the health care professions had seized the initiative earlier and established their own regulatory boards which operated under state authority. The hospital establishment had likewise created a national accrediting agency. Therefore, certification by one of these accrediting agencies was generally accepted as evidence of adequate performance and suitability to receive funds. Those groups that had not established such bodies were thus most likely to feel the brunt of governmental regulatory efforts. In addition to nursing homes, these included home health agencies, durable medical equipment distributors, and HMOs.

Even those professions that impose their own oversight can be strongly affected by regulation. Regulation for quality control establishes standards for care that affect eligibility for payment and the amount of that payment; also, sanctions may be imposed. The other regulatory control comes from determining what will be covered. Services provided by an authorized group will be covered but not those provided by some other agency. One form of provider (for example, a physician) will be covered but not another (for example, a nurse).

At different times these regulations have been labeled as restraint of trade. The whole notion of professional control has been challenged. There is no question that many actions carried out in the name of quality health care are self-serving. On the other hand, controlling the right to treat has been a major method of assuring high-quality care. Although some groups become impatient with the lengthy review and approval process required to release a new drug (and strong political pressure has occasionally forced some drugs, such as those for AIDS, to be approved without a full set of experimental evidence), most observers agree that such oversight is critical for protecting the public's health. Likewise, although there is growing enthusiasm for so-called nontraditional methods of care, most people would be uncomfortable if just anyone could declare him or herself a healer and demand payment from Medicare.

As programs are shifted away from a central, federal mandate, the rationale for national policies fades. Economies of scale would dictate that evaluation of therapies should be performed centrally, but states' rights do not require that such advice be heeded. Beyond its role in directing federal programs, technically, the federal government's authority for many regulatory activities is tied to the Interstate Commerce Act. For example, drugs used only within a single state do not have to be approved by the Food and Drug Administration (FDA). In practice, few products can succeed without a national market, but services might.

The federal government's role in Medicaid has laid the grounds for national standards. Most observers would agree that the Omnibus Budget Reconciliation Act of 1987 (OBRA 87) raised the expectations for nursing-home care in most states. The establishment of this common floor certainly reduced the variation in regulatory efforts across states. Forfeiting the gains made in establishing such programs would mean a great loss in quality of care. Conversely, providers argue that these higher standards lead to higher costs. States left to pay the bills may be unwilling to accept an external agency dictating standards of care. The discrepancies that already exist and are being addressed, however slowly, by the imposition of national norms, will likely widen again.

The changes needed in regulation have less to do with who is regulated than with how they are regulated. Less attention should be given to assessing the adherence to arbitrary standards that have not been established by empirical research and more to measuring how well various providers attain the desired outcomes from the care they offer. Managed care provides a means to focus on these outcomes. The health status of defined groups can be monitored. Of course, as long as enrolled populations self-select their providers, adjustments for differences in risk will be needed.

Placing the emphasis on outcomes has another important advantage: it facilitates the growth of knowledge about what works and what does not. Systematic data collection and analysis permits the use of epidemiological techniques to identify which treatments are most effective for defined conditions. Only after such knowledge is available should strict mandates, or guidelines, be issued indicating what should be done. Premature codification of care principles otherwise represents the enforcement of professional dogma, much of which may be based on a fundamental, but unsubstantiated, belief in the value of individual professional skills.

The same outcomes analyses can be further used to identify those providers that are doing a better job.[2] Once the initial analyses determine the treatment components that produce the best results, one can ask the next logical question: does this relationship occur more often in the hands of certain providers than in others?

Some elements of care may not manifest themselves quickly enough to rely exclusively on outcomes for analysis. One does not want to wait for an outbreak of an infectious disease to recognize poor sterilization technique, for example. Likewise, some components of care, such as how people are treated, are important even though they do not affect outcomes. Courtesy, accessibility, and respect can be monitored by patient-satisfaction surveys.

Managed care is not a prerequisite for a focus on outcomes but it does offer some advantages. Patients can be identified at earlier stages of a disease and the treatment followed prospectively. Those who do not receive care can be tracked along with those who do to look for problems associated with underservice.

PREPARING

Both federal and state governments have supported education for health professionals in many disciplines. State-supported universities subsidize the education of health workers. Federal and state governments have provided loans and scholarships to allow poor students to pursue professional training. Some states have operated extensive programs designed to attract students into underserved areas by means of loan-forgiveness programs. The federal government ran the Health Service Corps as a means to attract physicians and other health workers to practice and, perhaps, settle in underserved areas. Special training grants are provided to encourage the development of trainees in areas presumed to be in short supply, such as family practice and geriatrics.

Some have argued that these hidden subsidies, such as those for graduate medical education described above, should stop. Physicians, who stand to earn large incomes, should be willing to invest more in their own education. Others fear that, without the support, only the wealthy would be in a position to afford medical training. Not only would access to such educational opportunities be denied to poor scholars, but the graduates would be less likely to work in underserved areas both because they would be anxious to repay the substantial debt they had acquired and because they would be less likely to share the ethnic origins of underserved people.

Through its support of medical research, the federal government pays the salaries of faculty and provides indirect payments to medical schools and other health-science endeavors. Reductions in these funding streams will have serious implications for the structure of academic medicine. Unlike in other countries, where faculty salaries are part of the institution's core budget (hence, there are limited numbers of faculty), many American medical schools have operated as operational shells for entrepreneurial researchers, whose salaries must be raised annually from external grant and contract support.

The challenge is to find a way to provide assistance without indiscriminately supporting a disadvantageous system. Transferring payments from institutions to students thereby allowing the latter to purchase an education at market prices would encourage more responsive institutional behavior, but they would most likely be responding to consumer demand rather than training the types of students who are most needed.

PROMOTING

Government has played an important role in health promotion. One of the great public-health success stories is the decline in smoking that has followed the 1964 surgeon general's report. Governmental actions, both educational and legislative, have been pivotal. Banning tobacco companies from advertising on many media and making smoking illegal in public places have certainly had a profound impact on smoking behavior. Likewise, federal labeling requirements for food packaging have supported educational campaigns to make people more aware of the role of diet in disease prevention.

Government agencies have promoted a variety of health-education campaigns. Some, like the Women, Infants, and Children (WIC) program, include services as well as education. A grand health-promotion strategy has been outlined in Healthy People 2000, a set of national health goals to be achieved in this century.

Governments with less direct responsibility for health care delivery may be more motivated to engage in health promotion. For example, the Canadian federal government became the champion of health promotion when the responsibility for supporting personal health care devolved to the provinces (LaLonde 1974). A similar pattern might be expected in this country.

Generally, health promotion represents a low political risk, but there are dramatic exceptions. Active advocacy can run afoul of economic interests, such as the tobacco lobby and even food producers. Campaigns for the use of condoms, either for birth control or in response to AIDS, can alienate the religious right.

POLICY MAKING

In the end, the real questions about the role of government in addressing health services boil down to policies and their underlying philosophies. Those who see health services as a form of economic investment would target those whose services are most highly valued. For example, on the basis of potential contribution to society, there is a constant bias in favor of children over the elderly, although some ethicists couch this preference as a response to children's lack of exposure to life's opportunities (Callahan 1987), and some political scientists see a societal bias against children, in part, at least, because they have no political constituency. But even such closet conservatives are not prepared to overtly suggest that services be denied to those who are not deemed productive.

Given a perceived (and probably real) shortage of resources, at least of dollars to support care, some type of rationing seems inevitable. The basic question is how to do it. Few policy makers seem to have the stomach for an overt approach like that used for some years in Oregon (Kitzhaber 1993). A more popular solution is to bury the rationing and detach it from governmental actions. Managed care emerges as an attractive strategy. Government can negotiate a fixed predictable sum for its obligations for health care costs. It can define for whom it will be responsible and can leave the painful distributional decisions to another group.

There are good reasons to believe that governments are not the best institutions to make hard decisions. They are politically vulnerable. Popularity is a crucial ingredient in politics. No one gains friends by saying no. Governments are more vulnerable to embarrassment. Potential scandals are worrisome. Governments are less likely to withstand pressure.

Efforts to make the government the primary force for health care reform have suffered serious defeats. There are too many established groups depending on the health economy to tamper radically with the system. On the other hand, just the threat of government intervention has spawned a revolution in health care planning, essentially within the private sector. Consolidations are occurring constantly. Basic ideas about what is necessary and how things work are being revised hourly.

Managed care as a reform movement has accomplished more than planning. Specialty distribution has been altered to emphasize primary care. Hospitals are ridding themselves of bed capacity. New forms of care are emerging.

The emphasis is now on the care system itself and not on its distributional elements. Cynics describe this period as one in which people are trying to make a fast buck. The focus is on price. Volume purchasing, negotiated discounts, volume controls, and selective contracting are all being used. Where it exists, price competition should reach its nadir soon. Then competition will be based on efficiency and especially on effectiveness. Organizational factors, information support systems, targeting, outreach, and the like will play a central role.

Can government become the foster mother of invention? Can it stay ahead of the curve and direct the development of health care, or is it better off responding to what is created in the private sector? At the very least we need a vision of where we want to go and a sense of priority about which elements are most important.

There is currently, in the United States, a strong belief in the values of the marketplace and a concurrent enthusiasm for competition as the best means of assuring value. Alas, such enthusiasm may be misplaced. Competition in business is different from that on the playing field. Business competitors do not necessarily play by a fixed set of rules. Even a casual glance at what happens in business reveals a different picture. Not all markets are equally attractive. Businesses compete for those that are most lucrative and easily avoid those that present special challenges. The methods of competition include less desirable practices, such as advertising, which is not the best source of information and is more likely to misrepresent or promote irrelevant aspects of a product. Competition frequently leads to one company buying out another to reduce competition and an industry becoming dominated by a few giants, who are more difficult to restrain because of their monopoly powers. Marketing techniques often place great pressure on dealers and distributors to treat one brand more favorably than the others.

This situation is hardly one we would wish to see for health care delivery. If competition is to become the major force in assuring value, then some institution—and what could be more appropriate than government—has to act as the referee, assuring that the goals are socially desirable and that the rules are followed. If competition is left unchecked, we may find ourselves in a situation similar to that of the early 1960s, when the elderly population was gradually excluded from the private health insurance market because risk rating allowed companies to compete more aggressively for the employed workers' business.

Who will stand up in support of a strong government role at a time that government is out of favor? The academic community might be expected to play such a role (if anyone thought them credible or influential). Unfortunately academe seems to be following in the footsteps of their predecessors of an earlier era, that of the Weimar Republic. Intellectuals are more likely to provide rationalizations for new political trends than to support unpopular but sound ideas.

The consolidation of power in health care has reduced the number of voices being heard. Those that are being heard seem more intent on assuring that their constituents get (or retain) a piece of the action than on improving the system in general. Adam Smith is in and Rawls is out. Spokespersons for the disenfranchised have found it increasingly difficult to advocate for those that private enterprise wishes to ignore. The current proposals to limit lobbying activities for nonprofit groups sound a warning about just how effective efforts to silence these protagonists may become.

FINAL THOUGHTS

A few nagging questions remain. Why won't anyone face up to the problems with the Medicare program? As things stand now, Medicare beneficiaries enjoy a better level of health insurance than many working Americans. They have free choice of providers when most people must look within a specified group of participating providers. They can disenroll from HMOs at will when most HMO enrollees are locked in for a year. Despite the assumption that Medicare is a national program with comparable benefits for all, there is enormous variation in its costs from place to place. This variation must be substantially attributable to differences in utilization because the costs of major components like hospital stays are fixed. Proposals to address Medicare's financial crisis by imposing across-the-board cuts or added beneficiary payments fail to recognize the extent of the current variation in Medicare costs. Why should care cost so much more in Miami than it does in Minneapolis? Why should beneficiaries in Minnesota be taxed to cover these excess costs? Would it not make more sense to differentially limit cost growth in high-spending areas? Moving to capitation under managed care will do nothing to address these discrepancies; they will simply be codified.

The discussions about making all or part of Medicaid exclusively a state responsibility raise serious questions about whether geography should determine care. There is already considerable discrepancy from one state to another in terms of both eligibility and benefits. Transferring full responsibility for Medicaid to states under some form of block grant would widen the gap even further.

NOTES

1. I am tempted to suggest a new set of Ps to describe current governmental activities around health issues: prevaricating, posturing, protecting, and postponing.

2. Provider in this context can be a given individual or, more likely, a group or institution. Most medical actions do not occur frequently enough to permit the gathering of an adequate sample on a given individual provider.

REFERENCES

Brown, R. S. et al. 1993. Do health maintenance organizations work for Medicare? *Health Care Financing Review* 15, no. 1: 7–23.

Callahan, D. 1987. *Setting limits: Medical goals in an aging society.* New York: Simon and Schuster.

GMENAC. 1981. *Report of the Graduate Medical Education National Advisory Committee to the Secretary,* Department of Health and Human Services, vol. 1, GMENAC summary report (1980–0-721–748/266). Washington, D.C.: Government Printing Office.

Institute of Medicine. 1988. *The future of public health.* Washington, D.C.: National Academy Press.

Kane, R. L., and R. A. Kane. 1981. Extent and nature of public responsibility for long-term care. In *Policy directions for long-term care,* ed. J. Melzer, H. Richmond, and F. Farrow. Chicago: University of Chicago Press.

Kitzhaber, J. A. 1993. Prioritizing health services in an era of limits: The Oregon experience. *British Medical Journal* 307, 373–377.

LaLonde, M. 1974. *New perspective on the health of Canadians.* Ottawa, Canada: Department of National Health and Welfare.

Mendelson, M. A. 1974. *Tender loving greed.* New York: Alfred A. Knopf.

Moss, F. E., and V. J. Halamandaris. 1977. *Too old, too sick, too bad: Nursing homes in America.* Germantown, Md.: Aspen Systems Corp.

Reich, R. B. 1987. *Tales of a new America: The anxious liberal's guide to the future.* New York: Random House.

U.S. Dept. of Health and Human Services, Public Health Service. 1991. *Healthy people 2000: National health promotion and disease prevention objectives.* Washington, D.C.: Government Printing Office.

Watt, J. M. et al. 1986. The comparative economic performance of investor-owned chain and not-for-profit hospitals. *New England Journal of Medicine* 315: 89–96.

Weissert, W. G. 1986. Hard choices: Targeting long-term care to the "at risk" aged. *Journal of Health Politics, Policy and Law* 11, no. 3:463–481.

Chapter 9

Outcome Measures for Persons with Disabilities as a Litmus Test for Quality in Managed Care
Robert Griss

The Clinton health care reform plan promised universal coverage through the expansion of managed care in the context of an administrative structure of regional alliances that would encourage competition among health plans while ensuring equal access to medically necessary services for all persons in a geographical area. The political defeat of the Clinton plan signaled that managed care could proceed with minimal government regulation. The government has been operating more as a buyer of health care than as a regulator. As a result, there has been greater attention paid to increasing the consumer's capacity to choose among managed-care plans than to ensuring the quality of health care within managed care. One of the groups most vulnerable in managed care are persons with disabilities. This chapter examines the use of outcome measures for persons with disabilities as a litmus test for quality in managed care.

With the rapid and largely unregulated transformation of the health care system toward corporatization, privatization, and managed care, people with disabilities have an important role to play as a litmus test for quality in managed care. In the traditional health insurance system with providers paid on a fee-for-service basis, the services which patients received from different providers were not always coordinated, necessary, or perhaps even

This chapter summarizes research in progress which is being conducted with support from the Robert Wood Johnson Foundation and from a project on measuring quality in managed care for persons with disabilities jointly funded by the Administration on Developmental Disabilities and the Centers for Disease Control and Prevention in the U.S. Department of Health and Human Services.

the most effective. But patients were free to choose other providers if they thought they were not being adequately served. Under managed care, on the other hand, patients are dependent on primary-care gatekeepers who operate within a health plan whose organizational processes are structured to contain costs. The challenges for policy makers are to ensure that managed care is used to capture savings in the health care system that are then redirected to serving persons who are uninsured or underinsured, and that managed-care plans' priority of cost containment does not override the objective of providing quality services.

PROBLEMS WITH MANAGED CARE

As more frequent users of health care services who consistently depend on specialists, often require different levels and types of services and equipment (sometimes on an ongoing basis) in order to maintain their health, and greatly value the choice of provider, persons with disabilities face three problems in managed care. One is that the primary-care provider (PCP) may not be sufficiently knowledgeable to determine what services a person with a disability needs, what services the plan has the expertise to provide, and what needs should be referred out to specialists or other essential community providers. In many managed-care plans, especially those that farm Medicaid recipients out to the lowest bidder, the PCP may have extremely limited discretion over what services the plan will pay for. A second problem is that the PCP and other plan providers may have financial incentives to limit health care utilization even when medically necessary. One of the main types of utilization that managed-care plans try to limit is referrals to specialists, which are often needed by persons with disabilities. A third problem is that the managed-care plan may be more concerned with limiting its costs than with improving the quality of its services. This concern may take the form of reducing utilization, imposing discount prices on health care providers and suppliers, and encouraging the disenrollment of persons with complex health care needs. As long as managed-care plans can make higher profits by collecting per-member, per-month premiums from low-risk people than by providing appropriate rehabilitation therapies to increase functional capacity or by reducing secondary conditions for persons with chronic health conditions, persons with disabilities will be vulnerable in managed care.

MEASURES OF QUALITY

A major appeal of managed care to health care payers is its potential to reduce the growth of health care costs. Insurers prefer managed care because it enables them to shape the behavior of the health care providers with whom they contract. Providers can be controlled through financial bonuses, profiling criteria, and the fact that patients cannot choose providers without a referral from the gatekeeper. This creates a tension between insurers and providers over loyalty to patients. Whether the interests of payers and insurers can be counterbalanced by the interests of patients in the quality of health care depends on a combination of consumer empowerment, quality assurance, and effective quality oversight. The problem is that health insurers often succeed in frightening government and employers, the two largest payers, by warning that regulation of quality necessarily increases health care costs. The challenge is to develop measures of quality in managed care which can be used to exert pressure on the managed-care plan to use its obligations under capitation to promote health care quality rather than profits.

There are three possible approaches to ensure that managed care promotes quality. One is to educate consumers by making available report cards that describe the performance measures of different health plans. A major weakness of this approach is that the consumer/patient may not have a choice of plans if the employer actually selects the managed-care plan based on cost considerations. A second approach is to rely on external oversight or regulation to ensure that plans provide quality care. The challenge here is to have sufficient leverage over the managed-care plan to ensure that quality standards are maintained. Some consumer advocates look to the contracts between public programs, like Medicaid, and the managed-care plans for the leverage to protect quality. In fact, the combined leverage of Medicaid and Medicare, which together account for approximately one-third of total health care expenditures, could create powerful precedents for public accountability that all health plans would have to adopt. A third approach is to rely on consumer protections within the managed-care plan to ensure that quality is not sacrificed to cost-containment objectives. In fact, these three approaches are not mutually exclusive; they can be combined. But all rely on different measures of quality. The next section will identify different measures of quality and consider their implications for meeting the health care needs of persons with disabilities.

Regulating managed care to improve quality can be especially tricky in the case of persons with disabilities for several reasons. First, in the absence of a consensus about treatment guidelines for many disabilities, it is difficult to determine whether appropriate treatment was provided. Second, because many providers have had limited experience treating persons with disabilities, they do not know what services are most effective. And third, the small numbers of persons with disabilities in a particular health plan introduce some statistical reliability problems in monitoring the quality of services provided. Nevertheless, there are different dimensions of quality that can be measured in managed care.

Structural Measures

One approach focuses on structural measures of a plan's capacity to deliver appropriate services. These are often determined by compliance with licensing requirements or accreditation standards and might include a certain array of qualified and experienced health care specialists, a grievance procedure, and an information system which can report on certain data collected by the plan. While structural measures may indicate whether a plan has certain descriptive characteristics, they may lack scientific validity as quality standards. In the absence of a scientific basis for requiring managed-care plans to provide a certain number of specialists, managed-care plans may be required to have contracts with qualified specialty providers in the community in order to ensure that their enrollees will have access to appropriate care. But it remains to be seen whether plans will provide referrals to out-of-network specialists when their own providers do not have the capacity to provide treatment of equal quality. Some structural features, like a needs assessment at the point of enrollment, contracts with a sufficient number of qualified specialized providers, physical accessibility to a doctor's office and to medical equipment in the office, and the absence of physician-incentive arrangements tied to reductions in utilization regardless of judgments about medical necessity, may be most important to persons with disabilities.

Process Measures

A second approach examines certain organizational processes within the managed-care plan that reflect the organization's performance measures such as waiting times for making an appointment or actually seeing a specialist. Another type of process measure is the percentage of people with specific diagnoses who receive particular services that are recognized as essential for quality care. Process measures, when appropriately used, may be good predictors of outcomes, but it is difficult to determine whether appropriate care has been provided without knowing the specific condition and unique needs of the individual. In fact, process measures tend to focus on common needs of all enrollees rather than on condition-specific measures.

Since persons with disabilities are usually a small percentage of the total enrollees in a typical managed-care plan, and since there is a tendency to provide process measures which are perceived as most meaningful to the largest number of enrollees, the process measures which are most relevant to persons with disabilities are often overlooked, especially when the disabilities are low-prevalence conditions. Information about the structural and process measures of health plans could be made available to enrollees through a standardized report card before they choose a managed-care plan. Whether this information about plan performance actually contributes to meaningful consumer empowerment depends on whether individual patients can choose their own health plans and whether the managed-care plan decides that it is cost effective to provide quality care to people with certain conditions. Cost-containment strategies need to be placed within a civil-rights context in order to ensure that quality of care is not sacrificed to corporate profits in the health insurance marketplace.

Outcome Measures

A third approach to measuring quality concentrates on health outcomes. Managed-care plans often use consumer-satisfaction surveys as a measure of their performance, even though these may be more appropriately viewed as process measures. A consumer-survey approach called CAHPS (Consumer Assessment of Health Plans Study) is being developed through the Agency for Health Care Policy and Research to measure consumers' perceptions of quality. It includes a series of questions on whether the plan or providers respect and listen attentively to the patient, whether any services have been denied that the patient thought were medically necessary and should have been covered by the plan, and whether the patient has been satisfied with the plan, primary-care provider, and specialists over the past six months.

While consumer surveys can measure important perceptions of quality that are not likely to be identified through the health plan's reporting system, many consumers will not have used particular services, lack the comparative experience with different plans and providers necessary to judge certain technical aspects of quality, and want to believe that their health plan and providers have their best interests at heart.

Another approach to health outcomes is to compare survival rates of patients for different providers or hospitals that have provided certain procedures like coronary surgery. For people with many chronic conditions, however, survival rates, though obviously important, may not be the most sensitive measure of quality. There is growing interest in ambulatory-sensitive conditions which reveal patterns of preventable medical complications when appropriate care has not been provided. For people with specific chronic conditions in a managed-care plan, measures for preventable secondary conditions might include hospitalization rates for people with asthma, blindness or amputation rates for people with diabetes, or rates of pressure sores for people with spinal-cord injury or other mobility impairments. These outcome measures must be risk adjusted in order to serve as a valid measure of quality between plans that may be serving populations with different levels of severity.

In comparing the health outcomes for people with the same condition at comparable levels of severity for all plans within a geographical area, the focus could also be on changes in health status and changes in the person's ability to perform certain activities, like going to work or school, taking care of personal needs, participating in community activities, or experiencing a higher quality of life. These health outcome measures at the level of the individual are different from clinical outcome measures at the level of the cell or the organ, which are often used for determining medical effectiveness.

The World Health Organization has developed an International Classification of Impairments, Disabilities, and Handicaps (ICIDH), which looks at the determinants of health status at the cell, organ, activity, and society levels. To the extent that the interventions that are needed to improve health outcomes for persons with disabilities or other chronic conditions often require changes at the activity or community levels, the search for clinical pathways for diagnosing, treating, and making more manageable many chronic conditions may not only be a long time in coming but may also be diversionary from the goal of effectively improving functional outcomes.

As one of the first chronic conditions that some of the more progressive managed-care plans have begun to recognize, the example of diabetes illustrates an interesting transition from treating symptoms at the cell and organ level to emphasizing the importance of interventions at the activity and community levels. While traditional indemnity health insurance has historically been unwilling to reimburse health care providers for educating patients with diabetes in order to influence their behavior in such lifestyle areas as diet, exercise, weight control, and smoking, managed-care plans are beginning to recognize the critical importance of this challenge for effective chronic-care management. On the other hand, managed-care plans are willing to explore these "new" interventions because they are viewed as cost effective for the managed-care plan. If managed-care plans can determine cost effectiveness in terms of the difference between the cost of providing or of not providing certain services in relation to the capitation payment that is collected, this raises a troubling question of whether managed-care plans would be as willing to provide comparable interventions for other chronic conditions if they were not cost effective from the managed-care plan's perspective. This problem is even more likely to be exacerbated by the growing use of subcontracting arrangements by financially successful managed-care plans, which are able to shift their responsibility for enrollees with disabilities to subcontractors or carve-out plans which may lack the financial capacity to provide quality care to higher-risk populations.

While managed-care plans may prefer to be held accountable for certain process measures that they can control, the quality of services depends on how the managed-care plan responds to the unique conditions of each patient. For persons with disabilities, the factors that may have the greatest impact on health outcomes are often environmental factors, which managed-care plans have tried to insulate themselves from through restrictive definitions of medical necessity and arbitrary utilization review criteria.

RESISTANCE TO OUTCOME MEASURES

Not surprisingly, health care plans generally do not want to be held accountable for outcomes that they may not be able to readily change through the clinical interventions that they are responsible for. After all, poor health outcomes may be due to environmental factors such as poverty or environmental pollution or lifestyle choices as well as to the impact of poor health care services from previous health plans and providers. While these concerns are understandable, it is important that health care plans have an incentive to provide the interventions that are most likely to produce desirable health outcomes. Interestingly, many of the interventions that have the greatest impact on the health of persons with disabilities and chronic conditions are often not strictly medical interventions. If public policy ensured that managed-care plans were rewarded for achieving higher functional outcomes for people with the same conditions at comparable levels of severity, then these plans would have an incentive to cooperate and coordinate with other community resources to increase the likelihood that appropriate interventions were provided. This process could encourage health plans to promote public-health approaches, which can often be more efficient for a greater number of people. In addition, if managed-care plans were prohibited from offering bonuses to health care providers for reducing utilization and were only allowed to provide bonuses for improving quality outcomes, managed care could become a powerful force for health care quality.

OUTCOMES AS MEASURES OF DISCRIMINATION

The outcomes for people with the same condition at comparable levels of severity who are enrolled in different plans within a geographical area can also provide an indication of whether persons with disabilities are being discriminated against in a particular managed-care plan. While managed care offers potentially beneficial flexibility which can be used to individualize services, that flexibility can also be used to reduce effective care in order to reduce short-term costs and encourage disenrollment of persons with disabilities. To the extent that compliance with practice guidelines has limited the effectiveness of utility as a measure of quality care for many people with chronic conditions, it may be more useful to compare outcomes for people with the same condition at comparable levels of severity in different health plans. Finding that certain plans have better outcome patterns than others may help to identify structures, processes, and interventions that are more effective.

This information can also be used to trigger an investigation of discrimination that managed-care plans may be practicing by denying equal access to covered services for persons with disabilities. Subjecting all enrollees to the same limitations in a managed-care plan may actually discriminate against persons with disabilities if it would require reasonable accommodations to effectively respond to their health care needs. Ironically, the practice of treating people with different health care needs the same does not guarantee the equal access to quality care which managed-care plans are obligated to provide to all enrollees. By relying on administrative mechanisms which are not risk adjusted, such as physician incentive arrangements; utilization review criteria; and arbitrary benefit limits on covered services, which limit the amount, duration, and scope of services provided to people with a particular condition regardless of what might be medically necessary, managed-care plans may be discriminating against persons with disabilities. This discrimination may take many forms, for example, denying meaningful access to covered services, imposing unequal access to qualified providers, or subjecting persons with disabilities to arbitrary limits on covered services in violation of federal civil rights laws. The Americans with Disabilities Act (ADA) could be used in new ways to challenge discriminatory administrative mechanisms that deny equal access to quality health care for persons with disabilities in managed care.

PUBLICLY ACCOUNTABLE HEALTH CARE

Finally, as long as managed care, which has become the dominant health care delivery system, is driven by market-based competition, plans are likely to cut costs to increase profits and are not necessarily likely to work to improve health outcomes. The potential for managed care to capture savings in the health care system that can be redirected to the uninsured population or to people who are underinsured is likely to be lost to excess profits for chief executive officer (CEO) compensation, stockholder dividends, and corporate takeovers. These "outcomes," which are studied by financial analysts but are often overlooked by quality analysts, are driving the transformation of the health care system. Ironically, this largely unregulated competition in the health insurance marketplace may actually weaken the health care system's capacity to serve the entire population in a geographical area, even though public funding actually accounts for the majority of total health care expenditures in the United States. When Medicaid and Medicare expenditures are added to other public health care programs, such as veterans' health benefits, the Civilian Health and Medical Program of the Uniformed Services (CHAMPUS), federal employees' benefits, and the public subsidy for employer-sponsored health insurance premiums, public funding accounts for over 52 percent of total health care expenditures.

If health care were recognized as a public utility, on the other hand, this investment could be directed toward services that promote productivity, improve community integration, and increase both the efficiency and effectiveness of health care delivery throughout society. Only by combining civil rights, public health, and health care as a public utility will managed care contribute to the provision of publicly accountable health care that ensures equal access to appropriate services for the entire population.

Chapter 10

Housing: Reconstructing the Federal Government's Role and Responsibilities

Michael E. Stone and
Chester Hartman

OCTOBER 1996: THE CONTEXT OF FEDERAL HOUSING POLICY

On the sixtieth anniversary of the passage of the United States Housing Act of 1937, this fundamental federal framework for low- and moderate-income housing is in danger of being repealed by Congress. The housing bill President Clinton signed in September 1996 calls for no increase whatever in the number of government-subsidized housing units.[1] Hundreds of thousands of units of public housing are slated for demolition without replacement; hundreds of thousands of units in privately developed and owned "expiring use" projects are no longer required to be subsidized for lower-income people; and hundreds of thousands of tenant-based rental certificates and vouchers are facing contract expiration without certainty of renewal. A recent *New York Times* report on federal housing policy concluded: "The federal government has essentially conceded defeat in its decades-long drive to make housing affordable to low-income Americans" (DeParle 1996).

These attacks and cutbacks are, of course, a substantial piece of the larger assault on federal social-welfare policies, but they also have their own character and context. Since the early 1980s, federal housing programs for low- and moderate-income people have been subjected to relentless ideological attack. Furthermore, the U.S. Department of Housing and Urban Development was subjected to scandalous and cynical abuse by Reagan appointees and cronies, from which it has never fully recovered (Dreier and

Atlas 1995). Yet during this very same period, the federal government has chosen to provide at least $500 billion, and possibly up to $1 trillion, in "social welfare" spending to bail out the failed savings and loan associations that were once the mainstay of the grand public/private partnership for middle-class home ownership (Stone 1993). And the federal treasury has continued to provide, through the Internal Revenue Code, ever increasing "social welfare" benefits in the form of tax deductions and credits, now totaling well over $100 billion a year, to housing developers, realtors, and upper-income homeowners (Dolbeare and Kaufman 1996).

These widely disparate magnitudes of federal financial housing assistance and the differences in substantive policies and political attitudes associated with the various categories of beneficiaries go back to the origins of large-scale federal intervention in the 1930s. When the economy collapsed into the Depression, the first and most substantial federal efforts in the housing field were to bail out and restructure the housing-finance system through creation of a central banking system for home loans, mortgage insurance to protect mortgage lenders against borrower default, and secondary mortgage markets to provide liquidity to mortgage lenders. The second priority was to support the home-building and brokerage industries through promotion of long-term, low-down-payment, federally insured mortgages. Job creation through federally financed construction came next in the order of concerns. The housing needs of the poor were not high on the list of public-policy concerns, despite President Franklin D. Roosevelt's recognition during his second inaugural address of "one-third of a nation ill-housed" (Stone 1993).

After World War II, rhetorical concern with housing needs found new expression. By the time that the traditional and now platitudinous National Housing Goal of "a decent home and a suitable living environment for every American family" was enshrined by Congress in the preamble to the 1949 Housing Act, more than a century of housing problems had left tens of millions of households living in physically deficient housing. Nearly five decades later, a much greater proportion of the U.S. population occupies what would be called a "decent home," but the ability to afford a decent home has become far more elusive.

Affordability has become the nation's foremost housing problem. In 1950, about half the households in the United States were "shelter poor," to use coauthor Stone's term (1993). By 1970, the proportion had declined to about one-third, reflecting the benefits to middle-income people of prosperity and federal support for suburban home ownership. Since 1970, however, there has been no reduction in the proportion of households that are shelter poor; it has fluctuated between 30 and 36 percent as the economy has risen and fallen, while the number of shelter-poor households has risen from 19 million in 1970 to 30 million in 1993.[2]

And the ultimate housing problem—no housing—is seemingly omnipresent and intractable. One recent study (Link 1994) looked at the incidence of homelessness over long periods (rather than the standard point-in-time survey) and found that over the five-year period 1985–1990, 5.7 million people had been literally homeless (sleeping in shelters, bus/train stations, abandoned buildings, and the like), while 8.5 million people reported some type of homelessness (staying with friends or relatives out of necessity). Lifetime homeless figures were 13.5 million people (literal homelessness) and 28 million people (any type of homelessness). These findings dwarf previous estimates and "counts" of the homeless and suggest just how massive and of longstanding duration has been the failure of the U.S. housing system.

As is now common knowledge, since the 1970s the responses of business and the government to the weakening international position of the United States and the associated squeeze on corporate profitability have produced widening income inequality, with those at the bottom experiencing declining real incomes and those in the middle barely keeping up with inflation while those at the top have very substantially improved their standard of living. What is perhaps not so well known is that during this same period housing costs have been driven to dizzying heights by unstable housing markets in many areas, perverse housing policies, and an increasingly volatile national mortgage market, as well as by demand for housing from ever richer households at the top of the income distribution.

This analysis contrasts with conventional explanations for the growing affordability problem. For example, emphasis on demographic factors tends to ignore the long-term persistence of shelter poverty and the institutional context of private, speculative interests in housing and land within which demographic trends are played out. Substantial problems existed before the baby-boom generation matured and before the new wave of immigration, and there is no reason to believe that such problems will "naturally" be resolved as the number of new households grows less rapidly in years to come.

Arguments regarding the changing role of cities in the affordability problem of the past two decades also tend to be incomplete. Within the context of uneven development by the overall economy, cities and regions have experienced their own forces of uneven development in which the private ownership and development of land and housing have long been crucial ingredients. The dramatic transformation of urban areas that began in the 1950s and has accelerated since the 1960s was not the inevitable outcome of an organic "maturing" of cities: it was the result of conscious choices by powerful actors with a predictably unequal distribution of costs and benefits. Many cities deliberately wrote off much of their declining commercial and manufacturing bases and tried to become regional, national, or international centers of high technology, medical services, finance, education, or tourism, with an employment structure of high-paying technical and managerial jobs on one side and low-wage service and clerical jobs on the other. The past generation has seen full fruition of the corporate/government partnerships fostering such changes.

The results for the residential communities within central cities and many older inner suburbs have been waves of disinvestment, demolition, and speculative reinvestment—at various rates and in various forms. In many cities this dynamic had already caused massive displacement of lower-income residents by the 1960s (LeGates and Hartman 1982). Most displacees ended up with higher housing costs in their new locations in addition to enduring social, psychological, and physical loss and pain (Hartman 1971). While the 1970s and 1980s saw soaring rents and sale prices, condominium and luxury rental conversions, and "upscale" arson (to clear out tenants and generate cash for luxury rehab) displacing lower-income urban residents, these processes were logical extensions of the earlier, publicly supported urban renewal and highway displacement and privately generated abandonment and "downscale" arson.

Meanwhile, local governments' dependence on property taxes and borrowing has caused continuing fiscal problems. Earlier revenue inadequacies often have not been relieved by a booming real-estate market, in part because of tax breaks offered to induce commercial development, in part because political erosion of state and federal tax bases has restricted revenue sharing and local aid. One result has been that many long-term homeowners have faced substantial tax increases as their assessed valuations rise with the market, leading to property-tax revolts and fueling antigovernment attitudes. The now-familiar trends and consequences of urban housing costs since the 1970s thus did not appear suddenly and unexpectedly. They have occurred within particular kinds of housing and land markets, in which high-level political-economic decisions have interacted with repeated private buying, selling, and refinancing, thereby greatly exacerbating affordability problems.

In addition, understandable anger and concern about reduction of federal government support for subsidized housing since the early 1980s have all too often ignored both the larger dynamics of affordability and the real flaws in past federal intervention. Even in the 1960s and 1970s era of considerable federal support for subsidized housing, the new housing created never fully replaced what had been lost to lower-income people, and rent subsidies were generally insufficient to bring rents down to what shelter-poor households realistically could afford. Much of the subsidized housing produced in that period provided windfalls to private developers in the form of tax-shelter benefits. Predictably, as the opportunities for private profit from operating such housing for low- and moderate-income people have run out in the late 1980s and into the 1990s, developers have been selling and converting the housing to market rentals or condominiums where demand exists, or, in less-desirable neighborhoods, simply defaulting on the mortgages and writing off their losses—except in those too-rare instances where the residents have organized effectively to maintain their developments as low- and moderate-income housing.

No discussion of the nation's housing problems can ignore the centrality of race. The housing conditions and affordability problems of African-American and Latino households are markedly worse than those for Whites. And while there has been considerable expansion and suburbanization of the Black middle class, a substantial segment of the nation's Black population is, in Massey and Denton's (1993) term, hyper-segregated and pejoratively labeled the "underclass." Numerous studies document persistent "redlining" by lenders (Squires 1992) and racial discrimination by real-estate agents, landlords, and other gatekeepers (Fix and Struyk 1993). And housing wealth is disproportionately owned by Whites (Oliver and Shapiro 1995).

Also, the widely publicized frustration and political rhetoric about diminishing opportunities for individual home ownership have tended to idealize ownership and overlook its downside. The attractions of home ownership are undeniable: most of us desire the security of tenure and control over our living space that only home ownership has seemed to provide in this society, along with the possibility of relatively stable housing costs, some equity accumulation, income-tax benefits, and a sense of community membership and social status that home ownership has promised. While high acquisition costs and interest rates have made it difficult even for upper-middle-income families to buy their first house, this is not the only, nor necessarily the most significant, problem manifested by conventional home ownership. The risks of mortgage foreclosure and tax foreclosure have undermined the security this tenure appears to offer. The popular home-owner tax benefits are highly regressive: more than two-thirds flow to households with incomes over $75,000 (DeParle 1996). And many home owners have placed the enhancement of property values above the enhancement of community, developing resentment toward those regarded to be of lower status and erecting legal and economic barriers, such as restrictive zoning regulations, that raise housing costs and preclude socially responsible development.

Finally, inherent weaknesses in the system of housing finance led to the expansion of secondary mortgage markets and financial deregulation, contributing to higher interest rates, inflation, and an explosion of debt far greater than the ability to repay it. These problems interacted with speculative investment in existing housing and shifts in production toward luxury housing, pushing housing costs and mortgage debt up to outrageous levels, leading to increasing numbers of mortgage defaults and foreclosures, and thereby adding to the forces bringing about the collapse of lending institutions.

THE RIGHT TO HOUSING

Neither the reversal of the cuts to existing programs nor the reengineering of these programs or even the devolution of housing programs to state and local governments can begin to alter the fundamental sources of the housing problem. Rather, efforts must be directed toward institutional change, not another generation of tinkering with existing institutions. Such changes are required, not only as the practical response to the economic failings of our society, but also in response to the moral failure to meet the housing needs of a great proportion of our people.

Rather than idealizing the market and serving as the handmaiden of private capital, federal policy must transcend the limits of the market and truly serve social purposes. Public action and social responsibility must move beyond the hollow promise of past policy to the establishment of a legally enforceable and publicly secured right to housing (with "housing" encompassing community as well as shelter).

The right to housing is an idea that builds upon the communitarian tradition of the commonwealth, in which personal advancement is not at the expense of the community and there is a social obligation to assure all people of having the necessities of life. It builds as well upon the recognition that political rights and civil rights have little practical meaning or utility for those among us whose material existence is precarious.

Slowly, without any coherent strategy, and to a limited degree so far, the rhetoric of a right to housing has begun to percolate into the realm of organizing and political action. Throughout the United States, organizers and activists more and more often speak of a right to housing in the context of housing organizing. Considerable work has been done to develop a policy framework for fundamental and long-term changes to realize the right to housing—a framework that can also guide new kinds of progressive and responsible public policies for the current period (Institute for Policy Studies' Working Group on Housing 1989; Stone 1993; National Housing Law Project 1995).

IMPLEMENTING A RIGHT TO HOUSING

Implementation of a right to housing could only occur over a period of many years, not all at once. It is certainly to be expected that implementation would involve increased public expenditures for housing. However, such a mandate would not merely or necessarily involve a quantitative expansion (or restoration) of current housing programs. Rather, it would lead to an evolution in our concept of housing and the nature of the housing market. Achievement of a right to housing would actually lead to a far more cost-effective use of those public dollars that are appropriated for housing, as it would require a more rational, integrated, and comprehensive approach to meeting housing needs than the ad hoc and piecemeal approaches that have existed heretofore.

What are some of the major policy ingredients that might be most central to a new federal role of working toward realization of the right to housing?

Expansion of Nonspeculative Social Ownership

1. Expand substantially the amount of housing under nonspeculative ownership to ensure long-term affordability, community viability, and responsible use of public resources. The term "social housing" is not widely used in the United States (although it is common in Europe) but is coming more into use to describe housing that is permanently outside of the private speculative market; it includes not only public and nonprofit ownership, but such forms as low-equity/no-equity cooperatives as well as mutual housing associations, community land trusts, and limited-equity individual home ownership. Social housing is also referred to as "nonspeculative" or "forever affordable" housing.

Until now in the United States, this stock of housing has been created mostly through new construction. We would argue, though, that the most efficient and effective policies for addressing the primary problem of affordability and moving toward a right to housing would involve acquisition and conversion of existing housing occupied by low-income families into nonspeculative or social-ownership housing. While costs vary, average per-unit costs for acquisition and conversion are at most half of the cost of new construction and in many cases much less.

Residents of such housing would not only have their affordability needs addressed (in many instances, where they currently live), but would also achieve long-term security of tenure as well as the possibility of substantial control over and responsibility for their housing—values integral to the concept of a right to housing.

While it is not possible to develop them in detail here, there are two basic policy approaches under which a substantial fraction of the existing housing stock could be brought under some form of nonspeculative ownership over the course of several decades as part of a right to housing program, namely,

- financial assistance to low- and moderate-income home owners who are shelter poor or facing foreclosure, in return for their agreement to transfer their residence to nonspeculative ownership;
- the buyout of a substantial proportion of the stock of unsubsidized private rental housing occupied by low- and moderate-income people, of absentee-owned rental housing through negotiated sale or eminent domain, and of owner-occupied private rental housing through voluntary sale or as part of estate settlement after death.

Social Tenure and Allocation of Nonspeculative Housing

2. *Implement, in nonspeculative housing, a model of tenure that provides the security, autonomy, control, financial benefits, and sense of community membership promised by home ownership.* Social tenure offers housing at much lower cost than conventional home ownership and without the risks of foreclosure, but also without the possibility of speculative gain.

3. *Allocate nonspeculative housing equitably and efficiently through a "social market" that would maximize choice for households in the nonspeculative sector and would reveal consumer preferences for planning purposes* (Stone 1993). One of the principal concerns often expressed about the prospects of a large sector of nonspeculative housing is about how decisions would be made regarding who gets which units. If housing is not allocated through the private market, does this inevitably imply big bureaucracies, inefficiency, and inequity? As long as nonspeculative housing comprises only a small share of the total housing stock, it will be necessary to use social criteria (for example, low income, homelessness, displacement) to determine eligibility, as well as administrative procedures, such as waiting lists, priority categories, or point systems, as are used now, in order to determine which eligible household receives an available unit. By the same token, as long as the social sector remains small, there will continue to be the same problem of horizontal inequity that exists at present with subsidized housing, that is, only a small proportion of needy households receive any benefits, while the benefits per subsidized household are quite large.

If, however, there were to be a commitment to a large-scale nonspeculative housing sector, in which it would be possible to realize the notion of housing as a universal right, then the situation looks quite different. Under circumstances where there is no opportunity for private profit, where there is an adequate supply of decent housing, and where everyone is assured of the means to afford at least some of the available supply of decent housing, a market might actually provide a degree of allocative efficiency that is never, in fact, realized in the capitalist housing market, and without its inequities.

Within the framework of an extensive, but decentralized, nonspeculative housing sector, the putative benefits of markets and of vouchers might indeed be realized, but in ways that are equitable and cost effective in contrast to their weaknesses and contradictions under current institutional arrangements. A social-housing market could also serve as a valuable tool for democratic planning, revealing through consumer behavior the types of housing various types of people prefer to live in when they have reasonably adequate (but not unlimited) resources available for meeting their needs.

Financing Nonspeculative Housing

4. Finance the acquisition, rehabilitation, and production of nonspeculative housing increasingly through direct public capital grants rather than mortgage debt or bonds in order to reduce both the affordability burden created by mortgage payments and the instability of the financial system.

5. Reform the financial system in order to deflate the credit bubble, reduce speculative uses of credit, and assure an adequate supply of credit— to complement capital grants—for productive investment in housing as well as infrastructure and job-producing industry. All private capital-market participants should be required to make below-market payments into a national housing trust fund to finance nonspeculative housing and community development. Credit-allocation authority and incentives should be used to steer private savings to community loan funds, state housing finance agencies, and mutually owned savings institutions.

6. Reform the housing tax loopholes and incentives in the Internal Revenue Code to create a more equitable tax system, reduce speculative incentives, and provide another source of revenue for a national housing trust fund.

7. Establish employer accountability and financial responsibility for helping to meet the housing needs of their workers and communities. Under an amendment to the Taft-Hartley Act, unions may (and should) negotiate for housing trust funds as part of their members' benefits. Private commercial and luxury developers should make linkage payments or meet inclusionary housing requirements. Other employers should establish voluntary housing programs or make payroll-tax payments into housing trust funds (Brooks 1994).

CONCLUSION

Even though the prospect of fully realizing the right to housing through fundamental changes in the institutions of housing provision is unlikely in the immediate future, these principles provide a framework for identifying and evaluating efforts already under way as well as defining a new federal role in housing that moves policy making in the right direction.

The possibility of actually creating a large and viable social-housing sector requires that nonspeculative housing be defined in more than just economic and legal terms. One component involves matters of process. Social ownership and financing must be linked with decentralized and democratic control and responsibility for housing—even though resources and standards may largely come from the federal government. Contemporary visions of nonspeculative housing are intimately interwoven with the ideal of participatory planning and design, along with resident and community oversight (if not actual control and responsibility) in the development and operation of such housing.

Nonspeculative social housing also offers a means of creating housing forms and facilities that are more responsive and adaptable to emerging and diverse household types and living arrangements by including the provision of supportive services as well as physical housing. The movement for nonspeculative housing has, as well, always been associated with the concept of community development—encompassing economic and social opportunity as well as infrastructure and municipal services.

Many informal groups and community-based organizations, a number of localities, a few states, and even bits and pieces of federal programs have been experimenting with some of the housing concepts we have described, although in a necessarily limited way due to the lack of an adequate federal policy framework and significant federal financial support. The growing infrastructure of social housing, along with grassroots organizations and state and local leaders and governments, have the potential to exert great leadership and initiative for a new understanding of the housing problem and thus, for new directions for federal policy aimed at effectively achieving a right to housing.

NOTES

1. During the Reagan years, net new budget authority for assisted housing decreased by more than 80 percent (in inflation-adjusted dollars). But because of the long funding pipeline for housing and because large amounts of new budget authority for housing had been appropriated during the Carter years, which Reagan was unable to get Congress to rescind, annual outlays for assisted housing actually increased each year during the 1980s, as did the total number of subsidized units (Dolbeare and Kaufman 1996).

2. Recognition of the interaction among incomes, shelter costs, and the cost of nonshelter necessities leads logically to an affordability standard that is a sliding scale rather than a fixed percentage of income. A household paying more than it can afford on this standard is shelter poor, the squeeze between its income and housing costs leaving it with insufficient resources to meet its nonshelter needs at a minimum level of adequacy. The shelter poverty affordability approach provides dramatic and compelling evidence of the inadequacy of the conventional 25- and 30-percent-of-income standards—and any other universal percentage—for shelter affordability. It provides a quantitative standard that can be readily adapted and applied to a whole range of programmatic, policy, and analytical purposes. Strikingly, the shelter poverty analysis does not reveal a more extensive housing affordability problem than does application of the conventional percent-of-income concept, but it does suggest a rather different distribution: the housing-affordability problem among lower-income households and among larger households is much more severe than indicated by the traditional standard but is less severe among middle-income and smaller households. About one-quarter of White, one-half of Black, and one-half of Latino households are shelter poor. The shelter poverty

affordability gap—the deficit between the amount shelter-poor households are paying and what they can afford—is about $100 billion a year (Stone 1993).

REFERENCES

Brooks, Mary. 1994. "Housing trust funds." In *The affordable city*, ed. John Emmeus Davis, 245–64. Philadelphia: Temple University Press.

DeParle, Jason. 1996. Slamming the door. *New York Times Magazine*, October 20.

Dolbeare, Cushing and Tracy Kaufman. 1996. *Housing at a snail's pace—The federal housing budget: 1978–1997*. Washington, D.C.: National Low Income Housing Coalition, August.

Dreier, Peter and John Atlas. 1995. Housing policy's moment of truth. *The American Prospect*, Summer, 68–77.

Fix, Michael and Raymond J. Struyk, eds. 1993. *Clear and convincing evidence: Measurement of discrimination in America*. Washington, D.C.: Urban Institute.

Hartman, Chester. 1971. Relocation: Illusory promises and no relief. *Virginia Law Review* 57: 745–817.

Institute for Policy Studies Working Group on Housing. 1989. *The right to housing: A blueprint for housing the nation*. Washington, D.C.

LeGates, Richard and Chester Hartman. 1982. Gentrification-caused displacement. *Urban Lawyer*, (winter): 31–55.

Link, Bruce et al. 1994. Lifetime and five-year prevalence of homelessness in the United States. *American Journal of Public Health* (December): 1907–12.

Massey, Douglas and Nancy Denton. 1993. *American apartheid: Segregation and the making of the underclass*. Cambridge, Mass.: Harvard University Press.

National Housing Law Project. 1995. *Housing for all: Keeping the promise*. Berkeley, Calif.

Oliver, Melvin L. and Thomas M. Shapiro. 1995. *Black wealth/white wealth*. New York: Routledge.

Squires, Gregory D. 1992. *From redlining to reinvestment: Community responses to urban disinvestment*. Philadelphia: Temple University Press.

Stone, Michael. 1993. *Shelter poverty: New ideas on housing affordability*. Philadelphia: Temple University Press.

Chapter 11

Welfare Reform: Fixing the System Inside and Out

Jared Bernstein and
Irwin Garfinkel

WELFARE COMES WITH CAPITALISM

The market forces that create economic growth and a tide of winners also create recessions and the occasional losers who need assistance. But since the creation of the English poor laws in the fourteenth century, welfare programs have been controversial. While they reduce insecurity, they also cost taxpayers money and reduce reliance on work and the family as sources of economic support. This inherent tension has, at different points in U.S. history, fueled intense debates. Welfare policy inevitably forces a choice between our values of compassion and community on the one hand and self-reliance and self-interest on the other. As a result, the generosity of welfare programs fluctuates with the resolution of each round of reform.

Having made a campaign promise to "end welfare as we know it," welfare reform was high on the Clinton administration's policy agenda in the first term. The administration initially proposed a plan that would limit cash assistance for those able to work to two years and provide work relief after that. The plan that he ultimately signed into law, however, reflected a more punitive approach championed by congressional Republicans. Under the new plan, welfare provision is terminated after a five-year period, with no provision for those who are unable to find work. Furthermore, financing is shifted to a block grant approach, and states will be given leeway to implement shorter (but not longer) time limits.

The authors acknowledge the helpful comments of Sheldon Danziger, Heidi Hartmann, and Christopher Jencks.

These reforms address a number of concerns about welfare that, even though they are continually invoked by policy makers and widely held by the American public, are for the most part not true. Chief among these myths are the following:

- Few people on welfare are truly needy; rather, government handouts entice able-bodied people away from the workforce and into the system. Once there the living is easy and dependence becomes long term.
- Subsidies for children have created an explosion of out-of-wedlock births, seriously threatening the stability of American society.
- Runaway welfare spending is one of the chief culprits behind ballooning federal deficits.

Yet myths can be powerful, and in the case of welfare reform their tenacity is leading us down a path on which we risk exacerbating some of our most serious social problems and solving none of them. Such a result, however, is far from inevitable, particularly if we take this opportunity to broaden the focus of welfare reform.

The key to reforming welfare lies not within the system but outside it—in the labor market and social institutions that are creating economic insecurity and fostering dependence on welfare. If we ignore these needed institutional reforms and only reform welfare from within, we will once again be faced with the impossible trade-off that has bedeviled every round of welfare reform. If we simply make welfare more generous, thus reducing economic insecurity, we run the risk of increasing dependence. Yet, if we reduce access to welfare or further reduce benefits, we reduce economic security, increase poverty, and, as we shall see, do little to reduce the number of births to unmarried teenagers.

This is not to say nothing needs to be done about the welfare program. In conjunction with progressive reforms outside welfare, the Aid to Families with Dependent Children (AFDC) program should have been converted to a time-limited cash-relief program culminating in eligibility for work relief. Long-term cash relief is an inappropriate tool for aiding those capable of work; a work-relief program that provided eligibility to intact as well as split families would have served to reinforce both work and family.

THE MODERN HISTORY OF WELFARE IN THE UNITED STATES

Although AFDC has gotten a tremendous amount of attention from policy makers and the media, it is but a small part of the modern American welfare state, representing just 9 percent of total social-welfare expenditures and 1 percent of the federal budget.[1]

AFDC was created in 1935, as a minor part of the landmark Social

Security Act, to aid the children of widows and other single mothers.[2] President Roosevelt and the other architects of the act believed that government should both provide relief to people who needed it and prevent as many people as possible from needing that relief. Assistance programs like AFDC were intended to act as a safety net to relieve the poverty of single mothers and temporarily support victims of market failures in times of severe economic stress. At the same time, public education and social insurance programs were expected to *prevent* poverty and recourse to the safety net.

Work Relief versus Cash Relief

The creators of the Social Security Act considered work relief to be more appropriate than cash relief for those that were expected to work—that is, able-bodied men. Thus, in the depths of the Great Depression, the federal government launched the Works Progress Administration, providing 3.33 million work-relief jobs.[3] AFDC provided cash assistance because poor, single mothers were not expected to work; it was designed to help these mothers imitate the child-rearing practices of the middle class—that is, to refrain from market work and stay home to raise their children.

Although AFDC was expected to shrink in importance once survivors' insurance was enacted (1938) and matured, its caseloads instead grew as divorce, separation, and out-of-wedlock births increased. Criticism of welfare grew as well. By the early 1960s, AFDC was criticized for providing inadequate benefits, discouraging work and independence (since benefits were reduced by a dollar for each dollar earned), and, by failing to cover two-parent families, encouraging marital dissolution. These critiques have driven every round of welfare reform since.

The Kennedy administration agreed that AFDC discouraged work and marriage, and it proposed the provision of social services to promote work and independence and the extension of eligibility to unemployed workers.[4] Congress enacted legislation first to encourage and then (under Nixon) to force AFDC mothers to work and become independent. Under Reagan, access to the welfare rolls was tightened through the imposition of more stringent eligibility standards, and stiffer work requirements were imposed.[5]

Despite stronger laws, the compulsion to work has been weak for a number of reasons. State governments have been unwilling to spend the necessary job and training funds to implement a work requirement. Demand in the labor market for workers with the skills of the average welfare recipient has been weak. The difficulty and expense of child care have precluded the option for many parents willing to work. And, since time limits have not previously been a requirement, lack of employment has never been used to force recipients to leave the welfare rolls.

The emphasis on work represents an important shift in AFDC policy. In retrospect, this new emphasis is not surprising. By the 1960s, the child-rearing practices of middle-class mothers were in the midst of a revolution. At the beginning of the century, less than 10 percent of married mothers with children worked. This percentage has grown consistently since then, reaching 68 percent by 1993 (Bergman 1986; U.S. House of Representatives 1994). Hence, the model for motherhood on which the AFDC program is based is no longer that of a parent staying home to raise the children. When the overwhelming majority of mothers work, it becomes politically indefensible to argue that poor, single mothers should not have to. Furthermore, there are both economic and psychological reasons for encouraging work among recipients: abstaining from work increases the isolation of welfare mothers and their children from mainstream society and reduces their opportunity to improve their economic and social status.

Similarly, in light of the shift in AFDC caseloads from widowed mothers to divorced, separated, and never-married mothers, it is not surprising that welfare policy has increasingly emphasized child-support enforcement.

Trends in Welfare Benefits

Between 1960 and 1970, the average AFDC cash benefit grew by about 35 percent. Medicaid was added to the welfare benefit package in 1965 and food stamps in 1972–1974. Starting in the mid-1960s, the efforts of welfare-rights organizations and progressive lawyers helped to make AFDC more accessible than ever before. By the mid-1970s, close to 90 percent of eligible families sought assistance; the share of female-headed families that were on welfare grew from 30 percent in 1960 to 54 percent in 1975.[6] All of these effects, combined with the growth in single motherhood, resulted in a dramatic growth in AFDC caseloads, from 0.8 million in 1960 to 3.5 million in 1975.

During the last two decades, the value of welfare benefits has declined. The value of AFDC plus food stamps fell 27 percent between 1972 and 1992 (almost all of this decline is due to the fall in the real value of AFDC benefits). At first, real benefits declined because state legislators failed to increase them to keep pace with inflation. Lately, however, many states have actually cut benefits. As the real value of benefits has declined, so too has the proportion of families headed by single mothers that receive welfare. Indeed, by 1992 the proportion of those families on the welfare rolls had fallen from 54 percent in 1975 to 42 percent.

Finally, both the increase in welfare benefits during the 1960s and early 1970s and the subsequent decrease since then were, given the benefit of hindsight, predictable. The average standard of living in the United States is the best single predictor of the need for welfare benefits. The 1960s were prosperous years, but since 1973 the real wages of most Americans have fallen, and families have been able to maintain their living standards only by increasing their hours of work. Welfare, then, takes a double hit: not only does the need for it rise, but, with most families struggling to keep from falling behind, public support for it falls.

THE LIMITS OF REFORM FROM WITHIN

The related goals of welfare reform are to reduce both poverty and dependency on public support. But reform that seeks only to change the incentives within the existing welfare system, while lowering caseloads, will not significantly slow the increase in single-parent families and will increase the poverty and deprivation of our most vulnerable families. Time limits, in the absence of low-wage labor-market reform, will also increase economic insecurity.

Welfare Benefits and Female-Headed Families

The growth in welfare caseloads has been driven by the growth in families headed by females. Some conservatives claim that welfare caused this growth and that eliminating welfare will reverse it. Both economic theory and common sense suggest that welfare benefits increase the ability of a poor, single woman with a child to live independently and to be selective about a new partner. Neither theory nor common sense, however, suggests how large the effect will be.

Compared with other factors—increases in employment opportunities for women, decreases in employment opportunities for men, and changing social values—government benefits account for only a small portion of the growth of mother-only families. (Improvements in employment opportunities for women appear to be the single most important factor.) A review of the literature reveals that government transfers have reduced remarriage but have had only a minor effect on divorce and out-of-wedlock births.[7] The increase in benefits that occurred between 1960 and 1975 accounts for, at most, 15 percent of the overall growth in families headed by women. Furthermore, although welfare benefits have declined since 1975, the share of families headed by a single mother has continued to grow.[8] Finally, while Canada, France, Germany, the Netherlands, Sweden, and Great Britain provide more generous government benefits to all families (including those headed by single mothers) than does the United States, the proportions of families headed by single mothers in all these countries is considerably lower than in the United States.[9] In short, the evidence indicates that even a substantial reduction in welfare benefits will result in only a small reduction in the number of families headed by single mothers.

Reducing Welfare Dependency

It is true that a substantial reduction in welfare benefits would lead to a notable reduction in dependence on welfare. In the extreme case, eliminating welfare eliminates welfare dependence. But substantial reductions in benefits also lead to increases in poverty. We have already performed the experiment, and the historical evidence is clear: from 1960 to 1975, as the welfare benefit package increased, the proportion of single-mother families on welfare rose—from 30 percent to 54 percent—and poverty rates for female-headed families fell. From 1975 to 1993, as the value of the benefit package fell, the proportion of single mothers on welfare shrank to 43 percent, and poverty rates rose slightly.[10]

What is the extent of welfare dependency? This fundamental issue has been the subject of much research, but the central finding is that a minority of welfare recipients are "long-termers." A classic study by Mary Jo Bane and David Ellwood in 1983 revealed that 30 percent of families were on welfare for eight years or more, including multiple spells. More recent research by LaDonna Pavetti (1992), using monthly rather than annual data, shows a significantly smaller share—15 percent—of long-term welfare dependents. Nevertheless, these families account for the largest share of recipients at a given point in time and are the most costly to the welfare system. Not surprisingly, those most likely to be welfare dependent are young, never-married, minority women who are high school dropouts.

Work and training programs are one way to simultaneously reduce poverty and promote independence within welfare. Controlled experiments conducted by the Manpower Development Research Corporation show that many of these programs are a good investment: within a few years the benefits exceed the costs for both recipients and taxpayers. Despite this success, the reductions in poverty and AFDC caseloads have been small to modest—usually well under 10 percent (Geuron 1991).

Placing a time limit on cash assistance and providing work relief thereafter are likely to reinforce the positive effects of work and training programs, although it will be some time before we know how significant the effect might be. Moreover, there are costs to substituting work relief for cash assistance.

To begin with, work relief is more expensive per recipient than cash relief. The work must be organized and supervised, and child care must be provided to single mothers with young children. Unless caseloads decrease substantially, time-limited cash assistance followed by work relief will be more expensive than pure cash relief. Also, work relief will reduce the standard of living of current beneficiaries. Cash relief allows mothers to spend their time in child rearing and other productive activities. Recent research indicates that most welfare mothers now supplement their welfare checks with part-time, off-the-books earnings (Jencks and Edin 1990; Spalter-Roth et al. 1995). Because a person cannot be in two places at once, work relief limits such opportunities. Work relief may also displace other public-sector workers and thereby lower wages (since work relief will pay less than public-sector jobs) and increase unemployment. This possibility calls for the involvement of local public-sector unions which can help organize local work projects that do not jeopardize their members' employment (Meiklejohn 1995).

Finally, any positive impact from time limits will be constrained by the condition of low-wage labor markets. Given their labor-market profiles, any unsubsidized employment former welfare recipients can find will invariably place them in the low-wage sector, which is currently characterized by weak demand. Among entry-level high school graduates, pretax hourly wages fell 29 percent for males and 18 percent for females from 1979 to 1993. Unemployment for young, female dropouts—a group disproportionately represented on welfare roles—was 18 percent for Whites in 1993 and 42 percent for Blacks (the national unemployment average was 6.8 percent). Another symptom of weak demand in low-wage labor markets is the steep decline in the proportion of young workers with a high school education or less who are employed (the employment/population rate). For young, Black, male dropouts (ages 25–34), this rate fell from 83 percent in 1973 to 52.4 percent in 1993. These figures, taken together, portray a very weak labor market that is unlikely to provide a useful foothold for welfare recipients.

Because substituting work relief for cash relief would reduce the economic well-being of an already vulnerable population, such a policy shift should not be undertaken without other changes that increase the economic well-being of poor, single mothers and their children. As part of a broader set of labor-market and social-policy reforms that make work pay, however, instituting time limits on cash assistance followed by work relief is a policy we ought to adopt. For those expected to and capable of work, welfare should be a temporary safety net, not a permanent source of income.

OUTSIDE WELFARE: REDUCING ECONOMIC INSECURITY, POVERTY, AND DEPENDENCE

Policy makers are clearly responding to the American public's demand to lower welfare caseloads. As noted above, reducing the value of welfare benefits is one way to accomplish the goal, but reducing welfare will increase poverty. The objectives of reform should be to lower welfare expenditures by reducing poverty and economic insecurity. This goal can be reached only by reforms outside welfare, specifically by reforming low-wage labor markets and the relevant social policies.

This broader approach to welfare reform is necessary because the problem of dependency is a poverty problem—a connection conspicuously missing from the welfare debate. And poverty has begun to do a strange thing. Up until the early 1980s, if the economy performed well and the rate of employment was healthy, poverty, as one might expect, declined. Around

1983, however, this relationship disappeared: in bad times as well as good, poverty has increased. One explanation for this new phenomenon can be found in the growth of wage inequality, in which the distribution of economic rewards has been skewed to the point where less-advantaged families are unable to benefit from overall growth.[11] As a result, fewer are able to avoid the clutches of poverty.

The impact of the decline in male wages and labor force participation on poverty and welfare caseloads has also received too little attention. Bernstein's study (Mishel and Bernstein 1994) of the determinants of welfare caseloads in seventeen states from 1960 to 1990 found that the wage trends of low-wage males had a larger impact than those of low-wage females. A branch of poverty analysis associated with William Julius Wilson has examined this relationship. Wilson's hypothesis is that, as males become less eligible as marriage prospects from an economic perspective, the incentive for women to marry weakens and more welfare-eligible families are formed. In a sense, the welfare benefit becomes a replacement for the contribution of male earnings to the household. Thus, taxpayers from higher up on the wage scale pay part of the price of the failure of low-wage labor markets to sustain a family wage.

If nothing else had changed, the decline in the value of welfare benefits after 1975 would have led to a decline in welfare caseloads. However, the number of families headed by single females continued to increase as the wage rates of those at the bottom plummeted. Thus, strengthening low-wage labor markets is integral to true welfare reform.

Labor-Market Policy

There are four primary reasons for the expansion of low-wage sectors of the labor market: the increased returns for education and experience (which place young, less-educated workers at a relative disadvantage); the deterioration of the real value of the minimum wage; the decline of unionization rates; and the shift from manufacturing to service employment (which reflects, in part, increased trade). If we are serious about "making work pay," these are the proper areas for intervention.

In this context, worker training should be seen as raising the human capital of welfare recipients so that they might benefit from the increase in education returns. This goal is at least rhetorically part of welfare reform already, but it has historically been underfunded.

Increasing the minimum wage to its 1979 value in real terms would have particularly strong effects for female workers, 58 percent of whom earned hourly wages at or below this level in 1993. (The current minimum wage is $4.75; to make it worth as much in 1996 as it was in 1979 would require raising it to $6.15) In fact, correcting the decline in the real value of the minimum would fully reverse the hourly wage loss experienced by high school–educated women (Mishel and Bernstein 1994).

Since unions are historically associated with higher wages for noncollege-educated workers, particularly women (Hartmann et al. 1994), labor-law reform that facilitates organizing will help turn around wage decline. Trade policies (like NAFTA) that pit our low-wage workers against labor forces with even lower wages both contribute to wage decline and hasten the shift from manufacturing to low-wage service jobs. Such policies should be avoided.

Finally, serious welfare reform should force us to rethink the concept of full employment. The labor-market policies of the Federal Reserve Board have reflected the belief that overall unemployment rates below about 6 percent will lead to hyperinflation. As noted above, the unemployment rate for young, female high school dropouts in 1993 was 18 percent for whites and 42 percent for blacks, while the overall rate was merely 6.8 percent. Thus, a monetary policy that enforces this level of employment is unlikely to reduce the need for welfare assistance.

Social Policy

Public-opinion polls consistently show that a large majority of Americans favor spending more on the poor but less on welfare, which suggests strong public support for aiding the poor outside the welfare system. Public opinion is consistent with the traditional social-democratic view: welfare is a necessary last resort, but large caseloads are undesirable and suggest that something is amiss in the broader society.

Welfare reform becomes the occasion for addressing these broader ills through social policy reforms. Of great importance in this regard are the earned income tax credit (EITC), universal health care, child care, child support, and child allowances.

Outside of public education and social insurance, the transfer system in this country as it affects children is split in two, with welfare benefits going to families at the very bottom of the income distribution and tax subsidies going primarily to families in the upper-middle and upper segments. Furthermore, the bulk of welfare benefits are targeted at the poorest of the poor because the payments are limited to single-parent families. The near poor, the lower-middle class, and even the middle class pay the price, and many are resentful. This system is not only inequitable, it also undermines work and marriage at the bottom of the income distribution.

The Clinton administration has said that the first objective of welfare reform must be to "make work pay." To this end President Clinton proposed and persuaded Congress to adopt as part of the 1993 budget agreement a substantial increase in the EITC. By 1996 the maximum annual EITC benefit for a family with one child equaled $2,094; it equaled $3,560 for a family with two or more children. President Clinton argued at the time that universal health care coverage had to precede welfare reform because, while welfare mothers are able to receive health care coverage from Medicaid, the working poor are forced to make do without health insurance.

Most Americans now believe that one objective of social policy should be equal access to health care. The benefits of such a policy extend far beyond improvements in health: some estimates indicate that a universal health care system would reduce child poverty by 20–30 percent (Kim 1993), reduce welfare caseloads by up to 20 percent (Moffitt and Wolfe 1992), and increase the probability of marriage by up to 2.6 percent (Yelowitz 1994).

To insist that poor, single mothers work is to strengthen the case for public subsidization of child care, and not just for single-parent families but also for two-parent families among the working poor. Mothers cannot work and care for their children at the same time, and few will maintain that poor, single mothers can afford to pay for adequate child care.[12] Subsidizing child care has the added advantage of reducing poverty and insecurity at the same time that it rewards work and independence. France and Sweden have the most universal systems of child care in the world, practically no child poverty, and lower rates of welfare dependence than does the United States (Garfinkel and McLanahan 1994).

Ultimately the case for subsidizing universal child care should be made at the most basic level. Nothing is more vital to future productivity than child rearing. The traditional method of providing child care—full-time care by the mother—is high quality but very expensive since the foregone market earnings of the mothers are enormous. As a consequence, most mothers of pre-school-age children now work. It is in the national interest to make certain that modern forms of child care are as high in quality as the traditional form.

Public subsidization of child care is also essential for achieving gender equity. In modern industrial societies, the responsibility for child rearing falls principally on the mother, and the foregone labor-market experience stunts her human capital growth. Such an arrangement is not only inequitable but also inefficient. A nation that relies only on its men for market work squanders half of its human potential.

Another social issue that is having an impact on welfare caseloads is the failure of our system of public enforcement of private child support. Only 60 percent of mothers with children who are potentially eligible for child support obtain legal entitlement to support. Of those, only half obtain the full amount to which they are legally entitled; a quarter receives nothing. If child support were perfectly enforced, payments in 1990 would have been about $50 billion instead of $13 billion, poverty among children potentially eligible for child support would have been reduced by about one-fourth, and AFDC caseloads would have been about 20 percent lower.

The Clinton administration is correct in trying to strengthen child-support enforcement, but it has not gone far enough. To redress the failings of our current system, we should add a Child Support Assurance System (CSAS) to our menu of Social Security programs. Under CSAS, child-support awards would be set by a legislated formula based on a percentage of the nonresident parent's income, and payments should be deducted from the absent parent's earnings, as with Social Security deductions. The government would guarantee a minimum level of support—the assured benefit—just as it guarantees minimum benefits in old age and unemployment insurance. The assured benefit would be financed from welfare savings and from a very small addition to the Social Security payroll tax.

The CSAS would increase the economic security of all children who live apart from a parent, rich and poor alike. Withholding a fixed percentage—17 percent, for example—from the paychecks of all nonresident parents would increase the amount and regularity of private payments. Even so, private support payments for many poor children would continue to be low and irregular, as are the incomes of their absent parents. The assured benefit would compensate by providing a steady, secure source of income for these children. It would more than double the reduction in poverty and welfare dependence achieved by private support alone.[13]

In 1984 and 1988 Congress took steps toward implementing a CSAS on the collection side by requiring states to adopt numerical guidelines for determining child support awards and to withhold child support from the paychecks of obligors. Tentative steps in the direction of an assured benefit were also taken in the form of waiver authority for Wisconsin and New York to experiment with variants of the concept. Wisconsin did not proceed with the test, but New York has been experimenting since 1988 with an assured benefit limited to families with incomes low enough to qualify for welfare.

Finally, the United States is the only Western, industrialized country without a children's allowance. During the 1992 presidential campaign, Bill Clinton proposed a middle-class tax cut that had, as its centerpiece, a refundable tax credit of $1,000 per child. After assuming office he backed off the proposal because of its cost, but he has since revived it as a nonrefundable credit of $500 per child. A nonrefundable credit is of little help to those who owe no taxes, but a credit is more progressive than the current child exemption in the income tax, and it will therefore be of help to the working poor and the lower-middle class.

CONCLUSION

Welfare can relieve, but not prevent, poverty. When welfare caseloads grow large, something in the broader society is amiss. Poverty and welfare dependence are now high because of the disastrous deterioration in the low-wage labor market and the inadequate development of social policies in the areas of health insurance, child care, child support, and tax treatment for families with children.

Reforming welfare from within can do little to reduce poverty. At best, work and training programs will make a small positive contribution. Cutting or eliminating benefits will reduce dependence on welfare but only at the cost of increasing poverty.

To eliminate both poverty and dependence on welfare requires solutions outside the system. Increasing the minimum wage, strengthening unions, promoting full employment, and providing universal child care, national health insurance, child support assurance, and child allowances are the essential ingredients of real welfare reform.

NOTES

1. Eliminating the program *entirely* would shave $17 billion, or about 10 percent, from the projected FY 1995 deficit of $170 billion and would trim the national debt by less than 0.5 percent. Proponents of reducing federal spending may consider such savings worthwhile, but they should not be deluded into thinking that these savings will eradicate deficits.

2. The program was originally called Aid to Dependent Children. The name was changed in 1950 when the program was amended to add benefits for the child's caretaker as well as the child.

3. Because of congressional opposition, President Roosevelt proposed neither a permanent work-relief program nor national health insurance.

4. In 1961 Congress gave states the option of extending eligibility for AFDC to families with an unemployed parent—AFDC-UP. Only about half of the states adopted AFDC-UP programs, and eligibility was severely restricted.

5. By tightening eligibility standards, the Reagan changes cut the welfare caseload by as much as 500,000 (Levitan 1990).

6. Our participation-rate levels differ from those in Moffitt (1992 table 3), apparently due to different data sources; however, the trends are similar. Our data for these rates come from the following sources: data on family cases headed by single parents are from various issues of *Characteristics and Financial Circumstances of AFDC Recipients* (U.S. Dept. of Health and Human Services, Administration for Children and Families, Office of Family Assistance); data on female heads of household with children are from the Bureau of Census (series P-60–185, p. 6).

7. See Garfinkel and McLanahan's 1986 review of empirical research in the United States.

8. The most recent comprehensive review of the literature by Robert Moffitt (1992) comes to the same conclusion: welfare has had very little effect on female headship.

9. See Smeeding and Rainwater (1991). That Sweden has a lower proportion of single-parent families than the United States may come as a surprise. This is because of the confusion between marital status and residence patterns. Children who live with unmarried mothers are frequently included in the Swedish count of

single-mother families. About half of these children, however, are living with their natural fathers as well and therefore these units should be counted as two-parent families (Gustafson 1995).

10. There are many other important determinants of the poverty rates for mother-only families. Our point is simply that cutting welfare benefits has never made these families better off, while increasing them has.

11. The ratio of the wage at the ninetieth percentile to the tenth percentile grew between 1979 and 1993, from 3.6 to 4.6 for males and from 2.7 to 3.8 for females.

12. Larry Mead, professor of politics at New York University, argues that the lack of child care is not a barrier to work for poor, single mothers because they can get adequate care from relatives. If he is correct, the cost of public subsidization will be slight because there will be few takers.

13. We acknowledge that CSAS could lead to an increase in divorce, though we suspect this effect would be small (see Garfinkel 1992). At any rate, with CSAS these newly divorced families would be less likely to need public support.

REFERENCES

Bane, Mary Jo and David Ellwood. 1983. *The dynamics of dependence: The routes to self-sufficiency*. Prepared for the U.S. Department of Health and Human Services, Washington, D.C.

Bergman, Barbara R. 1986. *The economic emergence of women*. New York: Basic Books.

Garfinkel, Irwin. 1992. *Assuring child support: An extension of Social Security*. New York: Russell Sage Foundation.

Garfinkel, Irwin and Sara McLanahan. 1986. *Single mothers and their children*. Washington, D.C.: Urban Institute Press.

———. 1994. Single mother families, economic insecurity, and government policy. In *Confronting poverty*, ed. Daniel Weinberg, Sheldon Danziger, and Gary Sandefur. Cambridge, Mass.: Harvard University Press.

Geuron, Judith. 1991. *From welfare to work*. New York: Russell Sage Foundation.

Greenstein, Robert. 1995. Testimony to the Subcommittee on Human Resources of the House Ways and Means Committee, January 13.

Gustafsson, Siv. 1995. Single mothers in Sweden: Why is poverty less severe? In *Poverty, Inequality and the Future of Social Policy*, ed. Katherine McFate, Roger Lawson, and William Julius Wilson. New York: Russell Sage Foundation.

Hartmann, Heidi et al. 1994. What do unions do for women? *Challenge*, July/August.

Jencks, Christopher and Kathryn Edin. 1990. The real welfare problem. *American Prospect*, no. 1, spring.

Kim, Y. H. 1993. *The economic effects of the combined non-income-tested transfers for families with children: Child support assurance, children's allowance, and national health insurance*. Ph.D. diss. University of Wisconsin, Madison.

Levitan, Sar. 1990. *Programs in aid of the poor*. Baltimore, Md.: Johns Hopkins University Press.

Meiklejohn, Nanine. 1995. *Work and training opportunities for welfare recipients*.

Washington, D.C.: American Federation of State, County, and Municipal Employees.

Mishel, Lawrence and Jared Bernstein. 1994. *The state of working America 1994–95.* Economic Policy Institute Series. Armonk, N.Y.: M. E. Sharpe.

Moffitt, Robert. 1992. Incentive effects of the U.S. welfare system: A review. *Journal of Economic Literature* 30: 1–61.

Moffitt, Robert and Barbara L. Wolfe. 1992. The effect of the Medicaid program on welfare participation and labor supply. *Review of Economics and Statistics* 74 (December).

Pavetti, LaDonna. 1992. *The dynamics of welfare and work: Exploring the process by which young women work their way off welfare.* JFK School of Government, Harvard University.

Peterson, George. 1995. *A block grant approach to welfare reform.* Urban Institute Welfare Reform Brief, no. 1.

Smeeding, Timothy and Lee Rainwater. 1991. *Cross-national trends in income poverty and dependency: The evidence for young adults in the eighties.* Paper presented at the Joint Center for Political and Economic Studies, Washington, D.C., 20–21 September.

Spalter-Roth, Roberta et al. 1994. *Income insecurity: The failure of UI to reach working AFDC mothers.* Washington, D.C.: Institute for Women's Policy Research.

———. 1995. *Welfare that works: The working lives of AFDC recipients.* Washington, D.C.: Institute for Women's Policy Research.

U.S. Department of Health and Human Services. Office of Family Assistance. *Characteristics and financial circumstances of AFDC recipients.* Washington, D.C.: U.S. Government Printing Office.

U.S. House of Representatives. 1994. *Green book: Background material and data on programs within the jurisdiction of the Committee on Ways and Means.* Washington, D.C.: U.S. Government Printing Office.

Weinberg, Daniel, ed. 1994. *Confronting poverty.* Cambridge, Mass.: Harvard University Press.

Yelowitz, Aaron S. 1994. *Will extending Medicaid to two-parent families encourage marriage?* UCLA, Department of Economics. Mimeographed.

Chapter 12

Federal Role in Establishing National Income Security for Children

Martha N. Ozawa

The federal government is confronted with a great challenge: to cut expenditures for welfare programs while investing more public resources in the nation's children. Such investment is necessary if the country is to have a future workforce with the skills necessary to compete in the global economy and to support the impending retirees of the baby-boom generation, each of whom will have only two workers to support them instead of the current three (Federal Old-Age and Survivors Insurance and Disability Insurance Trust Funds 1995). How the United States can meet this challenge and what the federal government's role should be are crucial issues to address.

The government's push to cut expenditures for welfare programs is in response to negative public attitudes toward welfare families, which are compounded by the fact that, increasingly, women are becoming dependent on welfare because they give birth out of wedlock as teenagers. In 1991, as many as 53 percent of the children on Aid to Families with Dependent Children (AFDC) had mothers who had never been married, as compared with 32 percent in 1973 (House 1993, 696). Of the $47.27 billion that were spent on all AFDC families in 1990—including AFDC, Medicaid, and food stamps—an estimated $25.05 billion (or 52 percent) were spent on AFDC families whose dependence was the result of teenage pregnancy and childbirth. The annual public expenditures to support each such family increased from $13,902 per year in 1985 to $28,123 per year in 1990, in 1990 dollars (House 1993, 1148).

Responding to the public's apprehension about welfare programs and their beneficiaries, Republicans proceeded to implement the Contract with

America as soon as the party gained power in both houses of Congress. In an attempt to reform welfare, the Republican-led House of Representatives passed, on 24 March 1995, the Personal Responsibility Act (House Resolution 4 [H.R. 4]) and the Republican-led Senate passed, on 20 September 1995, the Work Opportunity Act (H.R. 4). Although some of the provisions of the two versions of H.R. 4 are different, block-granting of AFDC (which is called Block Grants for Temporary Assistance for Needy Families [TANF]) and limiting its payments to two years per episode and five years during a woman's lifetime have become part of the new law, thus ending the entitlement principal. States are likely to be given the option of taking food stamps assistance as a block grant. Furthermore, supplemental security income benefits will no longer be provided to substance abusers and to children whose disabilities do not meet the severity requirements in the Social Security Administration's medical listing of impairments (Burke et al. 1995).

American children have enormous problems. Nearly 20 percent of those aged 3–17 had, in 1988, at least one developmental, learning, or behavioral disorder (Zill and Schoenborn 1990); and child abuse and neglect tripled between 1976 and 1986 (Bureau of the Census 1990, 176). In addition, only one in seven eighth graders had the math proficiency expected for that grade; and at age seventeen, half of the high school students in this country could not handle decimals, fractions, or percentages to solve simple equations (Applebee et al. 1989; DeWitt 1991). In 1988, thirteen-year-old American students scored lower on math and science tests than students of the same age from Ireland, Korea, Spain, and the United Kingdom (Department of Education 1991, 1143). Furthermore, the U.S. rank in infant mortality declined from thirteenth in 1960 to twentieth in 1988; and in 1990, the leading causes of death among fifteen- to twenty-four-year-olds were accidents, homicide, and suicide, in that order. In the face of the rapidly declining quality of life for children, the 1990 per capita social welfare expenditures for children were only one-eleventh of those for the elderly (House 1993, 1165, 1179, 1564, and 1567).

The declining economic status of children compounds the deterioration of their living conditions. Fuchs and Reklis (1992) demonstrated that, from 1960 to 1988, the median household income per child decreased from 67 percent to 63 percent of that per adult aged eighteen–sixty-four and from 84 percent to 68 percent of that per elderly person. In the meantime, the poverty rate of children surpassed that of the elderly in 1974 and reached 21.9 percent in 1992, a rate 1.7 times as high as that for elderly people (House 1994, 1158).

With that scenario as a backdrop, this chapter (1) explains why the current system of public transfers, particularly AFDC (or TANF as of October 1996), cannot be a means by which public resources are channeled effectively to children, and (2) advocates for the direct involvement of the federal government in establishing income security for children.

DEFICIENCIES IN THE CURRENT SYSTEM

The current system of public income transfers is inappropriate for and incapable of providing income security for children for three reasons: (1) AFDC (or TANF) dilutes the attempts of other programs to improve work incentives, (2) the allocation of federal funds (or block grants) to finance AFDC (or TANF) is inherently inequitable and counterproductive, (3) the philosophical underpinning of AFDC (or TANF) is incompatible with the ideology of investment in children, and (4) public income transfers fail to provide an effective safety net for children.

AFDC's Adverse Effects on Work Incentives

AFDC as it has operated reduces assistance payments dollar for dollar as beneficiaries increase their earnings. Because of the high benefit-reduction rate, which diminishes the value of work to zero in dollar terms, it is difficult to enhance work incentives through other programs. In addition, AFDC's objective of providing adequate benefits clashes with the goal of the earned income tax credit (EITC) to improve work incentives. Figures 12.1 and 12.2 depict the situations of three-member families (a mother and two children) in New York City and Texas who are on AFDC and are subjected to an EITC subsidy rate, the implicit tax rates in the AFDC and food stamp programs, and the explicit tax rates of the payroll tax and eventually of the federal income tax as their incomes increase. These figures illustrate what the financial situations of AFDC families might have been at various levels of earnings in 1994 if the EITC had been fully phased in as provided by the 1993 Omnibus Budget Reconciliation Act (OBRA).

It is clear from these figures that AFDC undermines the work incentive of the family in New York City, which provides generous payments, more than it does that of the family in Texas, which provides meager payments. The New York City family is subjected to cumulative implicit marginal tax rates ranging from 31.7 percent to 61.7 percent, except when its earnings are less than $120 a month, when a positive subsidy of 8.4 percent applies. In contrast, the Texas family enjoys the positive subsidy of 8.4 percent for a wide range of earnings levels—from $1–120 and $305–702 per month—that is, within these ranges, each dollar earned brings the family a net income of $1.08.

Although the EITC improves the work incentives of the New York City family to a considerably lesser degree than those of the Texas family, it enables the New York City family to escape poverty with greater ease. That

Figure 12.1
Effects of income transfers and taxes on net total family income, 1996 (in 1994 dollars): The case of families of three, Texas

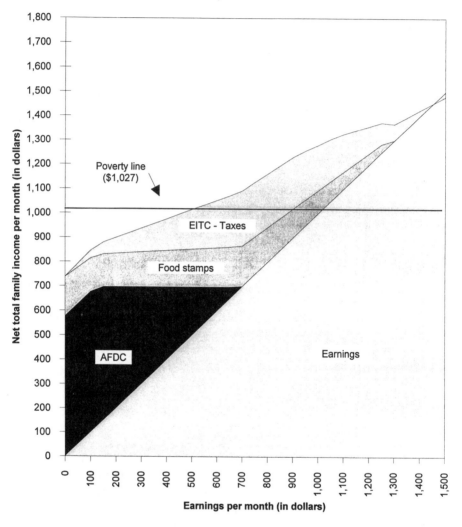

Source: M. N. Ozawa, "The Earned Income Tax Credit: Its Effect and Its Significance," *Social Service Review* 69 (December 1995): 568.

is, with the EITC, the New York City family needs to work only 126 hours per month, or 73 percent of full-time work hours, to achieve the same income level as the Texas family working 151 hours a month, or 87 percent of full-time work hours.

These examples demonstrate how the objective of providing adequate

Figure 12.2
Effects of income transfers and taxes on net total family income, 1996 (in 1994 dollars): The case of families of three, Texas

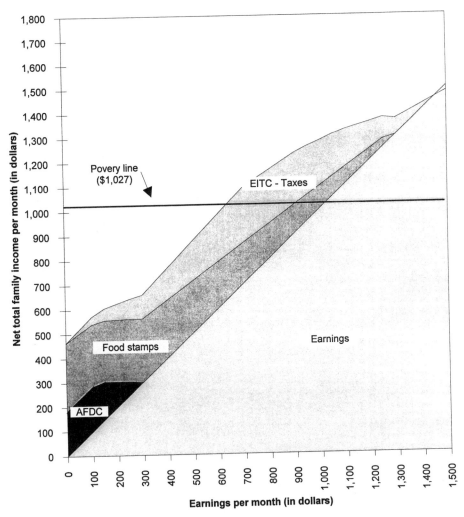

Source: M. N. Ozawa, "The Earned Income Tax Credit: Its Effect and Its Significance," *Social Service Review* 69 (December 1995): 569.

AFDC payments clashes with the intent of the EITC to enhance work incentives. This dilemma is keenly felt in New York City. Ironically, in states that provide meager AFDC payments, such as Texas, the EITC is much more effective in increasing incentives for AFDC families to work. Thus, policy makers always face a trade-off between adequacy and work incentives when they attempt to provide income support to low-income families through either means-tested programs or a combination of such programs and a wage-subsidy program. If the United States wishes to provide adequate income security for children without compromising the work incentive, it will have to do so outside the welfare domain.

Inequitable Allocation of Block Grants

Since the inception of AFDC in 1935, the federal government has participated in funding the program only indirectly. Because the Social Security Act of 1935 left the level of AFDC payments up to the states, the federal government uses the grants-in-aid to help the states pay for AFDC on the basis of a matching formula, which is slanted in favor of poorer states. The federal government has subsidized AFDC payments at rates ranging from 50 percent to 83 percent, depending on the per-capita income of a state. However, because AFDC payments are so low in many poor states, the use of the apparently progressive formula does not necessarily translate into larger average subsidies per recipient in those states. Moreover, because the AFDC payment levels are related to the percentage of African-Americans in a state, the average federal subsidies per recipient have also inadvertently become linked to race. In a 1991 study (Ozawa 1991), I found that states with low per-capita incomes and those with a high percentage of African-Americans receive smaller subsidies per recipient than do states with the opposite characteristics. Therefore, one can expect that the allocation of federal block grants for TANF, as prescribed in H.R. 4, which also uses the Medicaid matching formula, will be related to per-capita income and race in the same way.

Table 12.1 presents the 1996 allocation of federal block grants to states for the financing of TANF as described in H.R. 4. These data are presented in two ways: (1) the average block grant per recipient and (2) the average block grant per poor person. As the table shows, the average federal block grant per poor person would vary among the states even more than the average block grant per recipient. New York would have received the highest block grant per recipient ($1,938.35) and Mississippi the lowest ($477.75), with the median state, New Jersey, receiving $1,085.90. In terms of federal block grants per poor person, Alaska would have received the highest amount ($1,166.47) and Alabama the lowest ($123.42), with the median state, Montana, receiving $361.79. These interstate variations would have been far greater than the cost-of-living differences among the states.

Table 12.2 presents the results of a regression analysis of average federal block grants per recipient and per poor person. These two indicators of federal grants are regressed on the per-capita income of a state and the

Table 12.1
Average Block Grants for TANF, 1996

Per Recipient		Per Poor Person	
States	Amount ($)	States	Amount ($)
New York	1938.35	Alaska	1166.47
Alaska	1867.43	Dist. of Columbia	829.30
Hawaii	1723.23	New York	812.05
Vermont	1538.44	Massachusetts	756.71
Idaho	1499.07	Connecticut	745.11
California	1491.34	Rhode Island	728.18
Dist. of Columbia	1480.05	California	708.98
Connecticut	1429.17	Vermont	707.00
Rhode Island	1410.73	Washington	693.25
Massachusetts	1394.04	Hawaii	691.87
Washington	1388.92	Michigan	606.82
Oregon	1382.37	Wisconsin	561.26
Minnesota	1334.13	Ohio	505.08
Utah	1324.85	New Jersey	496.87
New Mexico	1308.91	Oregon	470.94
New Hampshire	1297.77	Minnesota	465.26
Wisconsin	1276.82	Delaware	460.11
Montana	1251.02	Maine	445.56
North Dakota	1245.58	Wyoming	432.04
Iowa	1210.17	Utah	427.49
Kansas	1161.13	Pennsylvania	417.85
Michigan	1131.26	Maryland	383.12
Arizona	1127.97	Iowa	378.51
Maine	1120.94	Arizona	376.76
Wyoming	1115.74	New Hampshire	375.65
New Jersey	1085.90	Montana	361.79
Oklahoma	1049.11	New Mexico	360.05
South Dakota	1019.95	Kansas	357.65
Nebraska	1008.00	Colorado	332.89
Pennsylvania	997.05	North Dakota	315.64
Indiana	997.02	Indiana	304.53
Nevada	989.76	Illinois	290.72
Maryland	982.53	Nebraska	288.46
Colorado	954.68	Georgia	273.87
Delaware	940.04	West Virginia	270.41
Ohio	936.70	North Carolina	266.61
West Virginia	900.54	Virginia	263.42
North Carolina	871.11	Missouri	258.03
Florida	824.38	Florida	253.03
Missouri	811.49	Kentucky	243.43
Virginia	806.09	Oklahoma	239.76
Georgia	802.12	Tennessee	198.69
Illinois	779.91	South Dakota	197.64
Kentucky	767.19	Idaho	187.26
Arkansas	739.13	Nevada	173.73
South Carolina	686.95	Louisiana	150.56
Alabama	621.81	Texas	142.90
Tennessee	609.14	South Carolina	141.17
Texas	574.34	Arkansas	130.05
Louisiana	565.40	Mississippi	127.77
Mississippi	477.75	Alabama	123.42

Source: Martha N. Ozawa, "Federal Role in Establishing National Income Security for Children," *Journal of Poverty: Innovations on Social, Political & Economic Inequalities* 1(2) 1997.

Table 12.2

Regression Analysis of TANF per Recipient and TANF per Poor Person, 1996

	TANF per Recipient		TANF per Poor Person	
	Coefficient	t value	Coefficient	t value
Intercept	−5.532	−3.029*	−20.340	−5.726***
Per capita income	1.317	6.941***	2.737	7.417***
Percentage of African-Americans	−0.143	−7.399***	−0.144	−3.816**
N		51		51
R²		0.637		0.555
F		42.152***		29.986***

*$p < .01$; **$p < .001$; ***$p < .0001$

Source: Martha N. Ozawa, "Federal Role in Establishing National Income Security for Children," *Journal of Poverty: Innovations on Social, Political & Economic Inequalities* 1(2) 1997.

percentage of African-Americans in a state. All variables are transformed into natural logarithms.

As expected from earlier studies (Ozawa 1991, 1995c), states with high per-capita incomes would have received considerably larger federal block grants per recipient than would states with low per-capita incomes ($t = 6.941$; $p < .0001$). The disparity in block grants per poor person between states with high and low per-capita incomes would have been just as great ($t = 7.417$; $p < .0001$). Translated into dollars, state *A* with a per-capita income that is $1,000 higher than that of state *B* would have received a federal block grant per recipient that is $91.72 larger. Similarly, state *A* would have received $70.81 more in federal block grants per poor person than would state *B*.

The amount of federal block grants per recipient that states would have received is inversely related to the percentage of African-Americans in the states. Federal block grants per recipient would have been considerably larger in the states with a low percentage of African-Americans than in the states with a high percentage ($t = -7.399$; $p < .0001$). The percentage of African-Americans would have exerted a slightly less—but still powerful—effect on federal block grants per poor person ($t = -3.816$; $p < .0004$). In dollar terms, state *A*, with a proportion of African-Americans that is ten percentage points higher than that of state *B*, would have received $147.31 less in federal block grants per recipient. Likewise, state *A* would have received $54.89 less in block grants per poor person than would state *B*.

These regression results indicate that the allocation formula of H.R. 4 is inherently inequitable. The formula will result in smaller federal block grants for states with fewer economic resources and for those with a high percentage of African-Americans, whether the block grants are per recipient or per poor person.

The Senate version of H.R. 4 attempts to rectify the inequitable allocation of federal funds. In particular, after 1996 a state would automatically qualify for an annual 2.5 percent increase in its grant if (1) its grant per poor person were less than 35 percent of the national average grant per poor person, or (2) its population growth from 1 April, 1990, to 1 July, 1994, exceeded 10 percent (Falk 1995). The House version of H.R. 4 simply distributes $100 million annually to states according to the growth in their populations from 1997 through 2000.

The adjustment in the allocation of federal block grants on the basis of the 1996 TANF payment levels, as prescribed by the Senate version of H.R. 4, would hardly make a dent in the great disparity among states that would have existed in 1996. According to my calculations, it would take thirty-three years for the federal block grant per recipient for Mississippi to catch up with the block grant for the median state if the block grant for Mississippi were allowed to grow at the compounded rate of 2.5 percent, as prescribed by the Senate version. Likewise, it would take forty-four years for the federal block grant per poor person for Alabama to reach the block grant for the median state. Moreover, adjusting the federal block grants according to growth in population would not change the interstate variation in block grants.

The interstate variation in AFDC payments (and in TANF in 1996 and thereafter) is a product of past social policies in the states that were antithetical to the public interest, which calls for investing in all children wherever they live. Thus, AFDC and TANF cannot possibly be the foundation for providing income security for all American children.

Absence of an Investment Ideology

Though at its inception in 1935 AFDC was a benevolent program designed to help widows raise their children, over time it has become an unpopular program. The increasing hostility toward AFDC stems from the fact that families with widowed mothers are now supported by survivors' insurance, and the rates of divorce and out-of-wedlock births have increased, thus most AFDC families are headed by never-married or divorced mothers. This attitude toward AFDC has been compounded by the new expectation that welfare mothers should work, as other mothers do.

The requirement that AFDC mothers must work was first incorporated into public policy in the Work Incentive Program of 1967. The 1981 OBRA made this requirement more explicit. The Job Opportunities and Skills Training Program—the centerpiece of the 1988 Family Support Act—capitalized on the experiences gained from the 1981 OBRA. Its goal was to have 20 percent of nonexempt AFDC mothers participating by 1995; however, this goal was not achieved, primarily because of the lack of available states' funds to match federal funds (House 1994, 356).

Wisconsin took the work requirement a step further. Under a federal waiver, Tommy Thompson, governor of Wisconsin, signed Act 99 into law on 13 December 1993. Entitled Work Not Welfare, the Wisconsin program requires mothers to start working for their benefits one year after they enroll in AFDC, and it terminates benefits one year later. The act also mandates the elimination of AFDC by 1999 (Ozawa 1994).

In the meantime, numerous states started welfare reform programs under the federal waiver, many of which include punitive sanctions. For example, California pays no more to new residents than the benefit level of their previous state of residence for one year, New Jersey does not pay benefits to babies born to mothers while on AFDC, Wisconsin reduces the benefit increase for a new baby, Maryland reduces benefits by $25 per month per child if families fail to follow a prescribed schedule of health care services, and Missouri terminates eligibility for AFDC when children fail to attend school for at least 80 percent of the school year (Burke 1993).

Thus, the AFDC program has ceased to be an income-support program for children. Instead, it has become a program for training AFDC mothers and moving them into the labor force—with punitive sanctions, if necessary. For the first time, the federal government is sending a message that children born to certain mothers are unwelcome. What is worse, children have become a political pawn in the struggle to control the behavior of low-income women who resort to welfare. In the political environment surrounding welfare, TANF will be an unsuitable program—both politically and practically—for investing in children.

Ineffectiveness of Income Transfers

In spite of the sizable amount of public spending on cash income transfers, which now approaches 9 percent of the gross national product (Bixby 1994; Bureau of the Census 1994, 446; Congressional Budget Office 1995, 22), this system of transfers is incapable of providing an effective safety net for the nation's children. Table 12.3 presents the results of a study by Ozawa and Lum (1995), which found that after receiving social insurance benefits (unemployment and Social Security) and welfare payments (all means-tested cash transfers, plus food stamps), the nation's poor children live, on average, at 66 percent of the poverty line, whereas the elderly poor live at 76 percent of the poverty line. Note that, although the economic status of poor children is much lower than many policy makers may wish to tolerate, it is welfare payments that are largely responsible for increasing the level of children's pre-transfer income (32 percent of the poverty line) to the level of their post-transfer income (66 percent of the poverty line). For the elderly, it is largely social insurance benefits that lift their pre-

Table 12.3

Effects of Public Income Transfers on Poverty Ratios of Poor Children, Adults, and Elderly Persons, 1991

Measure	Pre-transfer Income	Plus Social Insurance Benefits*	Plus Welfare Payments**	Total Percent Change
Poverty ratios				
Children	0.32	0.37	0.66	
Adults	0.32	0.40	0.60	
Elderly persons	0.09	0.64	0.76	
Percentage change				
Children		16	91	106
Adults		25	63	88
Elderly persons		611	133	744

*Includes social security and unemployment benefits.
**Includes all means-tested cash payments and food stamps.

Source: Martha N. Ozawa, "Federal Role in Establishing National Income Security for Children," *Journal of Poverty: Innovations on Social, Political & Economic Inequalities* 1(2) 1997.

transfer income level (9 percent of the poverty line) to the post-transfer level (76 percent of the poverty line).

(A separate analysis of the same data set used for the study by Ozawa and Lum [1995] shows that, among the three age groups—children, adults, and the elderly—the economic condition of children is the worst. The poverty ratio for all children is 2.56, compared with 3.06 for all elderly people and 3.66 for all adults.)

One major reason that American children fare so poorly in improving their post-transfer income status compared with children in other industrialized countries is that the United States does not have income-support programs that are specifically targeted to children—notably children's allowance and child-support assurance (Rainwater and Smeeding 1995). In the United States, transfer programs that involve large public expenditures do not affect the economic condition of most children. For example, as is clear from table 12.3, the Social Security and unemployment insurance programs, for which the United States spent as much as $301 billion in 1991 (Bixby 1994, 99), contribute little toward improving the income status of poor children. In addition, welfare programs in which many poor children participate involve relatively small expenditures and, thus, cannot effectively improve the economic status of children (Ozawa 1995a).

The inappropriateness of AFDC (and TANF) and the inability of the current system of income transfers to provide an effective safety net for children should lead concerned policy makers to look for alternative approaches to achieving income security for children.

FEDERAL ROLE IN ESTABLISHING INCOME SECURITY FOR CHILDREN

It is in the national interest for the federal government to play an important role in establishing income-security measures for children so that future generations of workers will be equipped to deal with this country's dual challenge: ensuring economic growth and supporting the growing elderly population. For these tasks future generations of American children must have sufficient cognitive capabilities and physical strength, the levels of which should not vary according to the racial, ethnic, and economic backgrounds of their parents, as they do now. To meet this challenge, the federal government must establish income security for children independently of the current Congressional initiatives to transfer the authority over many welfare programs to state governments.

There are strategic reasons for establishing such a policy as well. First, because the demographic compositions of states vary considerably, letting the states establish their own income-security measures for children places unequal burdens on the states. For example, states with large proportions of households with children will find it difficult to levy taxes on the remaining households. Thus, the horizontal redistribution of income from childless households to those with children can be implemented most effectively only if it occurs nationwide. Second, the nationwide redistribution of income from childless households to those with children can bring about the vertical redistribution of income from rich to poor states. Third, the national government alone has the power to collect enough revenues to ensure a national minimum income for all children.

The combination of a $1,000 refundable tax credit for all children and the EITC, as provided by the 1993 OBRA, can create this national income security. When the EITC is fully phased in in 1996, income security for a child who lives in a two-person family (one parent and one child) with a head who works full time at the minimum wage will be $3,156 ($2,156 from the EITC and $1,000 from the refundable tax credit). Likewise, the income security for each child who lives in a three-person family (one parent and two children) with a head who works full time at the minimum wage will be $2,782 ($1,782 from the EITC plus $1,000 from the refundable tax credit). Similarly, the income security for each child who lives in a four-person family (one parent and three children) with a head who works full time at the minimum wage will be $2,188 ($1,188 from the EITC and $1,000 from the refundable tax credit [Ozawa, 1995b]).

If annual earnings at the minimum wage ($4.25 × 2,076 hours of work = $8,823) are added to national income security for children, the income of the two-member family will be $11,979 (113 percent of the poverty line); of the three-member family $14,387 (114 percent of the poverty line); of the four-member family $15,387 (95 percent of the poverty line [Social Security Administration 1994, 151]).[1]

These calculations indicate that even a single-parent family with one or two children can escape poverty as long as the parent works full time at the minimum wage. Put differently, as long as the head of the family can meet his or her own economic needs through work (the estimated poverty line for a family of one in 1996 was $8,212 [Social Security Administration 1994, 151]), the family's income will be above the poverty line because the children will bring their own economic resources to the family through the national income security measures outlined here.

The amount of EITC provided under the 1993 OBRA is the same for all families with two or more children, assuming that the earned income is the same. Thus, children in large families will be provided for less adequately. The example just shown indicates that families with three or more children whose head works full time at the minimum wage will live below the poverty line. However, in 1993 only 9 percent of families had three or more children, and only 2 percent of families had four or more children (Bureau of the Census 1994, 64). Thus, if the federal government creates another bracket for families with three or more children and provides the EITC at a higher rate than for families with two children, the EITC will meet the economic needs of the vast majority of families with children. The unmet needs of the remaining large families can be dealt with through residual programs.

As illustrated, national income security for children can become a reality if the federal government (1) adopts the refundable tax credit of $1,000 for all children, as recommended by the National Commission on Children (1991), and (2) improves the EITC provision, as provided under the 1993 OBRA, by introducing another bracket for families with three or more children.

Providing income security for children in this manner would have no adverse effect on the work incentives for heads of households who work at the minimum wage. The $1,000 refundable tax credit would be provided to all children, regardless of their parents' work status or the amount of their earnings. Furthermore, in 1996, the EITC subsidized earned income at a stipulated rate until the annual earnings reach $8,910, in the case of a working head of household with two children, and $6,340 in the case of a working head of household with one child, thus providing positive work incentives for workers whose earnings are below these levels. Beyond these levels, the EITC stays the same (the maximum EITC) until the earnings reach $11,630 in both cases, thus creating no adverse effect on work incentives. Beyond the $11,630 level, the EITC begins to phase out, creating work disincentives. Thus, for a minimum-wage worker whose annual earnings are below $11,630, the EITC does not create work disincentives.

Income security for children will minimize the role of AFDC (or TANF). As a result, the United States can address the issue of income security for children with a nonwelfare, investment-oriented ideology and a strong national commitment to nurturing the nation's children. At the same time, freed from the concern of providing income support for children, each state government can concentrate on the administration of its residual income-support program, job-training program, and social service program to assist low-income families by using the standards and approaches that are compatible with the norms and aspirations of the people in the state.

Income security for children seems a realistic policy for the United States to adopt. However, obstacles abound. The Republican-led Senate and House are proposing several measures to scale back the scope of the EITC. For instance, they are attempting to freeze the EITC provisions at the 1995 levels instead of entirely phasing in the provisions as provided by the 1993 OBRA. In particular, the proposal would freeze the credit rate for families with two or more children at 36 percent instead of increasing it to 40 percent in 1996. In addition, the Senate proposal would increase the amount that the EITC would be reduced for each dollar earned beyond $11,630 from the current 15.89¢ to 18¢ in the case of families with one child, and from 21.06¢ to 23¢ in the case of families with two or more children. The House's proposal is even worse; it would increase the amount that the EITC would be reduced to 23¢ and to 28¢ for each dollar earned in these two situations, respectively (Storey 1995). If these proposals are adopted, then the income of families with children (a combination of earnings, the EITC, and the refundable tax credit) would be lower than the examples discussed earlier.

The $1,000 refundable tax credit for children also faces obstacles on two fronts. First, the recommended amount—$1,000—is twice the amount included in the Republican proposal (Calmes 1995). Second, the refundability of the tax credit may face political opposition. The public may argue that the tax credit exists so that taxpayers get back some of what taxes they have already paid in order to use their "own" money for their children, and thus, that nontaxpaying families have no right to receive such a credit.

Income security for children needs to be part of the political debate. Will the public support the scope of the EITC, as envisioned in the 1993 OBRA, so that working families with children can have more adequate incomes than wages alone can provide? Will the public support a further expansion of the EITC by introducing another bracket for families with three or more children? Is the public ready to double the amount of the tax credit for children and make the credit refundable so that it goes to all children, regardless of the taxpaying status of their parents?

CONCLUSIONS

As the United States shifts the authority over many social welfare programs from the federal government to the state governments, certain programs should stay under the federal government's authority. Income security for children is one of them. As this country meets the rest of the world in both economic partnership and competition, it will be in the national interest to make sure that as many children as possible have the health and skills necessary to hold high-paying jobs when they reach adulthood. Otherwise, future generations of workers will be unable to support the retired population adequately.

If the states were to develop their own income-security programs for children, there would be interstate variations in provisions, as has occurred with other state-developed programs, such as unemployment insurance. A federally developed income-security program for children would ensure that even children in the poorest state would have a minimum level of economic well-being, below which no child could fall.

Because income security for children is directly linked to the future of both the American economy and support for the elderly, the program should be pursued outside the domain of welfare. Both philosophically and programmatically, welfare programs are unsuitable for establishing income security for children. The most appropriate solution is to use the federal income-tax system to collect revenues nationwide and redistribute fiscal resources to children.

Establishing a national minimum income for children should be considered part of the national strategy for developing diverse skills that meet high standards. In the final analysis, the paramount issue will be how well Americans can perform the tasks at hand, whatever types of occupations they have chosen. This point cannot be overemphasized. The major challenge the United States faces is whether it can create, in its racially, ethnically, and culturally diverse society, future generations of workers, out of the current generations of children, who will have a consistently high level of capability.

NOTE

1. The projected 1996 figures for EITC were obtained from James R. Storey of Congressional Research Service, the Library of Congress, on 9 November, 1995. To calculate the 1996 poverty line, I inflated the 1993 figures at the compounded rate of 3 percent per year.

REFERENCES

Applebee, A. N. et al. 1989. *Crossroads in American education.* Princeton, N.J.: Educational Testing Service.

Bixby, A. K. 1994. Public social welfare expenditures, fiscal year 1991. *Social Security Bulletin* 57, no. 1: 96–101.

Federal Old-Age and Survivors Insurance and Disability Insurance Trust Funds. 1995. Board of Trustees. *The 1995 annual report of the Federal Old-Age and Survivors Insurance and Disability Insurance Trust Funds.* Washington, D.C.: U.S. Government Printing Office.

Burke, V. 1993. *Time-limited welfare proposals. CRS Issue Brief* (IB93034). Washington, D.C.: Congressional Research Service.

Burke, V. et al. 1995. *Welfare reform: The Senate-passed bill (H.R. 4). CRS Report for Congress* (95–991 EPW). Washington, D.C.: Congressional Research Service.

Calmes, J. 1995. House GOP clears the way for passage of ambitious tax-reduction package. *Wall Street Journal,* 6 February, 3.

DeWitt, K. 1991. Eighth graders' math survey shows no state of "cutting it." *New York Times,* 7 June, 1.

Falk, G. 1995. 2 October. *Memorandum of preliminary comparison of House- and Senate-passed H.R. 4 financing provisions for temporary assistance and child care.* Congressional Research Service.

Fuchs, V. R. and D. M. Reklis. 1992. America's children: Economic perspectives and policy options. *Science* 255 (January): 41–46.

National Commission on Children. 1991. *Beyond rhetoric: A new American agenda for children and families.* Washington, D.C.

Old-Age and Survivors Insurance and Disability Insurance Trust Funds 1995. Board of Trustees. *The 1995 annual report of the Federal Old-Age and Survivors Insurance and Disability Insurance Trust Funds.* Washington, D.C.: U.S. Government Printing Office.

Ozawa, M. N. 1991. Unequal treatment of AFDC children by the federal government. *Children and Youth Services Review* 13, no. 4: 257–69.

———. 1994. Women, children, and welfare reform. *Affilia: Women and Social Work* 9:338–59.

———. 1995a. Public spending on income-tested social welfare programs for investment and consumption purposes. *Journal of Sociology and Social Welfare.* 22: 132–46.

———. 1995b. The earned income tax credit: Its effects and its significance. *Social Service Review.* 69: 563–82.

———. 1995c. Medicaid matching formula, federal subsidies, and Medicaid payments. *Social Work Research* 19, no. 2: 89–100.

Ozawa, M. N. and Y. S. Lum. 1995. How safe is the safety net for poor children? Unpublished manuscript, Washington University, St. Louis.

Rainwater, L. and T. M. Smeeding. 1995. Doing poorly: The real income of American children in a comparative perspective. Unpublished manuscript, Maxwell School of Citizenship and Public Affairs, Syracuse University.

Social Security Administration. 1994. Annual statistical supplement. *Social Security Bulletin.* Washington, D.C.

Storey, J. R. 1995. *The earned income tax credit: Legislative issues in the 104th Congress, 1995. CRS Report for Congress* (95–340 EPW). Washington, D.C.: Congressional Research Service.

U.S. Bureau of the Census. 1990. *Statistical abstract of the United States, 1990.* 110th ed. Washington, D.C.: U.S. Government Printing Office.

———. 1994. *Statistical abstract of the United States, 1994.* 114th ed. Washington, D.C.: U.S. Government Printing Office.

U.S. Congressional Budget Office. 1995. *The economic and budget outlook: Update.* Washington, D.C.: U.S. Government Printing Office.

U.S. Department of Education. 1991. National Education Goals Panel. *The national education goals report: Building a nation of learners.* Washington, D.C.: U.S. Government Printing Office.

U.S. House of Representatives. 1993. Committee on Ways and Means. *Overview of entitlement programs: 1993 green book.* Washington, D.C.: U.S. Government Printing Office.

———. 1994. Committee on Ways and Means. *Overview of entitlement programs: 1994 green book.* Washington, D.C.: U.S. Government Printing Office.

Zill, N. and C. A. Schoenborn. 1990. Developmental, learning, and emotional problems: Health of our nation's children, United States, 1988. *Advance Data,* no. 190. Washington, D.C.: U.S. Department of Health and Human Services.

Chapter 13

Redefining the Role of Government: A Work in Progress

Robert Morris and John E. Hansan

By 1994–95 the participants in the Odyssey Forum had come to the conclusion that the changes in political and economic trends were more than transient interruptions on the road to creating an ever more perfect, and perfectible, welfare state in the United States based on the model initially adopted in the 1930s. The preceding chapters in this volume represent the results of our initial effort to explore alternative approaches to dealing with persisting social and economic problems

The months it required to produce the papers, and critique their recommendations, was a small-scale test of a belief that interested and informed citizens could help create a new social policy environment through their pooled, but uncompensated or unreimbursed, efforts to find alternatives to the two positions presented in public debate: (1) a fierce defense of the *status quo*, which is based on federal-government leadership and a reliance on steadily increasing federal funding; and (2) an equally fierce effort to replace that system with a wholly different model based on less federal responsibility and devolution of policy making to other sectors of society.

To sum up the purposes and guiding conceptions of the contributors to this volume, we can say, in midstream, that the authors share the following beliefs: (1) it may be unavoidable in the age of the information highway to look for consensus before a debate is conducted or rely on opinion polls and focus groups chosen for their likely production of bland consensus, but it is not sufficient; (2) it is unhealthy to be quiet in times such as these; (3) the public values bold ideas that may divide the nation as much as it seeks the quiet of centrist consensus; (4) public services can make a difference in the lives of people, and when they are not providing everything that is expected, it may be that they need to be reformed and redesigned rather than abolished.

Conventionally, individuals join in collective efforts around the promotion or protection of some shared interest. The Odyssey Forum recognized early on that there was already an abundance, a cacophony, an overload of ideas being offered. Choices among them would be made through an interplay of political forces representing specific interests—but what interests and whose? There already exist hundreds or thousands of advocacy organizations, think tanks, research centers, and academic organizations of one kind or another. Was the Odyssey Forum approach different?

Participants accepted the fact that they each had beliefs that guided their actions, but they wanted to approach a wholly new situation in social policy formation with the least possible amount of precommitment to solutions. They preferred to be as independent as possible from the positions held by the institutions that employed them, while keeping in mind the human needs that were at stake. The following guidelines were easy to articulate, but more difficult to act on:

1. The basic conditions for social policy have changed and will continue to change for the foreseeable future. Many advocacy groups have chosen to deny that anything basic has been altered and that their needs or special interests could not be met through increased public funding or a change in administration.

2. A strong role for the national government is necessary, although this role may be redefined.

3. The human needs of citizens will not disappear or diminish automatically. Some collective or collaborative effort must be sustained in the interests of the general welfare, but some of the existing efforts urgently need restructuring.

4. Sooner or later, ideas will find political leaders willing to "defy the tyranny of focus groups and resurrect the more ambitious kind of politics" (*Economist*, 24 August 1996, 23).

The group's first effort did identify alternative ideas for five areas: Social Security, welfare, health, housing, and work at better wages for more people.

Bearing in mind that the Odyssey Forum has operated through the pro bono efforts of individuals in several cities and wants to maintain the freedom this gives it, its members also began to put together other pieces of the complex mosaic which constitutes the policy arena for human needs. The following suggests this complexity but is offered with the present conviction that we lack both the proven technology and the civic will to engage in the massive governmental or private social engineering necessary to fit the pieces together by logical reasoning processes alone. The major ideological solutions available can be categorized as (1) some form of socialized state, which is not acceptable in a Marxist form today; (2) an unfettered free market of private forces, which has yet to prove that it can—unaided by public efforts—satisfactorily deal with economic, health, and human needs; (3) a reformed welfare state.

For such approaches, the underlying conflict between the eighteenth-century Enlightenment beliefs about freedom and equality is conceptually unresolved. This issue adds a philosophical element to the equation—how do we achieve both freedom and equality when human beings differ in their abilities and in their socially or economically determined means to realize their dreams? As citizens and as members of a "constitutional" society, it has become difficult to believe that we will not easily have both at once.

As a result, much of the political debate and public discussion concentrates on "proving" that this or that need is vital and requires public support. There is an underlying assumption that we live in a privileged era of great capacities and can have all that everybody wants and quickly. Evidence about possible limitations of resources is obscured by evidence that the resources we do clearly have are poorly allocated. The result is a proliferation of voices for expanding rights and wants that often conflict with each other, with little or no attention paid to the means for reconciling the needs and resources in a manner that is both equitable and consistent with the ideal of freedom for all these voices.

This, of course, is the stuff of elections and debate in an open society. The nation is in the midst of such a debate, opaque as it may seem to be. The opening chapter of this book, on the emergence of a conservative trend, describes how we unwittingly have been forced to confront the dilemma.

The participants in the forum have begun, in our way, to address this complexity step by step. The first of these steps is our acceptance of the reality that the diversity of voices raised over the *freedom* half of the philosophical equation need to spend more time on the strategies available to realize the *equality* half in an era when resources are inadequate for providing everything for everyone. This realization is happening after a forty-year span during which the necessity for making tough political decisions was postponed by a favored national economy and demographic conditions.

The conventional response to this dilemma has been that of political economy—the interplay of economic forces and political choices. But by 1980, two other factors made their appearance. The economic concerns of half of the population about seeing their incomes decline while the other half was doing very well were joined by an unfamiliar set of social concerns, not clearly or solely rooted in poor economic conditions. For example, the changed nature of the family, with more visible family conflict and new behavioral and sexual freedoms, and with the traditional family experiencing serial marriages, while others tried to rear infants without a father present.

Added to these concerns was a perception that personal security was threatened due to an increase in violent crime and the widespread use of addictive substances, especially drugs. The expanded belief in personal freedom also led to the replacement of institutional care for the mentally ill with medical and drug treatment outside of hospitals. The return of deviant behavior and the homeless to public view, whether or not they were in any way threatening, increased the concern about how to manage them. With no conclusive evidence, the perception grew that these essentially social and psychological or behavioral problems were increasing and were not being controlled or controllable.

While few of these social phenomena had any clear remedies, public belief that "government should be doing something and was not being effective" served to increase a growing sense of discontent with how government was functioning, laying the basis for a renewed conservative movement away from caring for the troubled or poor through national programs and policies. This position—the suspicion of an overly powerful government—was not new in American public life, but it began to have a greater influence on how the public expected the government to act. These doubts gave rise to an increased interest in devolving public responsibilities to either state governments or the private sector, which represented a complete reversal of the trend, begun in 1910, of shifting more authority and responsibility to the national government in Washington.

None of this has yet meant a clear retreat from public responsibility. Rather, voters have become unmoored from a clear belief about what they want government to provide and for whom, and what they or others should be expected—as a civic right as well as an obligation—to pay for in taxes.

On top of these concerns, the new electronic communication technology has added a less recognized dimension to the widely reported public discontent with (if not necessarily antagonism to) the way governments at any level have performed of late. Recent history has led to a belief in, or a wish for, quick solutions to complex problems, even when the causes are not understood. This wish for quick action, which would then free voters to go back to their private wants and interests, is very powerful. It leads to impatience.

But Odyssey Forum participants believe that more time is needed to move the country from distress about the serious changes occurring in the conditions people confront to a resolution that satisfies their desire for a balance between freedom and equality (of opportunity at least, if not of instant outcome).

So, in the 1990s, we have a four-sided equation, not a neat, two-sided, political-economic equation. Now choices involve (1) economic basics, the ability to balance fairly the supply and demand for material goods; (2) the social (and demographic) realities of circumstances such as a changed family structure, violence, deviant behavior, and a most diversified population that is also aging and producing greater retirement dependency; (3) the possible shift in public trust in government to do all the "heavy lifting" and a willingness to allow other institutions to handle some tasks through devolution of responsibility or funding; (4) the continual effort to find some acceptable balance between freedom and equality under a unifying vision for the nation (meaning its citizens) and an equal concern for all without discrimination against some.

The times do not encourage the undertaking of great tasks of social engineering that have been centrally developed and are administered within a hierarchal frame of rules and regulations. But a structure of new ideas for reforming institutions may, in time, constitute a coherent agenda that will reach the same ends as the great centrally planned designs of the depression era and the post-depression years of optimism.

The contribution of a new, atypical organization like the Odyssey Forum has not yet been established. But in this time of fundamental shift in the environment for social policy making, the established intellectual institutions may be changed or joined by new institutions—just as the past produced the likes of policy centers at universities, such at the Heller School for Advanced Studies in Social Welfare at Brandeis University, and freestanding policy centers such as the Brookings Institution, the Urban Institute, the Economic Policy Institute, and the Heritage Foundation. We and the other authors consider this book to be the initial test for discovering whether another type of idea-producing institution is feasible or useful.

Appendix: List of Participants at the Odyssey Forum Meeting, 26–27 January 1996, Washington, D.C.

W. Andrew Achenbaum, Ph.D., Deputy Director, Institute of Gerontology, and Professor of History, University of Michigan, Ann Arbor

Martin Berdit, Columbia, Maryland

Jared Bernstein, Economic Policy Institute, Washington, D.C.

Cheryl C. Bluestein, Doctoral Intern, School of Policy Sciences, University of Maryland-Baltimore County

Yung-Ping (Bing) Chen, Ph.D., Frank J. Manning Eminent Scholar's Chair in Gerontology at the University of Massachusetts-Boston

James R. Dumpson, Visiting Professor, School of Social Work, Fordham University, New York

Joe R. Garcia, Jr., Executive Director, Greater Cleveland Neighborhood Centers Association, Cleveland, Ohio

Thomas P. Glynn, Deputy Secretary, U.S. Department of Labor, Washington, D.C.

Robert Griss, Director, Center on Disability and Health, Washington, D.C.

John E. Hansan, Ph.D., Publisher, *Aging Network News*, McLean, Virginia

Chester Hartman, Executive Director, Poverty and Race Research Action Council, Washington, D.C.

Robert L. Kane, M.D., Minnesota Chair in Long-Term Care and Aging, School of Public Health, University of Minnesota, Minneapolis

Eric R. Kingson, Associate Professor, Graduate School of Social Work, Boston College

James A. Krauskopf, R. J. Milano Graduate School of Management and Urban Policy, New York

S. M. Miller, Director, The Joint Project on Equality, Commonwealth Institute, Cambridge, Massachusetts

Robert Morris, D.S.W., Emeritus Professor, Brandeis University, Waltham, Massachusetts

Martha N. Ozawa, Ph.D., Bettie Bofinger Brown Professor of Social Policy, George Warren Brown School of Social Work, Washington University, St. Louis, Missouri

Merrill Peterson, Professor of History, Emeritus, University of Virginia, Charlottesville

Juan Ramos, Ph.D., Associate Director-Prevention, National Institute of Mental Health, Rockville, Maryland

Alvin L. Schorr, Emeritus Professor, Mandel School of Social Sciences, Case Western Reserve University, Cleveland, Ohio

William Whitaker, Ph.D., Professor and Baccalaureate Program Director, School of Social Work, University of Maine, Orono

Index

A-Corp, 68 n.49
Adams, Charles Francis, 54–55
Adjusted average per capita costs
(AAPCCs), 113
AFDC. *See* Aid for Families with Dependent Children
African-Americans: AFDC benefit levels, 166–68; housing discrimination,
139; shelter poor, 144; unemployment rates, 153
Agency for Health Care Policy and Research, 129
Aid for the Aged, 6, 9. *See also* Cash
relief; Public welfare
Aid for the Blind, 6, 9. *See also* Cash
relief; Public welfare
Aid for Dependent Children. *See* Aid
for Families with Dependent Children (AFDC); Cash relief; Public
welfare
Aid for the Disabled, 9. *See also* Cash
relief; Public welfare
Aid for Families with Dependent Children (AFDC), 2, 9, 14, 17, 19–20,
26, 77, 115, 148–71. *See also* Temporary Assistance for Needy Families
AIDS (Acquired Immune Deficiency

Syndrome), 10; health promotion,
121; new drugs, 118
America Works, 26
Americans with Disabilities Act (ADA),
132
Anderson, Elijah, 32
Apprenticeships, 36. *See also* Youth
apprenticeships
Atomic bomb, 17

Bane, Mary Jo, 152
Beveridge Report, 72
Bill of Rights, 13, 72
Bingaman, Jeff, 61
Bishop, John, 40
Blacks. *See* African-Americans
Block grants, AFDC, 147, 162–71
Bluestone, Barry, 30
Brandeis, Louis D., 55
Britain. *See* Great Britain
Bureau of Labor Statistics, 31
Burns, Arthur F., 22
Burtless, Gary, 31, 78

California, 170
Canada: government benefits to families, 151; health promotion, 121

Carter, Jimmy, 37
Cash relief, 149, 153. *See also* Public welfare programs
Chandler, Alfred, 56
Child allowances, 155, 157–58, 171
Child care, 24, 155–58
Child support, 155–58; child support assurance system (CSAS), 157, 171
Children: declining economic status, 161–62; economic security, 161–74
Civil War, 9
Civilian Health and Medical Program of the Uniformed Services (CHAMPUS), 132
Clinton, Bill: administration, 40, 157; health care reform, 76, 92–93, 96–108, 125; housing bill, 135; increasing EITC benefits, 155; welfare reform policies, 147
Cold War, 7
Communitarian tradition, 140
Community Reinvestment Act, 25
Comprehensive Environmental Response, Compensation and Liability Act 1980 (CERCLA), 63
Comprehensive health planning agencies, 110
Concord Coalition, 76
Constitution, 13; contracts clause, 46
Constitutional conventions, 50
Consumer Assessment of Health Plans Study (CAHPS), 129
Consumer price index (CPI), 86–87
Contract with America, 161–62
Corporate welfare, 2, 8; tax benefits, 4
Corporations, corporate duty, 43–44; history, 44–65; negligence, 51–52; public duty, 48
Cost-of-living adjustment (COLA), 77
Council of Economic Advisors, 31

Defense Highway program, 22
Delaware, favorable environment for corporations, 58
Depression. *See* Great Depression
Developmentally disabled, 2
Devolution of federal responsibilities, 11–13

Disabilities: children with, 162; outcome measures for persons with, 125–33; persons with, vulnerable to managed care, 125
Disability insurance, 2, 15, 72. *See also* Social insurance
Discrimination: housing, 139; toward persons with disabilities, 131
Disproportionate share hospitals, 111
Dostoyevsky, Fyodor, 17
Drucker, Peter, 22

Earned Income Tax Credit. *See* EITC
Economic policies: macro, 21–25; micro, 25–26
Economist, 4, 18, 35
Education, 2, 15, 25, 32, 65
Einstein, Albert, 17
Eisenhower, Dwight D., administration, 22
EITC (Earned Income Tax Credit), 24, 33; an alternative means to social insurance, 76; Clinton's efforts to increase, 155; improving, 39–40; as income security for children, 172–74; relation to work incentives, 163–64
Ellwood, David, 152
Employment, 17–27, 29–40, 158
English Poor Law system, 9, 147

Family Support Act of 1988, 169
Farber, Henry, 31
Federal Bureau of Corporations, 57
Federal Employers' Liability Act, 54
Federal Reserve Board, 21–22, 33, 155
Federalist Papers, 13
Fee-for-service health care, 100, 125
Food and Drug Administration (FDA), 118
Food stamps, 9, 14, 39, 73, 150. *See also* Means-tested, programs; Public assistance
Forbes, Steve, 34
Fortune, 29
France, government's approach to means testing, 77–78, 156

German Greens, 18
Germany: apprenticeship system, 35–36; government benefits to families, 151; Weimar Republic, 123
GI Bill of Rights, 2, 7
Glennerster, Howard, 76
Gore, Albert, Jr., 60
Graduate medical education (GME), 111
Grameen Bank, 25
Granger laws, 54
Great Britain, 72; government benefits to families, 151; means testing, 76; social policy approach, 77–78
Great Depression, 5, 57, 72, 136, 149
Great Society legislation, 117
Gross domestic product (GDP), 7
Gross national product (GNP), 1, 4, 7–8, 13; slow down in growth, 10
Guaranteed income, public's opposition, 37
Guaranteed jobs, public's favor, 37

Hansen, Alvin, 22
Health care industry, 9
Health care rationing, 121
Health care reform, 91–108; single-payer system, 97
Health insurance, 15, 24, 125, 130. *See also* Universal health insurance
Health maintenance organizations (HMOs), 99–101; continued growth, 106; regulations, 123. *See also* Managed care
Health promotion, 120–21
Health Service Corps, 120
Healthy People 2000, 109
Heller, Walter, 21
Hispanics: households, 139; shelter poor, 144 n.2
HMOs. *See* Health maintenance organizations
Hobsbaum, Eric, 1, 8
Homelessness, 137, 142
Hoskins, Dalmer, 74–76
Hospital construction, 2
Housing: federal policies, 135–39; non-speculative ownership, 141–44; right to, 140–41; subsidies, 2
Housing Act of 1937, sixtieth anniversary, 135
Housing Act of 1949, National Housing Goal, 136

Illinois Supreme Court, 50
Income security for children. *See* Children
Income tax: federal, 175; progressive, 7
Indiana Supreme Court, 46
Individual retirement accounts (IRAs), 73
Institute of Medicine, 110
Internal Revenue Code, 136, 143
International Classification of Impairments, Disabilities, and Handicaps (ICIDH), 130
International Social Security Association, 74
Interstate Commerce Act, 118
Interstate Commerce Commission (ICC), 54–55
Interstate highways, 2
IRAs (Individual retirement accounts), 73

Jacksonian Democratic-Republicans, 45
Japan, 17
Job Corps, 34
Job Opportunities and Skills Training Act, 169
Job Training Partnership Act, 34
Johnson, Lyndon, 27

Kennedy, John F., Jr., administration's welfare policies, 149
Keynesian model of economics, 21
Korean War, 7

Labor market, low-wage sectors, 154
Laissez-faire theories, 45
Latino. *See* Hispanics
Long-term care, 116
Lugar, Richard, 34

Maine, 36

Managed care, 65, 99, 107, 111–23; measuring quality, 127–32; persons with disabilities, 125

Managed (health) care organizations (MCOs), 114. *See also* Managed care

Manpower Development Research Corporation, 152

Marcotte, Dave, 31

Maryland, 170

Massachusetts Railway Commission, 54

Means-tested: payments, 82; programs, 73–78, 166; public assistance, 9. *See also* Aid for the Aged; Aid for the Blind; Aid for the Disabled; Aid for Families with Dependent Children; Food stamps; Medicaid; Public welfare programs; Safety net; Supplemental Security Income

Medicaid, 2, 9; allows choice, 101; devolving to states, 123; federal government's role, 118; not available to working poor, 155; part of safety net, 73; proposed cuts, 81; a public health program, 132; support for long-term care, 115–16; a welfare program, 150

Medical savings accounts (MSAs), 108

Medicare, 2, 9; analogous to Clinton's health care proposal, 97; benefits, 113–16; connection to long-term care, 116; controlling costs, 113–17; example of reform process, 92, 104–5; facing up to the problems, 123; freedom of choice, 101; Hospital Trust Fund, 107; opposition of beneficiaries, 98; privatization, 107–8; problem of funding, 107–8; proposed cuts, 81; regulations, 118; as social insurance, 72; support for home health care, 111; a vehicle for other projects, 111. *See also* Social insurance

Medigap insurance, 115

Michigan, railroad war, 49–50

Minimum wage, 73, 154, 158

Minneapolis, 26

Minorities: apprenticeship programs, 36; job problems, 32; youth unemployment, 5

Moynihan, Daniel Patrick, 40

Nash, Nathanial, 40

National Commission on Children, 173

National Commission on Social Security Reform, 77

National Football League (NFL), 62

National Housing Goal, 136

National Institutes of Health, 2

National responsibilities, 13–14

Netherlands, government benefits to families, 151

New Deal, 1–2, 6, 57. *See also* Roosevelt, Franklin D.

New Hampshire Supreme Court, 49

New Jersey, 170

New York, influence on other states, 25

New York City, income for family of three on AFDC, 163–65

The New York Times, 4, 40; report on federal housing, 135

Nixon, Richard: administration, 149; universal health insurance, 91

Nonspeculative housing, 141–44

Nursing home regulations, 118

Occupational Safety and Health Administration, 54

Odyssey Forum, 179–83

Offe, Claus, 18

Ohio, railroad war, 50

Ohio Supreme Court, 50

Old Age/Survivors Insurance (OASI), 6, 72, 157. *See also* Social security

Omnibus Budget Reconciliation Act of 1987 (OBRA 87), 118; 1993 (OBRA 93), 172–74

Oregon, rationing health care, 121

Organisation for Economic Cooperation and Development, 81

Osterman, Paul, 32

Outcome measures, 125–27
Ozawa, Martha, 78

P corporation. *See* Public corporation
Pavetti, LaDonna, 152
Pennsylvania, 36; Supreme Court, 46
Pension systems, pay-as-you-go, 82
Perloff, Harvey, 22
Personal Responsibility Act, 162
Planning: government, 95, 110; health and social services, 109–10; housing, 142; New Deal, 6; regional, 110
Policy making, health and social services, 109, 121–23
Poor Laws, 9, 147
Poor relief, 6
Poverty and Race Research Council, 25
Preferred-provider organization (PPO), 100. *See also* Managed care
Primary care provider (PCP), 126. *See also* Managed care
Private sector, 3, 5; devolving responsibilities, 11; source of uncertainty, 43
Privatization: health care, 125; Medicare, 107; social security, 83–86, 89
Progressive Era, 53–54
Progressive Policy Institute, 40
Prospective payment system (PPS), 113
Public assistance, 18–19, 26, 83, 115. *See also* Aid for the Aged; Aid for the Blind; Aid for the Disabled; Aid for Families with Dependent Children; Food stamps; Means-tested, programs; Medicaid, Public welfare programs; Safety net; Supplemental Security Income
Public corporation, 43; reviving, 60–62; "P" corporation, 63–65
Public duty. *See* Corporations
Public education, 2, 15, 25, 32, 65
Public good, 2; search for, 53
Public health: departments, 112; public utility, 133
Public hospitals, 112
Public housing, 2, 73
Public jobs, 38
Public purpose, 44–54

Public welfare programs, 6, 20, 78; controversial, 147; history, 148–50; reducing dependency, 151; reform, 148; trends in benefits, 150. *See also* Aid for the Aged; Aid for the Blind; Aid for the Disabled; Aid for Families with Dependent Children; Food stamps; Means-tested, programs; Medicaid; Public assistance; Public housing; Supplemental Security Income

Racial discrimination, 10; in housing, 139
Railroads, 48–51; war, 49–50; immunity, 49
Reagan, Ronald: administration, 58; appointees, 135; budget for assisted housing, 144 n.1; fiscal policy, 95; welfare policies, 149
Reconstruction Finance Corporation, 24
Redlining, 139
Refundable tax credit, 172
Reich, Robert, 30, 61
Retirement. *See* Social security; Social insurance
Retirement age, 87
Roosevelt, Franklin D.: administration, 1–2, 5, 27, 72; second inaugural address, 136; support for universal health insurance, 91, 149
Roosevelt, Theodore, 57
Russell, Bertrand, 18

Safety Applicance Act, 54
Safety net, 11, 14, 73–74, 83. *See also* Aid for the Aged; Aid for the Blind; Aid for the Disabled; Aid for Families with Dependent Children; Food stamps; Means-tested, programs; Medicaid; Supplemental Security Income; Public housing; Public welfare programs
School to Work Opportunities Act, 36
Scocpol, Theda, 14
Scottish Common Sense, 45

Seamen, federal government's welfare role, 9

Securities and Exchange Commission, 63

Single-parent families, 4, 10; single mothers, 151. *See also* Aid for Families with Dependent Children

Smith, James, 79

Social compact, 71, 74

Social Darwinism, 72

Social Democratic Party, 81

Social housing, 141–44

Social insurance, 2; component programs, 72; concept undergirding social security, 85; reducing the role, 76; tax-based system for health care, 98; weakest protection for families with children, 74. *See also* Social security; Social Security Act of 1935

Social safety net. *See* Safety net

Social security: beneficiaries, 9; retirement program, 15, 71–89; 157, 171. *See also* Social insurance

Social Security Act of 1935, 2, 6, 148, 166; initial premises, 12

Social Security Board of Trustees, 80

Social services, 6, 15, 109

Sociological jurisprudence, 53

Soviet planning, 95

SSI, 2, 9, 14, 78, 83

Superfund law, 62–63

Supplemental Security Income (SSI), 2, 9, 14, 78, 83

Supreme Court. *See* U.S. Supreme Court; *various state supreme courts*

Survivor's insurance, 149. *See also* Social insurance; Social Security Act of 1935

Sweden: government benefits to families, 151; Social Democratic Party, 81; universal child care, 156

Taft, William Howard, 57

Taft-Hartley Act, 143

Tax incentives, 61

Teenage pregnancy and childbirth, 161

Temporary Assistance for Needy Fami-

lies (TANF), 162–171. *See also* Aid for Families with Dependent Children

Tennessee Valley Authority (TVA), 24

Texas, income for family of three on AFDC, 163–65

Thompson, Tommy, 170

Totalitarianism, 95

Transitional Employment Enterprises (TEE). *See* America Works

Truman, Harry S., support for universal health insurance, 91

Trust fund, 76. *See also* Social security

Ultra vires doctrine, 46–47, 60

Unemployment Insurance (UI), 6, 15, 25, 72, 157, 171, 175. *See also* Social insurance; Social Security Act of 1935

Unions: associated with higher wages, 155; decline, 154; strengthening, 158

Universal child care, 24, 155–58

Universal health insurance, 91–93, 125, 155–56. *See also* Health insurance

Urban renewal, 2; as "Negro removal," 23

U.S. Children's Bureau, 10

U.S. Department of Health and Human Services: Public Health Service, 109–10; Social Security Administration, 162

U.S. Department of Housing and Urban Development, 135

U.S. Employment Service, 40

U.S. Supreme Court, 46–47, 57

Veterans: education, 2; federal government's welfare role, 9; housing subsidies, 2

Veterans Administration (VA): health system, 132; hospital system, 111

Vietnam War, 7

Virginia Supreme Court, 44

Welfare. *See* Public welfare programs

Welfare advocates, 3

Welfare reform, 38, 147–60

Wharton, Francis, 51–52, 59
Wilson, William Julius, 38, 154
Wilson, Woodrow, 57
Wisconsin: influence on other states, 25; Work Not Welfare program 170; youth apprenticeship, 36–37
Wisconsin Auto Dealers Association, 37
Women, Infants, and Children program (WIC), 121
Work Incentive Program of 1967, 169
Work Opportunity Act, 162
Work relief, 149, 152

Workers' compensation, 14; origins, 53; as social insurance, 72
Workfare program, 38, 65. *See also* Work relief
Works Progress Administration (WPA), 38, 149
World Bank, criticism of social security programs, 81–85
World Health Organization, 130
World War II, 7, 72, 136

Youth apprenticeships, 33, 35

Zevin, Robert, 21

About the Editors and Contributors

JARED BERNSTEIN is a labor economist with the Economic Policy Institute in Washington, D.C., where he specializes in the analysis of wage and income inequality, with an emphasis on low-wage labor markets and poverty. His articles have appeared in many popular and academic journals. Between 1995 and 1996, Dr. Bernstein held the post of deputy chief economist at the U.S. Department of Labor, where he worked on the initiative to raise the minimum wage. He is coauthor of *The State of Working America*.

YUNG-PING CHEN holds the Frank J. Manning Eminent Scholar's Chair in Gerontology at the University of Massachusetts-Boston. He was a delegate to the 1995 White House Conference on Aging, as well as a consultant and delegate to the 1971 and 1981 White House Conferences on Aging. Dr. Chen served on the Panel of Actuaries and Economists of the 1979 Advisory Council on Social Security. Recent publications include *Income: Background and Issues*, *Unlocking Home Equity for the Elderly*, and *Social Security in a Changing Society*.

RASHI FEIN is Professor of the Economics of Medicine in the Department of Social Medicine at Harvard University Medical School. Professor Fein is a charter member of the Institute of Medicine in the National Academy of Sciences and a founding member of the National Academy of Social Insurance. He earlier served on the senior staff of President Kennedy's Council of Economic Advisors and was a senior fellow at the Brookings

Institution. His most recent book is *Medical Care, Medical Costs: The Search for a Health Insurance Policy.*

IRWIN GARFINKEL is the Mitchell I. Ginsberg Professor of Contemporary Urban Problems at the Columbia University School of Social Work and director of the New York City Indicators Survey Center at Columbia University. He is the author or coauthor of more than one hundred scientific articles and eight books on poverty, income transfers, program evaluation, and child support. Professor Garfinkel's most recent book is *Social Policies for Children*, which he coedited.

ROBERT GRISS is Director of the Center on Disability and Health in Washington, D.C., a public policy institute devoted to health care reform from a disability perspective. The center conducts policy analysis and research and advocates making managed care more publicly accountable. He is Cochair of the Consortium for Citizens with Disabilities. One of Mr. Griss's priorities is to use the Americans with Disabilities Act as a tool for challenging discrimination in the health insurance marketplace and in health care delivery systems.

JOHN E. HANSAN is a retired social worker and a coordinator of Odyssey Forum. He was formerly Director of the National Conference on Social Welfare and Interim Executive Director of the National Association of Social Workers. Between 1971 and 1975, Dr. Hansan served in the state of Ohio, first as Director of the Department of Public Welfare and later as Chief of Staff to the Governor, the Honorable John J. Gilligan. His most recent publication is *365 Ways . . . Retirees' Resource Guide for Productive Lifestyles* (Greenwood Press, 1996).

CHESTER HARTMAN is President/Executive Director of the Poverty and Race Research Action Council in Washington, D.C. From 1981 to 1990 he was a fellow at the Institute for Policy Studies in Washington, D.C. Dr. Hartman's most recent books include *Double Exposure: Poverty and Race in America* and, with Michael Stone and others, *Housing: Foundation of a New Social Agenda.*

ROBERT L. KANE holds the Minnesota Endowed Chair in Long-Term Care and Aging at the University of Minnesota School of Public Health. He is a professor in the Division of Health Services Research and Policy. He directs the university's Center on Aging and the Clinical Outcomes Research Center. Dr. Kane has a special interest in assessing the outcomes of care and has published widely about aspects of care for older people, including coediting *Quality Care in Geriatric Settings* and *Essentials of Clinical Geriatrics.*

ROBERT I. LERMAN, Director of Human Resources Policy at the Urban Institute in Washington, D.C., is an economist on leave from American University, where he chaired the Department of Economics. His research deals with youth employment and training, income inequality, child support, early fatherhood, and welfare policies. His most recent publication is "Building Hope, Skills, and Careers" which appeared in *Social Policies*.

S. M. (MIKE) MILLER is Research Professor of Sociology at Boston College and Senior Fellow at the Commonwealth Institute in Cambridge, Massachusetts. Formerly Director of the Joint Project on Equality, he is now Senior Advisor to United for a Fair Economy/Share the Wealth. He has been an advisor to community action, social policy, and poverty organizations in Ireland, Britain, France, and the United States. He is a member of the Board of Directors of the Poverty and Race Research Action Council and is coeditor of *Poverty: A Global Review* (1996).

ROBERT MORRIS is Kirstein Professor Emeritus at Brandeis University and Cardinal Medeiros Lecturer at the University of Massachusetts-Boston. Dr. Morris is a former president of the Gerontological Society of America and a fellow of the American Association for the Advancement of Science and the American Public Health Association. Among his publications are *Rethinking Social Welfare: Why Care for the Stranger?* and *Testing the Limits of Social Welfare: International Perspectives on Policy Changes in Nine Industrial Countries*.

MARTHA N. OZAWA is the Bettie Bofinger Brown Professor of Social Policy in the George Warren Brown School of Social Work at Washington University in St. Louis, Missouri. Her recent research has focused on the structure of financing and the provision of benefits under various income security programs, particularly as they affect children and the elderly. Dr. Ozawa's publications include three books, fourteen chapters in contributed volumes and more than one hundred articles. She serves on the boards of numerous academic journals.

ALVIN L. SCHORR is Leonard W. Mayo Professor Emeritus in the Mandel School of Applied Social Science at Case Western Reserve University. He was formerly General Director of the Community Service Society of New York, Dean of the N.Y.U. School of Social Work, and Deputy Assistant Secretary of the U.S. Department of Health, Education and Welfare. Among his publications are *The (British) Personal Social Service—An Outside View* and *Common Decency: Domestic Policies after Reagan*.

HOWARD SCHWEBER is a Ph.D. candidate at Cornell University, where he also teaches law and politics. Mr. Schweber practiced law for five years before deciding to return to an academic setting to pursue the historical development of American private law and its relation to political ideology. He has published and presented papers on early American law, nineteenth-century politics, and the role of the First Amendment in cyberspace.

MICHAEL E. STONE is Professor of Community Planning at the University of Massachusetts-Boston. Professor Stone has been involved for more than twenty-five years in research, policy analysis, program development, and advocacy on housing issues. He is the author of numerous articles and monographs, among them the widely cited report *One Third of a Nation: A New Look at Housing Affordability* (1990). His most recent book is *Shelter Poverty: New Ideas on Housing Affordability.*

ISBN 0-86569-266-1

EAN

9 780865 692664

90000>

HARDCOVER BAR CODE